THE
JOYS OF
TROUT

ALSO BY Arnold Gingrich

Arnold Gingrich

THE
JOYS OF
TROUT

CROWN PUBLISHERS, INC.
New York

Certain portions of this book have appeared, or will appear, in
somewhat different form: specifically, portions of Part One have been
included in the anthology *Fishing Moments of Truth,* prepared for
Winchester Press by James Rikhoff and Eric Peper; a portion of
Part Two, pertaining to The Anglers' Club of New York, formed part
of an entry in the *International Encyclopaedia of Fly-Fishing* prepared
for *Rainbird Reference Books Limited,* in England by Bernard Venables;
the items in Part Three concerning Bergman, Bethune, Curtis, Gill,
Green, Hallock, Henshall, Hewitt, Horne, Jennings, LaBranche,
Mottram, Norris, Prime, Rhead, Roosevelt, and Young were adapted
from entries prepared for the revised edition of *McClane's Standard
Fishing Encyclopedia,* published by Holt, Rinehart & Winston; the
Schaldach item was adapted from the introduction to *The Wind on
Your Cheek,* published by Freshet Press; the Brooks, Grove, and
Schwiebert items were adapted from reviews in *The Flyfisher,* the
journal of the Federation of Fly Fishermen, and the Schwiebert item
also incorporates material from the introduction to *Salmon of the World,*
published by Winchester Press; the McDonald item was adapted from
a review of *Quill Gordon* in *Book World,* in the *Chicago Tribune*
of November 26, 1972; the Ritz item appeared in part in *Trout,* the
journal of Trout Unlimited, as well as in the introduction to the new
edition of *A Fly Fisher's Life* published by Max Reinhardt at the Bodley
Head in London 1972 and by Crown Publishers in New York in 1973;
the Sage item is adapted from the introduction to a new edition of
The Ristigouche and Its Salmon Fishing, privately printed by the
Angler's and Shooter's Press, Goshen, Conn.; the Wulff item appeared
in the issue of *Field & Stream* for December 1971, as well as in the
introduction to *Fishing with Lee Wulff,* edited by Edward C. Janes,
published by Alfred A. Knopf, Inc., New York 1972; the section on
A. J. McClane appeared in the August, 1973, issue of *Field & Stream.*

Library of Congress Catalog Card Number: 73–82458
ISBN: 0–517–505843

Manufactured in the United States of America
Published simultaneously in Canada by
General Publishing Company Limited
Designed by Shari de Miskey

The assistance is gratefully acknowledged of
Bayard Schieffelin and Walter Zervas of the New York Public Library,
of Herbert Michelman and Nick Lyons of Crown Publishers,
and of Mrs. Jed Braun of the *Esquire* magazine staff.

To Adele Marie Louise Jennings
—in memory of Preston

Contents

Prelude

THIS IS MY FIRST FISHING BOOK IN EIGHT YEARS, AND though it is issued at nobody's invitation or request, to me at least it seems long overdue. Hardly had the type been set on *The Well-Tempered Angler* when a lot of things about fishing, and particularly my kind, which is fly-fishing, began to change.

This is odd, because fishing is one of those things you think of as hardy perennials that have been around since long before you and I were and will be long after we're gone.

True as that is in the long view, in the shortened perspective of our own times fly fishing has undergone considerable change, and it has been change for the better.

I don't, of course, know how far back you can remember, though the odds are pretty steep against your being able to hark back any farther than I can, but that doesn't really matter, because today the keenest fly fishermen I know are all under thirty, and some of them barely out of their teens.

They show a greater aptitude and degree of addiction for the sport than their fathers, and to me this is one of the few heartening signs of our era.

They can't remember, as perhaps you can and I certainly do, the nightly nuisance of drying silk lines and soaking gut leaders, in those now distant days when snelled wet flies were still to be seen, and nymphs were something new. They were in playsuits and rompers in those dingy days right after the Second World War when the fly rod seemed destined to extinction, as the advent of the fixed-spool reel made spinning appear to be the way of the future.

So they've never had to feel defensive about sticking to the old fly rod, when all their peers were taking up the newest thing. They have simply discovered, for themselves, that wielding a fly rod is the most fun you can have standing up. Nobody's had to tell them that its use is or isn't the thing to do.

Only a few years back, those of us who fly-fished were inclined to give ourselves airs, as members of a brave but beleaguered band, trying to conduct what we considered—or at least hoped to make—a dignified and orderly retreat from engulfment by the onrushing onslaughts of barbarous hordes.

Today, to our bemusement, we find that what we thought of as a determined rearguard action has since somehow been transformed into the straggling tail end of a gigantic new parade, marching to a different drum, and now we'll have to step lively to keep up with it.

Fly fishing, which had appeared to be undergoing an eclipse—it was never anywhere nearly total and now turns out to have been only temporary—is again vigorously on the increase. It has new organizations and publications going for it, and some of us who were its apologists are now rather awkwardly trying to adjust to the realization that it never needed our apologies.

It's a little like going to make a sympathy call, posies in hand, on an invalid who gets up to knock you down.

Part One

A BALM
FOR
FISHLESSNESS

WHEN YOU'RE HAVING A BLANK DAY IN FISHING IT doesn't mean, of course, that you're doing nothing that day. The chances are you actually work harder, change flies more often, agonize over every aspect of what you're doing to see whether there's anything you shouldn't be doing that you are or that you aren't doing that you should, and as far as you're concerned, the only ones who are doing nothing that day are the fish, because you're doing everything that you can think of.

(Surprisingly often, the one way to snap out of a prolonged spell of fishlessness is to try something—almost anything—that you haven't tried for a long time. If you can find a fly in your box that you haven't used for the last four seasons, that may do it. Sometimes it even works to find a fly of which you can say, in all honesty, that you've never yet caught anything on it. Fish are so perverse that they'll go to almost any lengths, to prove you wrong, even in that extreme instance.)

Similarly, when we say that our minds are a total blank, it's almost never true, unless we're asleep, and even then dreams keep the motor idling, so to speak, even if we don't remember the dreams when we wake up. Remembering that this is supposed to be a contemplative pastime, I sometimes try to check up on myself while I'm fishing, to see if I can get any inkling of what I'm contemplating, and I have yet to be successful at it. (All I get is me thinking about why I'm not thinking or if I am thinking or have preempted the thought process by interrupting through wonder about what it was I thought about when I last had a thought.)

Sleepless nights, or white nights, as the French call them, are pretty much the same thing. Nights we'd swear we haven't shut an eye, scientists assure us that we have, without realizing it, and they have devised various instruments that will prove it to us if we persist in our doubt. It's just that we think we're not sleeping, as we so often think we're not thinking, when of course we are.

By the same token, solitude is the norm in sport fishing, even for those who are frightened by the very thought of being alone. Most people I know have fishing partners, without whom they wouldn't dream of going off alone on even the briefest of trips. But what they forget, in all the togetherness of meals and lodging and entertainment activities that take place before and after fishing, is how little actual fishing time they spend together. Each has his own section of stream to fish, and normally they are either out of each other's sight or at least out of anything less than shouting distance apart. The actual fishing, even for people who wouldn't dream of going to a movie or a restaurant alone, is a solitary act.

But what if the two of you share a guide? Doesn't that puncture all this solitude?

Well, unless there's a new breed of guides that I don't know about, he figures you'll each assume that he's with the other if he isn't with you, so after dropping off one of you and then the other, and seeing that you're all set to fish, he's off picking blueberries. After that, finding him is about as easy as catching a waiter's eye.

So anyway, there you are alone with your fishing, alone with your thoughts, except that most of the time you aren't even aware of having any thoughts, and your only companionship is afforded, optimistically, by the fish, or pessimistically by whatever other wildlife you find yourself unable to avoid.

Well, what do you *do,* all this time you're supposedly fishing . . .

Lady, if you have to ask questions like that, you're not only in the wrong book, you got it off the wrong shelf. What you do when you're fishing, unless you're Lee Wulff or A. J. McClane or, in your case, Mrs. The Same, is just the best you can, knowing that it's hardly ever good enough, and that even when it is, it won't last—the fly that takes today, out of the dozens you try, and the hundreds of casts that you make trying them, is almost guaranteed not to take tomorrow. And even the experts can get skunked, and often do, even as you and I. It's just that they figure we'd be bored hearing about it, I guess, that keeps them from devoting more of their time to that aspect of the subject.

Goodness, I had no idea—but if it's so terrible, then why do you keep coming back . . .

Oh, madame, would that I could give you the definitive answer to that. Herbert Hoover said it was for fun, and to wash your soul, and I don't say he was altogether wrong, but I can't forget that he was less than altogether right about a number of things. Many others have supplied a variety of answers to this one question of why should a man go fishing, not once but again and again, as long as he is able, and while seeing some truth in all of them I don't find in any a strong enough mainspring, as a propellant to action, to account for the insensate desire to go fishing, not only every so often, but as often as possible.

I don't gamble, but I realize that many do. One woman at a time has always been all I could wholeheartedly devote myself to, though I know many men who collect them as I have collected books and fiddles (and oddly enough, those men invariably had the most heartbreakingly beautiful wives). Nor have I ever courted danger as some men do, even to the degree of a manic compulsion. In this respect, the example of my Mennonite forebears, with their abhorrence of violence, has filtered down to make me a logical candidate for the religious persuasion of Practicing Coward. But I recognize in these, and several other more or less similar drives, the same irresistible pull that keeps me, and so many like me, coming back for more, although the fish do their level best to persuade us that the game is not worth the candle.

What brings us back, I am convinced, is its glorious uncertainty. All of us, even the experts, would be bored blind in no time at all if all our little tricks worked every time we essayed them. It is the fact that they do work, just tantalizingly often enough to maintain our interest, but never with enough consistency to build up any sort of self-confidence, that keeps us coming back for more.

We do it, I know in my own case and in that of a number of others, when we have what most people would consider a lot of better things to do. We go right on doing it, though many of us become so discouraged that we swear, almost nightly, to give it up and go in for something like tatting instead, but we never really mean it, and we know it as we say it, just as we are not consciously invoking any deity every routine time we swear.

I fish most nights now, from April through October, and all weekend mornings the year round, since I have a fishing club not five minutes from my house. I am seldom skunked mornings, even in the depth of winter, but nights are another story. I'm sure that if a careful count were kept, it would show that over the last five years my evenings have been just a little more often fishless than not.

Since I never keep the fish I catch anyway, a realist might well ask what difference it makes. But the difference is enormous to me. When I have cajoled a trout of better than two pounds weight into taking my fly, what though it may have taken me ten minutes or more to revive him, after he has knocked himself out in an acrobatic display, to the degree that I can safely let go of his tail and let him swim away none the worse for the encounter, that night I will go home literally on wings of song and ready to lick my weight in no matter what. Conversely, if he and his peers have snooted all my enticements, over a stretch of three hours or more, I go home doubting every last and least fact of my entire existence, beginning with the fact that

I ever caught so much as a minnow in all my life. Memory is such a whimsical liar, telling us more often than not what we'd like to remember, rather than what actually happened, so I begin to doubt even the most memorable fish of my life. Maybe they all got away, and I never actually landed and released a single one of them, but just dreamed I did, including the four-and-a-quarter-pound brown trout that's mounted above the mantel in the one room in the house I call my own. How do I know he's real, and not an illusion, if I can't catch a damn thing now?

At moments like these, part of the mood that failure has induced is the firm belief that even if, unlikely as it now seems, I ever did catch a fish in my life, this in no way diminishes the now obvious certainty that I will never catch another.

For how else can I react appropriately to the awful ignominy of being skunked, as sometimes happens, for three nights in a row, on the very same water where I've sometimes, in the same three-hour span, taken and released as many as three dozen trout?

This ability to react with appropriate emotions, both to success and failure, is undoubtedly the greatest common denominator of all the assorted odd fellows who fish for the salmonids, trout and salmon, and their near-equals, though at times actually far their superiors in moodiness and unpredictability, the black bass.

If it weren't for the very real and always present possibility of complete and abject failure, these fish would long ago have lost the lifelong fascination with which they enthrall those who fish for them.

So great must our respect for our quarry become, through years of finding out how hard it is to repeat our successes with them, that even at the headiest moments of successful fishing, there is bound to be some awareness of the fact that this much joy must have its price, that will be paid in future periods of protracted fishlessness.

Last week, for instance, I was lucky enough to take a trout of better than four pounds on each of three successive evenings, and in fact two of them on the second night of the three, for as good a run of luck as anybody has a right to expect. But even as I saw the fly slurped up, each of those four times, I could see in my mind's eye, just as vividly, the sight of that same fish, in that same spot, under the same conditions, turning his head away from that same fly, with a movement exactly as deliberate as the one with which he now took it. And sure enough, this week, for three nights running, I haven't been able to stir up a strike from so much as a sunfish, though I've tried everything—in fact, much more than I had to try—that I did so successfully those three nights last week.

Wouldn't you think that frequent enough repetition of such patterns of performance and behavior would in time bring a philosophical acceptance, that would let defeat be shrugged off as lightly as victory? Well, yes, you would—if you weren't a fisherman. But any angler knows that we have to keep going back, to the stream or the lake or the pond, wherever it may be that out hearts are hung up, if only to put to proof the deep-seated conviction that we're going to get skunked again.

I remember my father's amused report of a fellow worker's remark, when I was knee-high to next to nothing, "Well, here it is Saturday, and I'll be going out to get drunk tonight, and, gee, how I dread it."

It didn't mean anything to me at the time, which must be the only reason I would have filed it away in my then uncrowded memory for future reference, but today I can see how it would jut with meaning, for a drunk or for an angler, or I suppose—though here I lack the feel—for a compulsive gambler. Probably all three of the addicts here bracketed could say with equal conviction, "Why, hell, I could quit just like that, if I had to."

As Mark Twain said of the ease of giving up smoking, "Nothing to it—I've done it again and again."

But while it's true that the only certainty in angling is its uncertainty, still it must be an oversimplification to attempt to ascribe all its charm to that one rather bleak fact. If that's all there is, then we could all get it over with much more quickly, by the simple expedient of taking up Russian roulette instead.

So for another try at a one-word isolation of the germ, I'll take a chance on *companionship*.

Part Two

THE COMPANIONSHIPS OF ANGLING

HERE AGAIN, IT'S NOT AS SIMPLE AS IT SOUNDS. SOME of the best anglers I know would have to be given very low odds in the Curmudgeon Sweepstakes. You can hate almost everybody and very nearly everything and still be a born fisherman. Look at Thoreau. Probably one of the greatest againsters of all time.

As a case of trying on the shoe to see if it fits, I look at myself as a prospective angling companion. Though I might rate myself as Sunny Jim incarnate, still I've had enough of my own company, over almost all of the allotted three score and ten, to realize without any very extensive comparative shopping that there must be better bargains around. Yet I go fishing all the time. Surely it can't be for the joy of my own company, which in any case I could have under much less strenuous circumstances.

But as Uncle Thad Norris best pointed out, better than a life-time ago, in the chapter devoted to "The Pleasures of Solitary Fly Fishing" in his 1864 volume, *The American Angler's Book,* and as we've all seen in actual practice, fishing is essentially a solo sport. What comes before and after may not be, but the fishing itself is.

Although I fish alone much more of the time than when there's anybody else around and have never felt that fishing had to be shared to be enjoyed, still I must admit that, if there were some practical way to count and measure my thought processes while I fish, it would show that I think much more about other people than I do about myself. And I'm sure I'm not unique, or even unusual, in this respect.

We all tend to do a certain amount of reading about any subject in which we have developed more than a casual interest, and also there's a certain inevitability, if you do anything long enough and often enough, that you're going to meet a number of people who are doing it too. So unless you're hiding out somewhere as a fugitive from justice or are a downed airman on an atoll, living off a survival kit, you don't have to be either a chronic joiner or a rampant extrovert to find that there's an inescapable element of companionship in your fishing, however solitary you may be in its actual practice.

I never, in a sense, fish alone, in that a good share of the time, even before dawn and after dark, I'm apt to be fishing "with" somebody. It may be somebody I've never known, nor ever will, or it may be somebody I have known but will never see again. Since it's with somebody who is in any case absent from the actual scene of my fishing, my own more than middle age and the law of averages team up to furnish the likelihood that it is somebody who is no longer living. But that's only natural, in any event; you can learn more from the dead than from the living, if only because there are so many more of them. But I still don't mean that all my fishing is "down among the dead men." I'm as ready as the next to take a tip from a passing stranger, when I'm somewhere out on a stream. And a great deal of my fishing is done with people, dead or alive, with whom I have fished in the past and, in the latter instance, undoubtedly will fish again, but are in any case not around right now.

Lately, for instance, I've fished quite a lot with Preston Jennings. Tiny, his widow, knows this, and I think rather wistfully envies me for it. She gave me his own copy of *A Book of Trout Flies,* but that will have to be between us, because she made me promise that I wouldn't tell anybody that she had done it, and except for this I really haven't. There were so many guys around hounding her for it that she solved the dilemma by giving it to me. But she more or less abrogated the secrecy pact herself by inscribing it to me for him, as naturally he hadn't autographed his own copy. My own copy of *A Book of Trout Flies* is the original Crown reprint, which was all I could find back in 1953 when he first gave me some *Isonychia bicolor* nymphs to try on the Esopus, and his copy of it constituted my sole Derrydale Press item in my motley collection of well-thumbed and dog-eared books on angling, as I was always interested in fishing books for "eating on the spot," so to speak, rather than as collector's items. I always felt the same about flies, for that matter, which is a pity because I long ago used up the original Jennings nymphs, which the Museum of American Fly Fishing would today be ready to give an arm for, doing with them what Preston tied them for and meant me to do with them, which was fish with them. I did have the sense, after Jennings died in February of 1962, to have some more tied up. Dick Kahil, at the Rainbow Lodge in Mount Tremper where Preston first gave me one to try at night after dinner, remembered the pattern, and he had Dick Grossenbach make me some. I've since been supplied with copies of these copies by Dave Washburn of Ridgewood, but that was only after my "rediscovery" of the fly this past winter.

I keep things like a magpie and I'm never surprised, if I rummage long enough in my vest, to come across flies that are anywhere from ten to twenty years old. (What am I saying, I found some spiders in an inside pocket the other day that were last used—and to get a double on them at that—in Austria in 1956.) So shortly after four in the morning, with the air temperature at four degrees above zero and the water temperature in our spring ponds at the Joe Jefferson Club in Saddle River at its year round fifty-five degrees, I found myself wondering what fly might tempt a trout that would be as big an idiot as I to be up and about at that hour. It was the twenty-second of February, and a holiday, so I had several hours in which to try to resolve the question.

At first I tried streamers, on the logical assumption that nothing else could be expected to convey much verisimilitude to the trout at that hour and that temperature at that season. I persisted longest with a size twelve Royal Coachman streamer, because it was the only thing I tried on which I felt any sort of bump as I retrieved it. It could have been a twig or a clump of fallen leaves, of course, but on the other hand it just might have been a fish. Normally you can see a fish following a streamer in this particular pond, but not between four and five of a February morning, when the fishing is pure Braille.

Encouraged by the bump on the Royal Coachman streamer, at a time when, for all you or I could tell the difference, any streamer might be any color, like a Model T Ford, so long as it was black, I thought of Preston Jennings's theories about the relative low visibility, in the eyes of fish, of the red end of the spectrum, and remembered how I had stained the kitchen sink of the house in Greenwich Village, dying leaders with purple Tintex, trying to prove his contention that a reddish leader tippet of 2- or 3X was no more visible to a trout than a transparent one of 5- or 6X.

All the experiment ever proved, in my experience, was that trout won't take anything, no matter how fine the tippet or what color, when they're not taking, and that they'll take anything, no matter how coarse the tippet is or what color, when they're determined to take. In this trout show a strong family resemblance to salmon, which will elude your fly though you practically foul-hook them with it, until the moment they decide to take it, when you couldn't get it away from them fast enough to avoid their seizing it if you tried.

Ha, I thought, I've caught old Preston in a contradiction, because if he's right that they can't see red as well as other colors, then how come he touted the *Isonychia bicolor,* a reddish nymph, which he insisted was "the nymph phase of the Royal Coachman," for a time of failing light?

At this hour the light was worse than failing; it was failed. I had to go up to the clubhouse to get warm, anyway, and while I was there

I could take advantage of the light in the kitchen to hunt through my flies. I decided to give the search as much time as it would take to heat the water for a cup of freeze-dried coffee, and sure enough, before it had approached the boil I had found one of Dick Grossenbach's copies of the Preston Jennings *Isonychia bicolor*. It had been over ten years since they had been tied, and probably well over half that time since I had last tried one. They had never really worked for me again, at least not with that marvelous efficacy they possessed the first time I had used one, that night below the Five Arch bridge on the Esopus back in 1953, and I had gradually got out of the habit of using them.

I tied one on now and went back down to the spring pond, where I could barely see the bare branches of the trees on the opposite bank, toward which I now cast. The first three slow retrieves failed to elicit a touch, and I was about to give up when I remembered that Preston had spoken of the *Isonychia bicolor* as a free-swimming nymph, and I decided to try retrieving it at the cantering mid-speed you would give a wet fly, as opposed to the fast trot to gallop that you would give a streamer. This time it drew a bump, though of such an inconclusive nature, more of a touch than an actual tug, that it could easily have been caused by brushing past some underwater obstacle. But on the next try all doubt was dispelled by the fact that a soft tap was followed by a strong pull, as a really heavy fish began to move away with my fly. I let him go, without tugging to get any feel of his size, but knowing that I could safely prod him a bit whenever he stopped, because in the predawn streamer fishing I had started out with a 4X tippet that I had not fined down now in putting on the nymph. From the vigor of his first pull I figured him to be a fish of perhaps fourteen to fifteen inches, but I was unprepared for the huge heave that he gave, jarring my shoulder through the slender length of my little Hardy bantam rod (the one-ounce, four-and-a-quarter-foot Royal Crown Phantom that alas they've stopped making), followed by a splash that sounded like the belly flop of a two-hundred-pound policeman. It was still too dark to see him, though I could make out the white of where the water boiled about fifty feet from the bank where I stood, but I still had to sense rather than see his next two jumps, although each time I could see the water go white.

I laid the rod down now, feeling pretty sure that after surviving three jumps the hold of the hook could be trusted while I ran to get the net in the little lean-to shelter where it is kept, and fingered the net's throat as I came back with it, to make sure I had the right one, with the built-in spring scale, so I could get some idea of his weight if I managed to land him.

I had to let him run five times before I could get him close enough to even try to net him, and the first two runs were worthy of a grilse. By the time I finally had him, it was just light enough to make out the markings on the clockface of the scale at the base of the net's handle, and I saw that the scale registered zero. In other words, this fish that I was pretty sure was the biggest I'd ever caught in five years of fishing these ponds, was a weightless wonder. It weighed zero pounds and no ounces.

I was just beginning to wonder whether perhaps I might not in fact be home in bed and dreaming such a surreal impossibility as that, when it dawned on me that, of course, at four degrees, the scale's spring was either frozen or its indicator needle was. I tried, first, to free the spring by slapping the net's handle smartly, but nothing happened, so I tried freeing the needle, from its adherence to the zero mark, with my fingers, and all that accomplished was to snap the needle right off.

Now that it was too late, it occurred to me that it would have been more sensible to try heating the scale with my cigarette lighter's flame, but now that the needle was gone there was no way left to indicate the weight, even if that idea had proved to be more practical than the first two things I'd tried.

I couldn't let a fish of this size go back into the water without first obtaining some vital statistic about it, so I decided to settle for its length, and got out a pocket tape measure from my fishing jacket.

Before risking removal of the fish from the net, however, I thought it would be a good idea to take it up to the upper right-hand pond, the only one of the three the club has that it restricts to fly fishing only. I didn't want to put it back only to have it caught again, on a salmon egg or a spinning lure, by somebody who might regard it as a suitable centerpiece for a fish dinner.

When I had it out on the bank of the upper pond, I began to doubt the evidence of my senses again, as I had to uncoil the steel tape past eighteen, nineteen, twenty, twenty-one, and even twenty-two inches, before reaching a point that spanned from jaw to tail. It was still not light enough to make out the fine lines of the fractional markings of the inches, so holding my finger on the exact spot, I had to light my lighter to read it. It was just a quarter of an inch short of the twenty-three-inch mark.

My best previous catch had been a rainbow, like this one except that it was a male, on opening day in 1970, that had measured twenty-one-and-five-eighths inches. There had been a lot of clamoring for that one, as there always is for every fish of any size on opening days, so I had let it go, to be taken home by whichever claimant wanted it most, and never had a chance to learn its weight. But the one fish Janie ever had mounted for me, a deep-bodied brown, ran four-and-a-quarter pounds although it exceeded the twenty-inch mark only by one-eighth, so that gives you some idea of what this fat female rainbow might weigh that went from one pond to another in the freezing dawn of Washington's Birthday, 1972. Certainly a lot more than four pounds, on a four-degree day.

Trout that size go into much deeper shock, after expending their much stronger efforts to get away, than the little ones do, and it was nearly twenty minutes, after first easing this one into the water, that I first felt confident enough of her future well-being to let go of the grip I had on her tail. Too often, in their addled state of confusion, like a just-knocked-out prizefighter, they will still come to enough to experience a panicky realization of being in some alien grasp and will try to swim away before they are really fit to travel alone. That's all right when you're wading in a stream, because you can almost always go along behind them and right them again if they keel over and hang helplessly below the surface, after swimming groggily some ten or twelve feet, but not in a pond where that puts them beyond your reach with a net or even a rake.

It was only after I had let this one tug a half-dozen times to shake its tail free from the clamp of my grip that it occurred to me that I had neglected to get its girth, along with its length, so that's an omission

I'll have to correct whenever I'm lucky enough to catch that fish again.

I've been trying ever since, before daylight, and again just before dark, whenever the failing light suggests the use of an *Isonychia* nymph, and more often than not, that fly will produce a strike, at those in-between moments of emerging and receding daylight, when it's really more night than day, though it very seldom seems to elicit any interest at any other time. But in those two changeover times, when the fishing generally seems to show something of a lull (unless it's one of those off days when it's so bad that you have no way to notice any difference), the *Isonychia bicolor* does seem to possess some unique attraction, and I won't let that moment pass, at either end of the day now, without giving it a chance.

Preston Jennings didn't include his dressing for it in *A Book of Trout Flies* because he hadn't figured it out by the time of writing that, but he did give it in an article he wrote for *Esquire* (July 1956) called "There *is* a Royal Coachman," and if it's any use to you, here it is:

TAIL:	Brown partridge
BODY:	A mixture of claret and dark-red seal's fur
THORAX:	Peacock herl
RIBBING:	Round gold tinsel
HACKLE:	A few turns of red or furnace cock's hackle
HOOK:	A No. 8 or 9 Sproat

There's a certain conversational value in it, too, even if you never use the fly. It's such a great put-down item, just to answer airily, "Oh, *Isonychia bicolor*," with the optional additive of only a touch of a supercilious sneer, when some unlettered citizen asks you, "Hey, bud, what're they takin' mostly?" because it always seems to produce such a classic double take of puzzled, almost frightened, stupefaction. I suppose it would be a bit more prudent to be sure of pronouncing it properly, but on ears that have neither ever heard of it or anything anywhere near the like of it, such a nuance is probably not too important.

I'm not even sure that I say it right, come to think of it. I say *Eye-so-nigh-kee-ya high-ko-lor*, just because that's the way Preston Jennings said it, the night he first gave me one, but I've heard *Eee-so-nee-chee-ya bee-color* too, so maybe the difference is like that between the ways Englishmen and Americans pronounce Latin. Our professors have always followed the Germans in this respect, whereas the English are a law unto themselves in their system of Latin pronunciation. Nobody seems to know how the Romans pronounced it when it was new, so there's no obviously higher authority around to consult, unless you think contemporary Italians have an inherited superiority, and they all seem to Italianize Latin phrases. So it stays, as far as I can see, in the same category with *eether, eyether,* and *ayether.* Anyway, to anybody who's never heard of it, you might as well say *Ish kabibble,* for all the response you'll get to *Isonychia,* however you say it.

Its pronunciation is probably a lot less important than its presentation, in any event, and of course that goes for every fly in the box. Preston always stressed giving it a lively swimming action, as opposed to the dead drift in the current. But in pond fishing, such as my use of it at the club, there seems to be some value in slowing it down to almost motionless suspension in the water, some six to ten inches below the surface. The slightest of twitches, amounting in succession to the slowest retrieve ordinary human patience will permit, seemingly enhances its attraction where an unduly rapid retrieve only seems to arouse suspicion of it. As against this, however, I've had trout take it when I was reeling in, after deciding to call it a day—but who hasn't, and on practically any fly you can name?

The maddening thing, not only about this fly but sooner or later about virtually every fly you ever get to depend on too much, is that from one minute to the next it can lose its efficacy. After that cold Washington's Birthday morning, I beat the ponds to a froth with the *Isonychia,* to a point where I was becoming a Johnny One-Note, and probably making the trout heartily sick of the sight of it.

That was shortsighted of me, I should think, because it stands to reason that any fly's effectiveness must be reduced by overexposure, and particularly in ponds where fish don't see the ever-changing array of possibly edible objects that a stream carries, and especially at a premature time like February and early March before nature begins to provide the crowds of insect life among which the *Isonychia* could mingle and thus insure itself against becoming too conspicuous. But it did keep working for me, night after night and early Saturday and Sunday mornings, for the next few months, until finally, like any good thing, it began to acquire the contempt bred of overfamiliarity. For a matter of some weeks now it hasn't worked at all, however I manipulate it. Obviously it has earned a rest, but I will never again, after the success it has had this past spring, let·it lie in a box unnoticed for another half decade.

"Cast your fly with confidence" is probably the most valuable single thing Theodore Gordon ever said, if we but have the wit to interpret it in such a way as to benefit fully from its meaning. There's no question that your expectations of a certain fly are a large part of the reason why it will produce for you (when it does) and the same thing can work in reverse. We all tend, for insufficient reasons, to get too high on some flies and too down on others. I wouldn't give you the time of day for a Muddler Minnow, for instance, though I can remember a time when, stiff with Mucilin, and hence diving and bobbing on the surface in a fast retrieve, a Muddler had the effect of a veritable Pied Piper, leading swarms of rainbows to chase after it, and then one after another of them to pounce on it, like a cat on a ball of yarn, when it moved fast enough that it appeared to be about to get away. But I can also remember one night when Al McClane and I, in a canoe on a lake near the Upper Beaverkill, kept trying for hours to repeat that experience, and got an ignominious skunking for our pains. I've since watched other anglers fish a Muddler as if it were a nymph, with the slowest of slow retrieves, and pick off one rainbow after another. But let me just start playing Monkey See Monkey Do, on such an occasion, and even once or twice with the very same Muddler, and for me it goes on strike, and won't produce a thing no matter how I fish it.

"Moderation in all things," Theodore Gordon probably should have added, though perhaps he assumed we'd have sense enough to take that for granted. For it is one thing to "cast your fly with confidence," which probably helps you to make the cast with greater care, and keeps you more alert, as you fish it out, for the strike that you so confidently expect, but it is quite another to go on flailing the water with it for hours on end, determined to make it work again just because it worked yesterday.

Of the two extremes, it would probably be better to start out with the assumption that the very fact that it did work yesterday *reduces* its chances of working today, so it would be better to invest some of that confidence in a fly that you haven't given a fair chance, after this one has shown that it no longer possesses yesterday's magic.

About the only certainty, other than uncertainty, in fly fishing is that a fly won't catch fish if it stays in its box. There's no sure way to guarantee its success, but that's the one sure way to implement its failure.

Knowing this, I ought to try to pace myself to use some of the flies that I now consistently pass over, when I'm reaching for one of my favorites. If I would do this regularly, I feel sure it would reduce the number of my fishless nights. But my big trouble is that I overreact to both success and failure.

Let me catch a four-pounder on no matter what fly and I'm ready to make that fly the foundation of a new religion, and I'm chucking it at every poor fish in sight for the next month, until I make them all so sick of the sight of it as to obviate its last chance of enticing any of them. I've done this with the Montana nymph, the Zug Bug, the little Royal Coachman streamer, and most recently with a New Zealand streamer called Mrs. Simpson. The latter is one of three patterns featured in a mail-order offering that must have been made to all the fishing clubs in the country, and in the case of the Joe Jefferson Club, the treasurer, who gets all such mail along with the bills, gave it to me. He did it without saying why, but presumably under the assumption that I am the club's likeliest sucker for anything new, and sure enough I sent off the next day for a dozen of these "proven trout killers," as advertised, at a dollar apiece.

Better I should have sent them the twelve bucks as a nondeductible goodwill contribution, telling them to keep the flies, but of course

I had no way of knowing that at the time. Back they came, in the assorted selection, four each of the Red Setter, Mrs. Simpson, and Parson's Glory patterns.

Since it had top billing in the folder that came with the flies, I naturally tied on the Red Setter first, and I was underwhelmed by the reaction. Not a touch, not a swirl, and no least sign of a follow. So I switched to Mrs. Simpson, and each of the three ponds literally exploded. I took four big fish on as many casts, each in a totally different direction. It was a bitch in heat, bringing the hounds running from all sides, and Bob Traver, with whom I share the fishing most nights, yelled down from the far end of the upper pond.

"My God, what're you throwing at them, pellets?"

So I gave him one, and for the next hour there was hardly a moment that one of us wasn't fighting a fish, and most of the time we both were. The only pause was the momentary one, at about the halfway point, for him to pull out and me to pocket the twelve dollars for a dozen for him. (I decided I couldn't do with fewer than two dozen for myself.)

The next night Ricky was there, so I gave him one, too, and Mrs. Simpson's second night's performance, with three of us now sharing the fun, was almost as sensational as the debut. Rickenberg, whose first name is the most frequently encountered among fishermen everywhere, Charles, ties flies himself, as Traver and I don't, and he promised to hurry home and try to make some copies of the one I had given him. This was almost certainly going to be a needed precaution, as we were catching some pretty big trout, and inevitably one of us was going to be broken off on virtually any cast, as some of our biggest specimens can snap any leader fine enough to fool them as if it were made of wet Kleenex.

That happened the next night, when Traver hooked the Dean of the upper pond, an old brown so big that he constitutes the equivalent of a written warranty that the upper pond now harbors no little fish. That fish was close to five pounds when I put him in there a little over a year ago, when we were restocking it, but he must have elephantiasis, because now he sails in every so often, like a battleship joining a flotilla of cruisers, and he makes the others, that run from four to four and a half, look puny. The closest to an equal he has in that pond is my Washington's Birthday fish, but that's a rainbow, and I've never yet chanced to see them close enough to each other to have any very good idea of the extent to which he outweighs her.

So I gave Traver our one remaining Mrs. Simpson, on the understanding that he would keep it the hell out of that pond until the new order came or until Ricky could come up with some reasonable facsimiles of it.

This was proving difficult, as Mrs. Simpson's exotic plumage gives the overall impression of a pigeon's neck, and Ricky's fly-tying materials were relatively austere. He was unable to resolve this shortage at the time, and only overcame it quite recently when, having reached the conclusion that his need was for feathers of a millinery rather than culinary nature, he persuaded his wife to sacrifice an heirloom in the shape of a toque, a great-aunt's Edwardian hat.

But there are some pretty mammoth fish in the other two ponds, too, and all three of us had lost our Mrs. Simpsons to them before the new supply arrived the following week.

The reason we can be so sure of the size of the fish in the upper pond is that its spillway boards, connecting it to the lower spring pond, where the main spring is, gave way during a flash flood last year, when for a few hours all three of our ponds were submerged beneath an inundation that transformed their terrain into that of one great ugly brownish-yellow lake. When the waters went back to normal we found that all the fish in the upper pond had taken advantage of the break to crowd in around the big spring in the lower pond, which naturally was the first of the three to get its customary crystal color restored. That made it irresistible to the fish in the still clouded and crummy upper pond, and every night for weeks thereafter we toted every sizable fish back up to the empty pond that we caught in either the lower spring pond or the big pond that lies alongside both the spring ponds. That one, almost a city block long, is fed by both the smaller ponds and in turn flows over a dam into the adjacent Saddle River. Traver and Ricky and I kept count, and so did Gene Anderegg and one or two of the other members, and every time one of us put a fish into the upper pond, from either of the others, we informed the other scorekeepers, until we satisfied ourselves that we had restored more than two hundred fifty fish. After that we stopped counting, but we've all made it a practice, ever since, to put all the most noteworthy catches up there.

Every so often a guest, or even one of our own unreconstructed members, will haul out a prize of better than three-and-a-half pounds, and none of us can quite muster up the nerve to suggest that the upper pond, since it is restricted to fly fishing only, would afford the happiest of homes for it. The suggestion would almost always be academic, in any case, by the time we could bring ourselves to making it, since people who take fish on salmon eggs or spinning lures usually kill them at the moment of capture, in a follow-through act that appears to be a foregone conclusion.

When the new supply of Mrs. Simpson streamers came, although I had in the meantime taken a fish or two on the Parson's Glory—though never a thing on the Red Setter—Traver resumed taking fish with his, like one going on with a conversation in mid-sentence after an interruption, but I have yet to take another, on my own double portion of the treasure.

Last night, for instance, I stood watching, up to my eyeballs in envy, while he pulled in eight fish on it. Not that I stood idle; I was trying it myself, at least from his third fish on, but the trout seemed unaware of it, on the end of my tippet, while avid as ever for it on his. I might better have had a bare hook, as then I might have snagged one of them, on their way to keep the rendezvous with his.

Whenever this happens to me and it happens fairly often, I have only one recourse, and that is to get as far away as possible, both from the type and the size of fly, as well as the method of fishing it. In short, to start over—acting as if I hadn't been fishing at all up to this point, and choosing a fly as if it were my first choice of the day.

It used to be that I would "start over," to try to break this jinx of fishlessness, by simply going back to a Montana nymph. I had great success with that, both in size fourteen and in size ten, when I first joined the club, and I gave some to Traver and Ricky. Traver's luck with it was phenomenal, or call it skill if luck sounds grudging, but in any case he took more and bigger fish on the Montana than anybody else in the club was taking, including those who invariably after a dozen casts with a fly resorted to the use of the spinning rod and hardware. My original supply of Montanas had come from Orvis, but Traver began getting them tied by Dave Washburn, the local cop, and Ricky began making copies himself. Between these two new sources of supply, augmenting those I had been giving out myself, within a very short time everybody in the club who deigned to try flies at all had begun to use the Montana nymph, including some of the less fly-minded, who began to resort to it on those occasions when the trout consistently refused spinning lures. By the time Gene Anderegg joined, the use of the Montana nymph was so prevalent that he said, "That fly seems to be the Joe Jefferson worm."

I had started similar runs on the Zug Bug and the little Royal Coachman streamer, but they were short rallies compared to the sustained and continuing boom of the Montana nymph.

But each new member seems to have his turn acting as a sort of new broom, making a clean sweep with something the others haven't tried, or in any case haven't been concentrating on of late, and there's a consequent run on it, unless and until somebody else sets up a more successful competing attraction.

Gene Anderegg had been a junior member of the club back in the late thirties, when he won national casting championships in his teens, but I brought him in as an adult member, over thirty years later. When he first began to fish the ponds, covering every corner of even the largest one with his effortless tournament-style casts, he had everybody agog over his success with a small Mickey Finn. After casting it a country mile, he would retrieve it as fast as he could haul it in, setting up a momentum that was greater than the speed you reach when you reel in after you've decided to call it a day, and the procession of trout that would follow this spectacular attraction, like urchins milling about behind the calliope in the old-fashioned circus parade, would often be rudely broken up by some old lunkers, brought by the strange sight from their distant and secluded lies, literally bunting their juniors out of the way in their eagerness to capture the cause of all the commotion.

But though Gene Anderegg seems able to perform this feat

whenever he feels like trying it, most of the other members who tried it soon grew arm-weary of the constant rapid tugging that it takes. The gambit is still occasionally employed, but usually as a last resort.

Another new member, Vean Geyer, started a brand-new run on that old standby the Muddler Minnow, but by giving it the exact opposite of the treatment Gene accorded his flying Mickey Finn. In this instance, the trick was to retrieve the Muddler not like the streamer that it is, but as if it were a nymph, letting it sink, and then inching it back so slowly as to keep it barely suspended in the water by the line and moving just enough to keep it from touching the bottom.

Here again, however, the success of the technique achieved by those who took it up after watching Vean Geyer do it was never as great as that of the method's initiator. By contrast, in no time at all every man jack in the club was catching more on the Montana nymph than I was. This realization was brought home to me on opening day in 1970, when I was getting royally skunked while all about me were my peers pulling in fish, and most of them on Montana nymphs. I put on a Zug Bug, in the contest's waning minutes, and managed to pull in the fish that won, at twenty-one-and-five-eighths inches, just as Doc Dieter, an old British Navy man, was readying his Verey Light pistol to signify the end of the morning's fishing. There was a lively run on Zug Bugs, though not for very long, immediately after that.

The conclusion is inescapable that any fly, subjected through sudden overexposure to the static population of these sequestered ponds, will quickly lose the novelty of appeal that it has when first presented.

One answer to this is to bring in new fish. For a little while at least, after the ponds have had their resident populations increased by the addition of new arrivals which are, compared to the jaded old settlers, eager wide-eyed tourists, the fishing picks up markedly. The eagerness of the new fish seems highly contagious, and for a couple of weeks after the ponds have been newly stocked, the old fish are stimulated into striking much more readily. Then they too settle down, and the doldrums resume, as the new fish become blasé too.

There's no sure-fire solution to this dilemma. Some react to it by retreating to the terrace and pitching horseshoes. At least the horse-shoes are there and can be picked up without hours spent hunting for them, as is too often the case with the fish. And for some tempera-ments, getting a ringer in quoits is as satisfying as tying into a big trout. Others are content to sit on the porch, with Tom Collins or Jack Daniels or Johnnie Walker, of whom at least it can be said that they are showing more willingness to please you than those damn trout will ever exert. Still others are driven to the assumption that the fishing far away will at least seem better, as most far-off things do, than at home. So trips to Iceland or the Maritime Provinces, or Montana and Wyoming, or Alaska or Argentina, are always looming up, and when they eventuate they provide fodder for the visual beguilement of winter evenings, in the shape of movies and slides to be shown in the clubhouse on Wednesday nights after dinner.

But some of us would go on fishing these ponds, with or without encouragement from the fish. The feeling about fishing is a lot like that about sex, that of course it's better when it's good, but it's not bad even when it isn't.

And for some, it must be realized, there's even a lot of fun in thinking about it. This last element must account, in large part, for what keeps us everlastingly at it. The number of fishless days, it seems, can never be great enough to cure us of this addiction.

Of course, the more you fish, the sooner you reach that stage where you'd rather put the fish back, for somebody else to catch, or simply to catch them again yourself, than take them home to eat, or even to have mounted, for the subsequent amazement of all and sundry. Most wives, for one thing, are less than ecstatic over mounted fish as elements of home decoration, and, for another, people who mount fish are nowadays even harder to come by than fish that merit being mounted.

You'd think, then, that as long as we're not going to keep the fish anyway, going fishless wouldn't be such a dire fate as to warrant our being classified as hardship cases. What's so bad about being skunked, if you set out resolved to return as empty-handed as if you had been anyway? And why moan about the one that got away, when you were going to put him back again even if he hadn't?

Well, this is where the element of thinking about it enters in. It only matters, of course, if you think it does. And, boy, you find it very hard to think of anything, at least at that moment, that matters more. In fact, the great thing about fishing is that there are very few activities, that are open to all men on a virtually equal basis, that can provide you with occasions to feel quite so deeply, to care quite that much.

It's all very well for Izaak Walton to have settled the question centuries ago, on a purely philosophical basis, by reminding us that no man can be said to have lost that which he never had. On that basis, of course, there is no such thing as a lost fish. But if it doesn't exist, why does it hurt so much?

I've never felt such intense compassion for anyone in my life as I felt for Ernest Hemingway in Bimini in 1936, when a marlin, that looked the size of a tank car in the sun, got away after some thirty jumps, and the hand-forged hook, looking the size of an anchor, came back pulled out and straightened like a bent bobby pin. And if I felt that bad, then how bad did he feel?

Nature, in one of her few acts of kindness, is supposed to have made our memories of pain mercifully short. We can remember, as an abstract fact, that this or that experience caused us pain, but it is scientifically posited that our mental mechanism lacks the means of really reenacting the actual sensation of pain.

So, all right, it does stop hurting, but no man who has ever lost a truly noteworthy fish has ever forgotten it either.

By the same token, the pain of losing a good fish, after he has taken, and after you've had him on long enough to sample the fight that is in him, is a relative joy, a privilege, and an honor, compared to the awful ignominy and the bleak despair of casting hours on end and never once feeling the least tug or pull or slightest twitch, by way of response to your endless flailings.

Skunked indeed! A real live skunk, aside from being very pretty, smells downright sweet as against the ineffable stench of defeat in the fisherman's nostrils.

For the safeguarding of one's sanity under these circumstances, there are only two things to do. (Oh, I suppose there are three, if your psychic stamina as an angler is so frail that you can consider resorting, at such junctures, to the use of salmon eggs or live minnows or frogs or worms. So maybe we'd better put it on the basis that there are only two things to do that are thinkable in present company.)

First, you can go on doing what you're doing, trusting to the law of averages that after X many thousands of casts you're going to catch *something*. The only way for the sentient angler to do this indefinitely, against the steadily rising counterpressure of tedium, is by concentrating intently on the exact shape and color and size of fish you have caught in the past, making this very same cast with this very same fly in this very same spot or in a spot very nearly like this. If taking this mental inventory takes you no longer than it would take most of us, then five minutes is about all this exercise is good for. Sometimes, though very rarely, five minutes of this is enough to produce a strike. When it has happened to me, it has restored my belief in miracles. There is no reason why it should work, when for a period of anywhere from hours to days nothing has worked, but there actually have been a few times when it has. The mere routine of consciously "reenacting the crime," so to speak, of deliberately attempting to do again precisely what I have done on some previous occasion, has now and then, though admittedly very rarely, made some poor fish volunteer to serve as stand-in for that other fish that I once caught with that same cast of that same fly in that same spot. Maybe it has something to do with an unwitting resurgence of that feeling Theodore Gordon categorized in his dictum: "Cast your fly with confidence."

Much more often, of course, and in fact typically, nothing at all will happen after you've gone through this elaborate reevocation of the past, and you must resort to some other mental accompaniment to your continuing casting. So you start thinking about this fly you're using (or if that's just a dull drab nameless blob of fur or dubbing, then about this rod, or this reel, or this line or this leader) and where you got it, and who else you know who has one just like it, or where you've been when you've used it, and with whom, and what happened, or even what you've ever either read or heard about it, and before you know it you will have followed such a long trail, in this woolgathering, that you've almost forgotten where you are or what you're doing. No, you're not in anything like an actual trance, but just in pursuing a train of recollection you have shifted your concentration away from your previous intentness on the actual mechanics of what you were doing. You may, for instance, have neglected to retrieve your fly in quite as businesslike a manner as before.

This happened to me one of those afternoons in the doldrums, not long ago. I was fishing a fly, to no response whatever, when it occurred to me that I'd forgotten what it was called. It didn't matter much, since the fly was certainly doing nothing to make it memorable. But it bothered me just the same. I remembered that it was a western fly that I'd got from Peter Alport, and I thought it was called a Humpy but that it was a near twin of another western fly that had an unusual name—some sort of bug. The only bug I could think of was the Zug Bug, which I've used much more frequently than this relatively exotic number from Norm Thompson out on the coast. Bug, bug, a something bug, not a Zug Bug . . .

I even remembered using it once out west, fishing the Firehole, in Yellowstone Park, with Russ Peak, the Stradivarius of the glass rod, and remembering that I took a hell of a good brown on it, and how embarrassed I was to see Russ wince as I said so—having forgotten completely, with my language as completely unbuttoned as it always is out fishing, that Russ Peak, aside from being one of the best rod makers alive, happens also to be a minister of the gospel, and what a goof I'd made—

Goof! Goofus! That's the word, a Goofus Bug. That's the name for the other fly almost the same or even the same as a Humpy . . .

In my abstraction, trying to think of a word, I'd gone through the unconscious reflex action of taking out a cigarette and lighting it, cradling my rod in my arm as I did so, and now the rod started slithering away, the line hissing and the reel whining, and there was a splash out in the middle of the spring pond, as a three-pound brown cleared the water in what looked like a three-foot jump.

It startled me so much that for a moment I didn't realize there was any connection between the bizarre behavior of my rod and the antics of that leaping brown, and the rod was on the ground and moving rapidly toward the edge of the mall between the ponds before I had the sense to grab it and start to play the fish.

That Goofus Bug had probably been sitting there motionless on the glassy surface for somewhere between three and five minutes before that crazy brown took it into his primitive brain to jump it. From the splash, he might even have pounced down on it from above, the way trout arc down onto a spider on the surface, before taking off in that leap he was making when I first saw him.

It was only because I had become too engrossed in my thoughts, and the momentary diversion of lighting a cigarette, that I had stopped giving the Goofus Bug the intermittent twitching retrieve that I always give any dry fly on our ponds, and that I had been giving it for better than an hour before that with no result whatsoever.

There is virtually no current in our ponds, so any action a dry fly has on them must be imparted by the fisherman. Unless you twitch them, they just sit there utterly unanimated, totally unlike stream fishing where the current carries them along like little sailboats.

So a fishless day was redeemed, not by my efforts, but by my momentary neglect of them. The only fish I caught that afternoon was on the one occasion that I had for the moment stopped trying to catch one.

Normally, I'd bet that the last way to catch a fish on one of our ponds would be to throw out a dry fly like the Goofus Bug and let it sit there for a matter of minutes.

The perversity of fish can be likened, I think sometimes, to the perversity of cats. They won't come when you want them, but only when they're good and sure that it's their idea and not yours.

But that, too, was another abnormal break in the doldrums. What I normally do, when the ponds go so dead that I begin to feel like a becalmed sailor, is go over to a bench and spread out on it all the flies I've got on me, looking for the least likely candidate for success.

I never do this without musing on the habits of the magpie. I carry flies in such a snarled mass, or mess, that they might as well be worms. Those that are in my pants I stuff into those little round plastic tubes that pills come in from the pharmacy, with a plastic cover that snaps off as easily as it snaps on, with the result that a good share of the time the flies are out of the containers, and putting my hand in a pants pocket is like putting it into a briar bush. Those that are in my shirt are in a larger transparent plastic box with a hinged lid, of which the hinges are of course broken within a week after I start carrying the box, so that these flies, too, are spilled about as often as they are contained, but I keep thinking that it's handier to carry them that way than it is to keep them in orderly rows in proper fly boxes. I have the latter, too, mostly the Wheatley boxes in which, following my father's ideal of order, there is a place with a clip for each fly, and each fly is in its place. That's fine, and the pockets of my fishing vests are fitted with them, and so are those of my fishing jackets, some for trout and some for salmon, awaiting the day when I make a proper fishing trip, properly equipped.

But the trouble is that those boxes carry some thirty to forty flies each, in their rows of six or eight, whereas I can dump some three to four hundred in one shirt-pocket-size plastic box that doesn't have all those neatly ordered rows of clips. Besides, with a transparent box I can turn it over and get a "fix" on the approximate location of the particular fly I'm looking for a lot faster than I could possibly hunt through a dozen closed fly boxes.

Spreading them all out on the bench, I look for a fly that has never, to the best of my recollection, taken a fish—at least, for me—anywhere I've ever tried it. I figure that if the fish are now passing up every fly that is a logical choice for this time and place and season of the year, my one chance is to give them something utterly illogical, and to present it to them in as unorthodox a manner as I can dream up.

For example, one time in such a mood and such a predicament, I fished out a Strawman, from a tangle of other flies.

Now there, I thought, is a fly on which I've never taken a fish of any kind. Nor has Al McClane. Nor does either of us even know anybody who ever has. I remember asking Al this, and his saying that he had also asked a lot of other people. Yet we both revere the memory of Paul Young, who first devised it, and that alone would be enough, you'd think, to put the Strawman in that category of flies we would "cast with confidence."

Paul Young's been gone since early 1960, so this particular

Strawman that I tie on now must be anywhere from twelve to fifteen years old. I remember I always fished it as a nymph, which it is, giving it the slowest of slow retrieves. I remember Paul's saying that he made it in imitation of those little straw "shacks" that the caddis flies shed, as they leave the larval stage, so obviously it isn't something that ought to go skittering around like Mehitabel, but should be given as nearly no motion at all as you can possibly impart to a fly. It looks, in size and shape, about like a blackberry. He dyed them various colors, down to black, of which I remember one that was a peculiarly poisonous-looking purple, but the one I fish out now, taking a good minute and a half to unpuzzle it out of a cluster of flies with most intricately locked hooks, happens to be the natural straw color.

I decide to dap the damn thing, to give it the wildest remove from any conceivable natural behavior. I feel as foolish, for the first few minutes, as if I were plopping cherries in the pond. But as I go along the water's edge, *plop plop plop,* flailing the surface with it, I see more and more motion around it, and I keep on, working my four-and-a-quarter-foot rod up and down like a pump handle, causing the twelve-foot leader to flick the fly here and there as I go about six to seven feet out from the shore, where the water is about four feet deep. I gather, from the commotion I'm causing, that a lot of ten-to-twelve-inch trout are holding a series of meetings to consider this strangely persistent phenomenon. This is interesting in itself, not that it puts me any closer to the actual taking of a fish than I was before, when my slow retrieve of a Montana nymph was absolutely uneventful.

But stay—this next little meeting is rudely interrupted, as a mouth that could belong to a snapping turtle closes over my dapped Strawman, and a brown as long as your arm has got it and he's off with it. The yellow streak of my new Micro-Foam floating line lengthens after him until I think it's going to reach the backing, and well it might, because this is the big pond we're fishing now, and he could run for a short city block with nothing to stop him. Certainly not me, with my puny wisp of a one-ounce rod, with which I couldn't turn him even if the leader would hold for the attempt.

But just as I've enjoyed the longest run from a hooked fish that I'm likely to encounter between here and Canada, he changes direction, and from the way the line goes limp off the tip of my rod I have to assume that he's either off or coming toward me. He gives no jumps, to afford any clue, but that's good, because if he were off he'd probably jump at least once to celebrate his liberation.

So I reel in, wondering, after the slack has been taken up, why it is that I no longer feel him. There's tension on the line, but nothing like the throbbing kind there was on that first wild ride, and soon I see the reason, as out comes a clump of green gook about the size and shape of a volleyball. Peeling it away I find my Strawman in its center, good as new.

Gone is Mister Brown, who perhaps should be referred to more fittingly as Grampa Brown, but no matter. He's still there, and so am I, but my day has been made. I'm prepared now, in payment of my just debt to him, to go on casting from now until dark, without catching so much as a leaf or a twig, but the odd thing is that after an experience like this it's very seldom that I'm obliged to pay the debt that way.

When one trout has taken, particularly if it's a trout of any size, another take is very likely to follow, and within a matter of minutes now, even if there's been no action for hours. Sure enough, some thirty feet up the pond, dapping as I go, there's another interruption, and it's a solid take from a nice enough rainbow—not in the same league, of course, as the brown that just got away—and after three or four jumps he's in the net where he just barely fails to move the needle across the two-pound mark. That keeps him from qualifying for the upper pond, but he's a good fish and he'll be all right left where he is, because in the big pond they have a better chance for growth, with more natural forage than the upper pond can provide.

More or less the same thing may happen once or twice more, until Ricky comes and takes the Strawman, so he can go home and copy it. When he does, we'll have a run on the Strawman, lasting anywhere from a week to a month, and it will take fish, not only by dapping but even when fished conventionally. Then the day will inevitably come when that too succumbs to the doldrums, and it will take something else to break the jinx.

Meanwhile, Traver will show up and tie on a Montana nymph,

or some other old standby, and calmly haul in one fish after another just as if there never had been any doldrums, and in fact for him there very seldom are. Oh, I've seen him skunked, too, on more than one night, for no fisherman in the world is altogether skunkproof, but for him the fishless nights are few and far between. Some are simply luckier in this respect than others, and skill doesn't have too much to do with it. There are times when Ricky and I could kill him, as he pulls fish out from under our noses, with the very same fly that we've just found completely useless. Mrs. Simpson only happens to be the latest example, but there have been and will be others. That's all right. There's one in every club. You and I spend a great deal of time wiping the droppings off our sleeves and shoulders, but for him the birds only sing. But that's part of what keeps us coming back, for in all the uncertainty that keeps fishing endlessly fascinating, there is also the certainty that somebody will be taking fish, with the same fly and at the same moment, that you can't. Some guys have all the luck, it seems. But there has never been a time or place where it hasn't seemed that way. If the Travers of this world didn't exist, they'd have to be invented. They are needed, to keep our humility in proper balance. Traver, by the way, is his real name, but he is not to be confused with my other good friend, Judge John Voelker of the Upper Peninsula in Michigan, who first made that name famous when he wrote *Anatomy of a Murder* and later gave it renown in angling annals with *Trout Madness*.

This Bob Traver, who got me into the Joe Jefferson Club, stands six feet six and, though a grandfather now, was for many years the youngest member of the club. He is also the outstanding cook among the membership and has the same "luck" with his sauces and fillings and crusts and icings that he so consistently enjoys with his fishing. He is like an outsized Al McClane, who also very rarely gets skunked, either in fishing or in cooking.

I had thought, as so many have said, that the United States Senate was the hardest club to get into, but some of these fishing clubs must make that claim dubious. It took me three years to crack this one, and if Traver hadn't happened to be its president, I might not have made it yet. Its site is Saddle River, just above the town line of

Ho-Ho-Kus, and that's the back door of New York City. But that's only a facet of the fact that the city is what it has its back to, and as a city dweller that was something I had to live down. This I have been trying earnestly to do for the past five years, serving as the club's volunteer adjunct caretaker, feeding the fish on all weekends and holidays, working my tail off with rake and broom keeping the ponds' surfaces cleared, and in general seeking to deport myself as I always adjured my kids to do, like "a little gentleman," but there are times even now when I harbor the feeling that I might still be on probation.

The club takes its name from the fact that its grounds belonged, in the last years of his life, to the famous American actor (and fisherman) Joe Jefferson. Jefferson fished places like Henryville with the likes of Gifford Pinchot and Grover Cleveland. His name survives in the vicinity also through the existence of a local theatre group known as the Joe Jefferson Players, but as I'm kept busy explaining to people who drive in through the open gates, or call up on the phone in the lean-to down at the foot of the ponds, there is no connection between the two organizations.

The clubhouse was built in the early twenties, by Canadian loggers imported for the purpose, out of the hewn trunks of chestnut trees felled in the great blight of 1916. Jefferson himself died in 1905, and the club's one remaining link with him is slim and tenuous, in the now rather frail person of its oldest member, Charlie Ackerman, now edging up on ninety, who as a boy of nine was allowed, by Jefferson's personal permission, to fish his ponds. Charlie still fishes them, as he did then, with worms, and his favorite spot, then and now, is in the shade of a giant elm that overhangs the lower end of the biggest pond. The spillway between the spring pond and the big pond makes a little stream of current, particularly when the top board is taken off the dam that regulates the emptying of the ponds into the passing Saddle River, and it is at the foot of this great tree, on the edge of this little current, that Charlie takes his stand. Charles, as I've often mentioned, is the preeminent first name of fishermen, but Charlie harks back to old Izaak rather than to Charles Cotton, for he is and has been a meat fisherman, man and boy. He lobs his worm into that almost-current and waits for results. The rest of us almost invariably have to wait longer, including Traver, and old Charlie hauls out some mighty fish.

The club belongs to the Federation of Fly Fishermen, but not Charlie. An honorable exception will always have to be made for him. He not only doesn't fish with a fly, he doesn't even fish with a rod. Though I make ninety myself, I will always see at the foot of that tree old Charlie lobbing out his worm, and standing like a graven image, impassively waiting for the strike with not rod, but tin can, in hand. This strange device, of Charlie's own manufacture, is a retired Number Two can, of the kind canned peaches come in, around which Charlie has wound some hundred feet of eighteen-pound-test Dacron casting line, such as bait casters use when they go plug fishing for bass. To a fly fisherman this line is familiar only in the form of backing, around the core of a single-action fly reel, surmounted by the thirty yards of enameled fly line.

Charlie gives the can an underhand toss, like a pitcher in softball, or what we used to call indoor baseball, and the line goes flying, uncoiling off the can around which Charlie has wrapped it, in exact conformance to the principle of the fixed-spool spinning reel, which Illingworth invented in England and Bache Brown first popularized, around World War II time, in America.

Charlie, who finds this outlandish engine a great improvement over the conventional "fishin' pole," first got the notion from watching some "young fellers" fishing that way up in Canada, where until very recently he used to drive his trailer every summer. He is not precise about the age or origin of these youths, but whether they were fifteen or fifty-five the odds are overwhelming that they were poachers on salmon waters, fishable with fly only under Dominion law, taking advantage of the obvious fact that nothing is more expendable than an empty Number Two can, and that a coil of casting line and a hook are much more readily pocketable on the advent of a warden than any sort of fishing rod, including those pack rods, in one-foot sections, that they sell at places like Abercrombie & Fitch.

The club holds a morning fishing contest on opening day every spring, with entries classed in only two categories, fly and nonfly. Charlie Ackerman has won the latter as often as anybody.

There are other old members, too, as might be expected in a club that has been going for very nearly fifty years, and a number of second generation members and even, in one instance, a third generation member, Dave Beasley, Jr., whose grandfather was one of the founders. But not even he could say, as Charlie Ackerman still can, that he remembered Joe Jefferson.

In *The Well-Tempered Angler*, which Alfred Knopf asked me to write for his fiftieth anniversary list as "a book about the fishing life," I mentioned only one organization, aside from a passing reference to the then just-forming Theodore Gordon Flyfishers. That was in the chapter called "The Boys Upstairs at Manny Wolf's," devoted to the very informal Wednesday lunching group known for short as the Midtown Club. Its one resemblance to the Joe Jefferson Club lay in the fact that they both meet on Wednesday, weekly in the case of the Joe Jefferson club during that portion of the year when daylight saving time is in effect, and every other Wednesday night the rest of the year.

My own fishing life changed greatly not long after that other fishing book came out, with the consequence that much more of my time has been spent in connection with activities at the Joe Jefferson Club than was ever the case with Midtown. This is partly because Midtown changed more than I did.

Midtown's actual name, represented by the letters MTYPA in the emblems some of the members sometimes wore on their hats when they still wore hats, was the Midtown Turf Yachting and Polo Association. It was so named because of all the activities the members weren't very passionately devoted to, these were the ones to which they were devoted the least. Ostensibly comprised of men who were engaged more or less directly in the publicizing of hunting and fishing, the club had a roster of thirty members by the time I joined it in 1962, and was meeting in a little back room upstairs above the kitchen at Manny Wolf's restaurant on Third Avenue at Forty-ninth Street.

Formed originally as a small group of cronies of Jack Randolph, *The New York Times* outdoor columnist (he died when the club was still in its infancy), Midtown was something of an anticlub right from the start. It had no regular dues, but simply an agreement to pass the hat whenever it either became necessary or just seemed like a good idea. Since it was assumed that all the members would be likely to be engaged in a certain amount of outdoor activity anyway, whether by vocation or inclination, the Wednesdays were picked as the days when more of them might be expected to be in town than any other day. And the thought was that the weekly luncheon meetings could be devoted to talking shop, about the various sports activities that they might have in common, as well as to the planning of outings when they might engage in the further pursuit of some of these activities together.

John Groth, with whom I was doing a good deal of fishing, got me into Midtown, and as of that time there were, or at least had recently been, a number of such outings, and the weekly lunches were pretty well attended. A Wednesday gathering of around ten was par for the course, averaging about a third of the members present any given week. The head count might vary widely, for no very discernible or predictable reason, from say a low of five one week to as high as fifteen the next, but a median attendance of ten.

The food and the fellowship were both good. Members could either order drinks from downstairs, or stop in a neighborhood liquor store on their way to Manny Wolf's and bring their own bottles or half-bottles of wine, which the room waiter would either open for them and pour, or provide the facilities for serving themselves in this respect if they preferred. Hardly anybody ever showed up before twelve thirty or left much before two thirty. There was no set agenda, or programs or speeches of any kind, and while there was a president, his chief function was the capture of everybody's attention for the occasional routine announcement, such as the losing or finding of this or that item, and otherwise he neither monopolized, nor very frequently interrupted, the steady flow of conversation.

For most of the members, the club was a pleasant lunching habit, which they maintained fairly regularly unless they were kept away by an access of extreme pressure, such as a business or household crisis, or a spell of illness. A few members would grouse about some aspects of the club's service or ambiance and now and then somebody would get huffy over what he deemed the undue familiarity or excessive informality of the room's one regular attendant, the waiter Little Joe.

But there's usually something somebody takes exception to, in almost every fixed gathering place, and most of the members would have been content to go on to this day, spending most of their Wednesday noons together in the little room upstairs at Manny Wolf's.

In any case, those members who were most prone to make a scene, or raise hell about something, were the least regular in their own attendance, and the club would have suffered no irremediable loss if they had simply decided to stop coming altogether.

But no, on the principle that the squeaking wheel gets the most grease, these spoilsports were listened to, and indulged, and Midtown moved out of Manny Wolf's. It promptly began to disintegrate, because while only a few had ever been vocal in their dissatisfaction with anything at Manny Wolf's, almost everybody hated almost everything about all the places that were tried thereafter.

The first one, Janssen's, was big and busy and noisy as Grand Central Station, of which indeed it was, through one of its entrances, an integer. They kept promising to reserve a separate section of their balcony, but one Wednesday after another something unusual would happen, to prevent any one section's being set apart, and we would wind up with a couple of adjacent tables in the middle of the main floor, a fate comparable to trying to keep a couple of cockleshells bailed out and afloat in the middle of a howling storm on the open ocean.

When the patience of even the most optimistic was finally eroded, a succession of other places was tried, but none could ever provide a separate, or in any way isolated, small room that we could feel was our own, and not find ourselves dispossessed of with scant notice, if any. Midtown Manhattan is a hurly-burly on weekday noons, in which the only snug harbor is a club. We were a club without a clubhouse.

We finally found one, in the Williams Club, where Ted Rogowski had wound up, after a succession of disillusioning experiences similar to ours at Midtown, when he first splintered off from our Wednesday lunches the small group that ultimately became the Theodore Gordon Flyfishers. He and Gene Anderegg and Lee Wulff, both of whom had been as regular at Midtown as their frequent travels could let them be, had begun doubling up on their midweek habit of lunching together, finding some spot to have first a Monday, but then later a Tuesday, lunch as well. In this they were shortly joined by Ed Zern, who had given Midtown its one semblance of fame by referring to it frequently in his *Field & Stream* column as "The Madison Avenue Rod, Gun, Bloody Mary and Labrador Retriever Society." Before long this little nucleus had accreted new adherents to a point that its membership was several times as large as the parent body, Midtown's, had ever been. Their interest in Theodore Gordon had early led them to Guy Jenkins, one of the few remaining links with that frail little figure of the past who had since become so heightened by legend as the Sage of the Neversink. Jenkins, as a member of the Williams Club, was able to arrange for Rogowski and the rest to enjoy weekly guest privileges there, and the Theodore Gordon Flyfishers soon had a room there to themselves. They were allowed to decorate its walls, and fill its bookcase, with items of their own, and to treat it as the home away from home they had never found.

So, after a couple of years and a number of places since Manny Wolf's, Midtown, like the old man moving in where his more successful son has run interference for him, was finally enabled to hold its Wednesday lunches there, in the wake of the Tuesday lunches of the Theodore Gordon Flyfishers.

The trouble was that about half the membership of Midtown had by that time given up in disgust, with the result that its Wednesday lunches drew a fraction of the crowd that patronized the Tuesday Gordon meetings. The Williams Club, which had made a great pet of the Gordon group, soon found that in Midtown it had something of a problem child. They would set aside a smaller room for the Wednesday lunch, after only five had shown up for it the day after the flyfishers had had twenty, and the next week when the Gordon might have twenty-five (or even more, like the fantastic figure of forty who showed up the Tuesday I brought Charlie Ritz), the attendance at Midtown's lunch would have dropped to three, or even two. This wouldn't be enough to warrant reserving even a table in their dining room, much less one of their private rooms.

There was even a noon in one of the Williams Club rooms where nobody else showed up at all, and I had to put on the Chautauqua version of Lucullus entertaining Lucullus. The Williams Club found it even less amusing than I did.

I wrote a letter to the remaining fifteen of Midtown's quondam membership of thirty, ribbing them for letting such a thing come to pass. It was the end of the 1960s, and I had just recently come into a slight spate of extracurricular titles, and acting as secretary pro tem, I wrote the membership an account of what I presumed they would like to know of what was pretty obviously the last meeting of the Midtown Turf Yachting and Polo Association. I made it sound as if seven men—this one representing the Business Committee for the Arts, that one representing the New York Board of Trade, another the Magazine Publishers Association, and another The National Book Committee, and so on until it sounded like the stuffiest squad that ever had the misfortune to be inflicted on one another—had come to that last meeting of Midtown, along with the one guy they all knew, the publisher of *That Magazine,* and that a perfectly dreadful time was had by all. They all stood around sipping a drink, and not one of them said a blithering word, except once, in answer to the room waiter's query of whether anybody else was expected, and all *he* said was "I don't know."

After that, the attendance shot up one hundred percent, as Berni Schoenfield, shamed by my letter, kept me company the next few Wednesdays, sitting forlornly on a bench outside the guest dining room, where members of the Williams Club entertain the distaff side of their families, while a waiter looked to see if there might be someplace he could squeeze us in, as Midtown had obviously lost the right to even a table, to say nothing of a room.

So that, for a long time, seemed to be the inglorious end of Midtown, while the Theodore Gordon Flyfishers waxed ever stronger, and today has a membership up in the hundreds, after its beginning as a split-off from Midtown's onetime thirty.

The moral probably is that the Theodore Gordon Flyfishers, latching onto the mystique of one man's legend, were able to hitch it to the stars, so to speak, as the great ecology boom got under way. By playing up, and fanning, the latent interest in and concern with the environment, the Theodore Gordon Flyfishers could attract people who were not so much motivated by a desire to sit around in endless hunting and fishing bull sessions, on into the afternoon, as by an impatient urge to get something done about the way our streams and air have been befouled, and who thought they could see in the Theodore Gordon Flyfishers a ready means of expressing the feeling that they were at least and at last trying to do something about it.

Perhaps there's room for only one old-fashioned fishing club to a city, like The Anglers' Clubs, in New York and Chicago, and The Flyfishers' Club in London. Certainly there's a generation gap, as dramatic as any other, in the contrast between these older clubs and the newer organizations, such as the Theodore Gordon Flyfishers, which was begun only in the spring of 1963, and most of the groups that comprise the Federation of Fly Fishermen.

The latter, like a case of cellular division, was really in its beginning the offshoot of an offshoot. When Gene Anderegg and Lee Wulff went along with Ted Rogowski, to start having a lunch away from the lunch they'd been sharing midweeks at Midtown, they had a little more in mind than just another chance to sit around and shoot the breeze about ever heavier trophies and ever lighter tackle. They both had a feeling that there might be more to the future of fishing than paying ever higher prices for fewer stretches of preserved waters. And out of their feeling came the first concept of the Federation of Fly Fishermen which today, along with Trout Unlimited, is doing yeomen work, all across the country, in a desperate last stand against the despoilers.

Granted, this is a far cry from the old Herbert Hoover idea of fishing, as something to do for fun and to wash one's soul. Nobody need be against either of those admirable aims in order to take cognizance of the possibility that fishing has another dimension. It can also serve as something of a litmus paper, to show by the coloration of its condition whether this land of ours is sick or healthy. For it follows, as the night the day, that water that isn't fit for a trout won't much longer be fit for us.

Trout Unlimited has in its name that much of the aspect of handwriting on the wall. It didn't have, when it began out in Michigan in the fifties. Its name was frankly patterned after that of Ducks

Unlimited, which was Edgar Queeny's effort to safeguard the future of a sport of which he happened to be fond.

But trout and ducks, no matter how important they may be to some people, are of course of trivial significance against the larger concerns of the body politic. However, they are both symptomatic, in that their vanishing or their flourishing is a direct indication of which way the welfare of the whole human race is headed. In this light, their significance is no less than cosmic.

To me, all these organizations have their place in the larger concept of the companionships of angling. We fish because we love it, and like to talk about it and read about it, and hence we seek out, or are attracted by, people and books and clubs and committees or confederations that are as concerned with fishing as we are. Some of these people may be guides in the backwoods, some city dwellers whom we meet at business lunches and similar gatherings, and others we never meet and never can, except through the pages of books or magazines, but the one great common denominator that links us all is our love of fishing.

And if many of the contacts of our fishing lives are only mental, such as the remembered precepts that come back to us—from guides long gone, or now faraway fishing friends, or angling authors who today belong only to each other and the ages—as we face new fishing situations in actuality, then this is as it should be, since so much of fishing is purely mental.

But for the mental aspects of angling—the spiritual, the emotional, the philosophic—few of us would fool with fishing, once we had grown up and reached that stage at which one puts away childish things. The pole and the can of worms or bucket of minnows that comprised the appurtenances of fishing for most of us as kids must first be replaced by more sophisticated tackle, and then only, if we use these adult tools well enough and often enough to excite and sustain our interest, do we begin that progression through the phases of angling that culminates in the realization that success in fishing is not so much a matter of acquiring all the latest wrinkles in tackle and techniques as it is in the approach to fishing with a well-furnished mind.

Without the attractions of the mental side of it, certainly, none of us would ever, more than very casually, go in for such exasperating quarry as trout and salmon, or their near-counterparts in elusiveness, snook and bonefish, to say nothing of such a puzzler as the permit. In the upper reaches of angling, you get to the fish that can't be caught without study and that deserve and reward study once caught. For the angler's progress leads not to further bragging, but to an access of humility: the more we learn about fishing, the more we realize how much there is to learn and how little we know. It's the kid who's cocky about it. The mature angler knows that the biggest fish he catches was lying right next to a bigger one that he can't catch. It's the beginning of wisdom when you start to comprehend how much more there is to be known than you can ever, even in the proverbially long life of anglers, hope to learn. The best fishing makes you appreciate it.

And unless you're a case of arrested adolescence, your appreciation of this kind of fishing is never untinged with some concern over its future. Will it still be there for your kids to enjoy, assuming they have the wit to grow up enough to enjoy it? When such considerations begin to concern you, then you're ripe for the extension of your interest in fishing beyond the exchange of tall tales with the boys at the bar or around the table, and it's time to look into membership in the local or near-regional equivalent of an organization like the Theodore Gordon Flyfishers, or a local or nearby chapter of Trout Unlimited. The next step leads naturally to the national outfits, like the Federation of Fly Fishermen and Trout Unlimited, with their magazines *The Flyfisher* and *Trout,* respectively.

These magazines both provide a vicarious extension of your own angling experience, which will heighten the quality of your fishing wherever you fish. For that too is one of the joys of angling: the realization that you can do a better job of it than you have been doing, wherever you do it. I know I would rather have one new trick to try, with an occasional chance of succeeding, on my local trout than the most exotic and expensive fishing trip ever laid on for anybody. The one I can use again and again, while the other only whets my appetite for next time, which might be a long time coming.

It's customary, and practically obligatory for the sake of politeness, to say, "Boy, do I envy you," to the one who's about to set off for some fabled fishing somewhere. But Thoreau never got to go much of anywhere, and look at the good time he had. One of the best formulas for happiness I ever heard was the simple one, "making the most of what you've got."

Sure I love to go salmon fishing, but I'd swear off tomorrow if the price of going after salmon was promising never to look at another trout. Going salmon fishing is a lot like going to college. A lot of dopes get to go on whom it is largely wasted.

But it has been written about, in both instances, by men on whom not one moment of the magic of it was ever lost. I would a lot rather sit home and read Scrope's *Days and Nights of Salmon Fishing in the River Tweed* than go to the Tweed itself with some of the types who obviously go salmon fishing only because they've been told it's the thing to do.

Some of the world's best fishing is in the library, where it's open to everybody to enjoy vicariously, whereas in actuality some of it is preserved for poops who wouldn't know enough to miss it if they never had it.

Ironically, some of the great fishing may someday survive only in the library, if the present worldwide ecological crisis isn't surmounted in time. It may be true, as the wartime song so pathetically promised, that There'll Always Be an England, but it may also be true that something may still be rotten in the state of Denmark, metaphorically speaking, despite the present apparent willingness of the Danes to phase out their high seas fishing for Atlantic salmon.

The only good thing about the catastrophic decline of the Canadian salmon runs in 1971, which raised the hue and cry about the Danes to its highest decibel point, was that at least and at last it got the Canadian government to put an end to some of the netting that they ought to have ended two decades back.

"So it isn't only the Danes," I said to myself, when that news came from Canada, remembering reports made for the Atlantic Salmon Association over the past decade that kept calling the government's attention, again and again, to the enormous disproportion between the relatively puny revenues from the commercial netting that, over the years, kept threatening the vastly greater income to the country from sport fishing.

All along, when the haul of the Danes off Greenland was rising, as it did for a five-year period, in almost geometric progression, and the call for a boycott of all Danish goods was increasing in like proportion, I kept wondering if it wasn't an oversimplification to blame everything on the Danes. I couldn't help remembering, from my reading of old books, such as Grimble's volumes on the salmon rivers of the British Isles, what great fluctuations there had been in the salmon runs in the past. Grimble, writing over seventy years ago, had some tabulations of the eighteen sixties and seventies with fluctuations so severe as to make it look as if any day the British salmon runs would be over entirely, yet by his own Edwardian times, four to five decades later, the runs in those same rivers were enormous.

What had happened in those, roughly, corresponding years, of the last century? There were no Danish fishing boats around Greenland then to blame, and yet the runs went off as badly as if there had been. There was netting, and the nets were lifted. But obviously it was accountable only in part, because there were and have been fluctuations both before and since.

We know a lot more, about almost everything, than we did a hundred years ago, yet natural disasters keep occurring, around the world, as if we hadn't learned a thing.

Just as the Canadians were finally made to feel guilt over their netting, so have the Danes, after five years, and a world of pressure, made what is tantamount to an admission of guilt by agreeing to phase out their Greenland high seas fishery. But just as a confession doesn't necessarily solve a crime, though it may enable the prosecution to consider its case closed, so the mere signing of the Danish agreement is by no means enough to let the Committee on the Atlantic Salmon Emergency regard its work as ended. Richard A. Buck, its chairman, certainly knows this, and CASE is by no means closed.

It is very much "on the case," as the vernacular of the counter-culture puts it, and CASE is something worth your looking into, even if you never expect to do a day's salmon fishing the rest of your life. The cause of keeping the Atlantic salmon from becoming or remaining a vanishing species, as it has been more and more frequently termed of late, merits the interest and concern of every civilized adult. The Committee on the Atlantic Salmon Emergency will undoubtedly still have work to do for years to come, unless some miraculous Second Coming should suddenly end all pollution caused by commercial greed, or unless, indeed, the species should suddenly vanish.

I can't believe that will ever happen, no matter how bad the variations in the runs from one year to the next may be or remain. There are more horses in New Jersey now than there were before the automobile was invented. There are more deer in New York State now than there were in Revolutionary War days. And have you ever tried to rid a pond of bass, by draining it, as a preparation for stocking it with trout? Nature, which can cause some mighty upheavals and catastrophes, can also engineer some astonishing comebacks. A decade ago there was a lot of talk, during a spell of some seven years of severe droughts in the Atlantic states, of a receding water table, and people began to act as if water were our fastest-diminishing resource. Since then the area has been plagued by the opposite kind of trouble—record rainfalls and floods.

But eternal vigilance is the price of many things besides peace, and just because something hasn't happened yet is of course no guarantee that it can't happen, or never will. During the great Depression somebody asked Bernard Baruch if it would ever end, and his answer was that it would, based on nothing more than that "so far they always have." True, that was a pragmatic answer. But most of us base our lives on the probable, rather than the remotely possible.

Everything dies, in time, and ultimately the earth's hot core will cool. But most of us have many more immediate worries with which to concern ourselves. There isn't a species that may not eventually die, but meanwhile most of them are pretty hard to kill.

On the other hand, keeping them flourishing, as opposed to simply not vanishing entirely, can sometimes seem even harder than killing them off entirely. Look how many years it's been since the reintroduction of Atlantic salmon into those half-dozen Maine rivers first began. It has taken a decade to nurse their numbers up from the mere dozens into the still not very many hundreds.

The International Atlantic Salmon Foundation, headquartered in New York, and The Atlantic Salmon Association, based in Montreal, Quebec, but numbering as many American as Canadian members, are both vitally concerned with the future of this noble fish, and both are worthy of support. Contributions to each are tax deductible, for Americans, under present Internal Revenue rules, although in the case of the Atlantic Salmon Association, the first five dollars, in representing the yearly dues, would not be deductible. But since that part includes a subscription to *The Atlantic Salmon Journal*, which provides some of the best armchair salmon fishing to be found anywhere, it's not an unpleasant exception. It's been some years since I've been able to get away to go salmon fishing, but I wouldn't miss an issue of *The Atlantic Salmon Journal* for anything and think of it as one of the nicest of all the companionships of angling. (Actually, until 1973, membership was always fifteen dollars, but has been reduced to five in the hope of broadening public support, which makes *The Journal* a stupendous bargain.)

Since I am not allergic to my own company, as some people are, many of my own companionships in angling are enjoyed alone, either with the fish, while actually doing it, or with books or catalogs or magazines, in the days, and sometimes even the hours, away from it. Some men would rather hear about a thing from somebody else than undergo what they think of as "reading up on it," a term that for some would seem tantamount to a major operation. For them, of course, some form of fishing club constitutes their only means of keeping in touch with the world of angling.

That's all right. I'm not allergic to them, either. I belong to several. And I consider them just as central to the enjoyment of angling as any other of its many attributes. Sparse Grey Hackle, regaling his companions around the long table at The Anglers' Club in New York seems to be as legitimate a figure, in the landscape with figures that represents the angling of our time, as Elliott Donnelley or James Eriser, heading up such dedicated organizations as Trout Unlimited and the Federation of Fly Fishermen, or Gardner Grant, keeping the Theodore Gordon Flyfishers up to their eyeballs in conservation matters, or Bus Grove or Steve Raymond, with their respective editorships of *Trout* and *The Flyfisher*. For that matter, so does Charlie Ritz, with his International Fario Club in Paris, and all *they* do is sit down to dinner once a year. The world of angling is many faceted, and sometimes we get so involved with some of them that we tend to forget that its prime ingredient is supposed to be Fun.

I suppose you could say of fishing clubs what they say of old soldiers, that they don't die but just fade away. I know that's the impression I left of Midtown some pages ago, but there, too, a next to miraculous comeback has occurred.

After fading away from the Williams Club, the hospitable home of the thriving Theodore Gordon Flyfishers, poor old Midtown just went to pot, until the day a couple of years back when John Groth took it into his head to try reviving its weekly Wednesday lunches at the Overseas Press Club. A few of the old faithful rallied around, such as Dick Wolters, its last and indeed only president since Jack Randolph himself, and Berni Schoenfield, the secretary-treasurer who had a number of times lunched at Midtown only with me, and Jim Rikhoff of the Winchester Division of Olin, who began bringing more and more members of the then newly founded Winchester Press. Soon there was need for an ever-longer table, in the stately dining room of the Overseas Press Club, reached by a winding marble stair and overlooking the bench-bordered paths of Bryant Park, behind the New York Public Library. Pat Smith, who was doing a book with John Groth, for which I was doing the introduction, found it necessary to check things with me there a few Wednesdays, and before long Jack Samson, of *Field & Stream,* began showing up with an occasional contributor, and Bob O'Byrne, the chronic wine taster of the old Manny Wolf days, discovered that Betty, the waitress, could provide a passable red *ordinaire* in decanters, and Bill Pearsall took to dropping in with p.r. clients, and within a few months there were more guys than had ever squeezed in at once into the little room upstairs at Manny Wolf's.

But the Overseas Press Club, of which John Groth and I were the only members to legitimize the attendance of this swarm of animators of the erstwhile inert corpus of Midtown, now so remarkably *redivivus*, soon in its turn began to stagger from the slings and arrows of an outrageous fortune. Triggered by a treasurer's defalcation, the club's hold on its own building became more and more tenuous, and despite valiant efforts to hang onto it, the day came when the Overseas Press Club had nowhere to go but the benches in Bryant Park. The Overseas Press Club had never been on the street before, but that was nothing new to Midtown, which once again found its locale as imprecise as that of a floating crap game.

A succession of nearby clubs were tried as meeting places for Midtown, pending the possibility that the Overseas Press Club might find new quarters itself, and none of the stopgap solutions seemed much more than that, until Lee Wulff, who had resumed his old habit of turning up at Midtown every Wednesday he was in New York, provided a haven for Midtown at the Wings Club, on the first floor of the Biltmore. This is a flyer's club, of which Lee had been a member since the old days when he used to use his own plane to fly guests into the bush, at his camps on the River of Ponds in Newfoundland.

There the flickering flame of Midtown was once again re-trimmed, and since in this instance it could be worked out to take advantage of Lee Wulff's membership even on an absentee basis, the club was kept alive there for over a year while waiting for the installation of the Overseas Press Club's new quarters in the Time-Life Building in Rockefeller Center.

In the interim at the Wings Club, the Midtown Turf Yachting and Polo Association, which had begun life as Randolph's Irregulars, clung to it now with something of a pulmotor precariousness as the John Groth Marching and Chowder Society.

Most men you can walk a mile with, up and down Madison Avenue, won't know a soul and are no more likely than you are to be stopped en route, unless by a cop for going against a red light. But in the forties and fifties on Madison Avenue today, a walk with John Groth is not so much a walk as a progression. As the People's John meets and greets the populace, you'd think you were going not through the anonymous grim-faced crowds of midtown New York but of the villagers of somewhere like, well, let's say Nieuw Amsterdam, when everybody in it could be presumed to know everybody else and any stroll would be one big long hello.

Some are ex-students from the Arts Students League, some are art directors from the area's agencies and magazines, and some could be either or both; some are museum officials, others dealers, framers, printers, and lithographers and, for all I know, porters, connected in one way or another with various art galleries, and I suppose some would be models, as a lot of them seem to be women, but they all give, like a campaign slogan at a convention, the same greeting of "Hi, John."

Small wonder, then, that in one of Midtown's many phases it seemed to take on more of the semblance of a graphic arts group than a hunting and fishing gathering.

Since the reestablishment of the Overseas Press Club in the Time-Life Building, complete with the same old decanters, though lacking the greenery of the park view that was the other main attraction, at least for me, Midtown seems to be regaining much of its former stride, and the composition of the attendance is again more varied, partly perhaps because John Groth is himself away more often. He has either discovered Texas or it has discovered him, as he seems obliged to spend more and more of his time there. Having once, but briefly, had a Texas wife, I can think of fates for which I would envy him more.

But I would hate to see Midtown go down the drain again, if only because of the reflected glory in which it is entitled to bask. No great shakes in and of itself, it can be likened to the shiftless father of upstanding sons. Out of it came, more or less directly, both the Theodore Gordon Flyfishers and the Federation of Fly Fishermen, and that's no small claim to fame. True, this is like a small town's taking pride in the accomplishments of one of its natives, when the obvious fact is that he had to leave there before he could accomplish anything. Ted Rogowski, once he had the Theodore Gordon Fly-fishers alive and kicking, barely showed up at Midtown again, but of course by that time there wasn't much of any Midtown left to come back to. In any case, Ted soon moved away from New York, to go into legal work for the Department of the Interior, first in Washington and then, on a territory basis, out to the Pacific Northwest. As for Gene Anderegg and Lee Wulff, while Gene was doing his Johnny Appleseed cross-country act for the original organization of the Federation of Fly Fishermen he had no time left over to keep on coming to Midtown, but Lee did, and still does. He helped resuscitate Midtown again, after the Overseas Press Club went into its protracted eclipse, and now its Wednesday luncheons still have priority on his time when he's in New York, even ahead of The Anglers' Club, of which he has been a member for many years.

The Anglers' Club, of course, is beyond needing anybody's help, even that of such a peerless figure as Lee Wulff, whereas his occasional attendance at Midtown is a measurable stimulus to keeping it going.

Next only to, and probably today even on a par with, The Flyfishers' Club of London, The Anglers' Club of New York is Mecca to the fraternity of trout and salmon fishermen. In fact, for over fifty years there has been a special relationship between The Flyfishers' Club of London and The Anglers' Club of New York. Not only has reciprocal exchange of membership privileges prevailed between these two clubs since 1921, but it is undoubtedly safe to say that each of these clubs more nearly resembles the other than it does any other club in its own country. Alike they typify "a social organization of gentlemen anglers."

The English organization is senior to the American one by twenty-two years, since they were established respectively in 1884 and 1906, but even in this respect they are very much alike, as each of them is about equally junior to other associations of anglers—dating back to the 1700s—in their own countries. They are both purely social, and neither has ever acquired any club waters. In this latter respect they are singularly alike, in that this possibility has been kept under advisement, by both bodies of membership, for so long that this resemblance, too, is unlikely to be diminished within the foreseeable future.

The Anglers' Club of New York, like its English counterpart, has in its membership roster the overwhelming majority of the dominant angling figures of this century, and the list of its members' writings would serve as a practical guide to the angling literature of its time and place with few very conspicuous or noteworthy omissions.

At its inception, The Anglers' Club might more accurately have been called the Central Park Flyfishers, for it was there on Saturday afternoons, after a half day's work, that the nucleus of its membership met while engaged in casting practice, and the club's quarters, for its first decade, were a succession of leased rooms in Broadway hotels convenient to the Park's Seventy-seventh Street entrance, near which they had erected a casting platform. The original rooms were used chiefly to store the members' casting tackle. The club was first formed, with the intent of making it an angling club rather than an anglers' club, for the purpose of acquiring a suitable clubhouse on convenient waters. This was an idea that had occurred to Edward Cave and Perry Frazer, a couple of junior editors at *Field & Stream,* and it was in the magazine's offices, on November 20, 1905, that the first meeting was held to propose the idea, which after three meetings led to the club's incorporation on January 18, 1906. For the next fifteen years the club's activities largely consisted of casting in the park, with the organization and hosting of various tournaments, and the dinners at which the concomitant cups and prizes were awarded. In the First World War years, the tournaments were suspended and an annual outing became the club's only outdoor activity. The clubrooms, once mere conveniences for tackle storage, became oases of conviviality as the great drought of Prohibition settled over the land, and more frequent meetings than monthly dinners were deemed necessary, with the consequence that the uptown casting platforms were abandoned and by 1927 The Anglers' Club was moved downtown and turned into a luncheon club. Rooms in Hanover Street were obtained, where for the first time the members could gather around what has since become the core of the club's character, the Long Table. The quarters were tumbledown and the ambiance was shabby-genteel, and the food service was glacial in every sense, as orders had to be taken up the street to one of a succession of restaurants engaged to fill them. But the spirits were warming enough to compensate, and the club survived the Depression. In fact, in its darkest year, 1932, it even gave birth, on the distaff side, to The Woman Flyfishers' Club, which also still exists.

The club's present quarters, at 101 Broad Street, an address which is in London terms equivalent to being in the heart of the City, are an adjunct of the historic Fraunces Tavern, which means that they are eighteenth century inside and out. They appear to be an almost incredibly well preserved survival, but are actually a restoration, dating back only to 1940, when the club lucked into them through the fortuitous circumstance that the Sons of the Revolution, having acquired Fraunces Tavern and its adjacent structure for restoration as a museum, were looking for a suitable tenant for the second floor of the annex. But for a separate stairway leading from the street up to the second floor, The Anglers' Club rooms are actually in, though not of, the restoration of Fraunces Tavern, the space both above and below the club's rooms being used as integral parts of the museum. In this enclave of colonial New York in downtown present-day Manhattan, it is never the Londoner but rather the average New Yorker who feels the need, on first seeing the Long Table plain, of some sort of decompression chamber, to adjust to the shock of contrast with the world outside. (Provision for such a needed pause is thoughtfully provided, in the form of a self-service dispenser of sherry, near the head of the stairway where the visitor completes his ascent, and adjacent to the steward's desk at which members write out their luncheon orders.)

Here on the wall is a 1659 signature of Izaak Walton, next to a 1656 letter written by Charles Cotton to Isabella Hutchins shortly before their marriage. There is a large silver bowl, a Monteith, long known as the Home Pool, and so inscribed, and on the mantel there is a leaping silver salmon, by John Rennie, that he once devised for his own motor car and that subsequently became known as the Flyfishers' Mascot. Rennie was an honorary member of The Anglers' Club and after his death, as the base reads, this was "Presented to The Anglers' Club of New York by The Flyfishers' Club." Nearby are "the Hewitt chalices," a pair of silver goblets acquired by the late E. R. Hewitt, the club's president in 1917, when he won second place in the fly-casting championships on the platform of the Crystal Palace, some fifteen years earlier. And everywhere are trophies and books, all of the former awarded to and most of the latter written by present and past members of the club.

Outside, on Broad Street, over the wrought-iron balcony onto which the three French windows open, the club flag shows the familiar insignia, of fish and creel, that is also to be seen on the club tie. But it is on turning to the omnipresent bookshelves that The Anglers' Club's significance to the entire angling world is most readily realized. Here is LaBranche, with his *The Dry Fly and Fast Water* and *The Salmon and the Dry Fly*. He was one of the club's original members in 1906 and its president in 1911. Here is Hewitt, with his dozen books culminating in *A Trout and Salmon Fisherman for Seventy-Five Years*. And here, to be sure, is Skues, long one of the most active, albeit nonresident, members, contributing many of the club's most valued autographs, along with his own half-dozen volumes from *Minor Tactics of the Chalk Stream* through *Nymph Fishing for Chalk Stream Trout*. Here indeed is a whole long parade of some of the most formidable angling figures from the turn of the century onward, from John Atherton to Lee Wulff, with such stalwarts as Ray Camp, Eugene V. Connett, John Taintor Foote, Charles K. Fox, George Parker Holden, John Alden Knight, Henry Van Dyke, and Charles M. Wetzel in between. Nor should Sparse Grey Hackle be overlooked, as Alfred W. Miller has been known since 1954, when he wrote *Fishless Days* and took over the editorship of the club *Bulletin,* which has appeared since 1920, and became at the same time the club's historian. On him has fallen the mantle and he wears it with fitting grace, as his 1971 volume *Fishless Days, Angling Nights* attests. He typifies today not only The Anglers' Club but the representative American dry-fly man whose attitude, in contrast to that of his English counterpart, is fish the water, not the rise, and concentrate on the broken water rather than the smooth—and it matters not what fly you use, because all that matters is how you use it. In other words, which happen to be his own, "Sparse Grey Hackle is just an ordinary angler, even as you and I." But there are very few less ordinary anglers, just as there are very few less ordinary clubs.

In contrast to The Anglers' Club, which can be joined only through the customary private club practice, on invitation after election, the Theodore Gordon Flyfishers is as open to membership as, say, The National Geographic Society. In actuality the membership is largely confined to residents of New York, New Jersey, and Connecticut within the usual limits of commuting range. But there are notable, even glamorous exceptions, as in the case of Maxine Atherton Wyckoff, who lives in Vermont not far from the Canadian border, and Charles K. Fox of Carlisle, Pennsylvania, and Lee and Joan Wulff, who live at least nominally in Keene, New Hampshire, although at the behest of Garcia they are likely to be anywhere else. And the course of peregrination has led to a few memberships even farther off, like that of Founder Ted Rogowski, now three thousand miles away. But the contrast with The Anglers' Club, with which it has some overlap of membership, is even greater ideologically, because the Theodore Gordon Flyfishers is only incidentally social.

It began, or rather it tried to begin, as a chapter of Trout Unlimited, when TU itself was still pretty young. The charter dinner, so designated with underlining for emphasis, was announced on April 15, 1963, on the stationery of *Trout Unlimited,* and this first invitation to that event is the earliest written record that the organization now has of its own existence.

Beneath the Trout Unlimited letterhead is the typewritten line "N.Y. Chapter: Theodore Gordon Flyfishers," and beneath that are two lists of names, the one on the left appearing under the heading of "Charter Directors" and naming, in alphabetical order, Keith Fulsher, Arnold Gingrich, Walter Kehm, Roger Menard, Ted Rogowski, Ernest Schwiebert, Lee Wulff, Edward Zern. To these eight names is appended a ninth, out of alphabetical order because it is followed by the designation, "Honorary," and this last named of the Charter Directors is Harry Darbee.

On the right, above the date line April 15, 1963, three names are listed under the designation "Officers, pro tem," and they are Ed Zern, President; Walter Kehm, Vice President, and Ted Rogowski, Secretary-Treasurer.

The letter, after two paragraphs devoted to the nature and purposes of Trout Unlimited, announces that the Theodore Gordon Flyfishers, "a New York affiliate of this national organization," will hold its Charter Dinner on May 2, 1963, a Thursday evening, at the Gramatan Hotel in Bronxville, New York.

Four names are featured for this first after-dinner program: Lee Wulff, in a program of color movies; Guy Jenkins, "a long-time angling friend and correspondent of Theodore Gordon," in a short dedicatory address; and Ed Zern and Ted Rogowski, jointly setting forth the purposes, policies, and objectives of the Theodore Gordon Flyfishers.

The letter, as if aware of the fact that it might someday be called upon to serve as the cornerstone of the organization's written history, goes on to provide more information than would normally be expected of such an invitation.

It says, first: "Four hundred individuals in the metropolitan New York vicinity are being requested to join us on this significant evening, to participate in this signal event. You are one of these, and we ask that you attend with your wife, or male or female guest as you choose, in this first meeting of this new angling fraternity."

It goes on to say: "At the mailing of this announcement, forty persons in the metropolitan New York area have already become members of Trout Unlimited. If you are one of these forty, the Committee has received your name from the Trout Unlimited national secretary. Please, however, signify attendance on the return card, and we welcome your advance interest."

The other three hundred sixty to whom this invitation was extended were politely told that their acceptance for the dinner had to be accompanied by a filled-in membership application for membership in Trout Unlimited, which was also enclosed.

Adding only the now quaintly historic touch that the dinner charge would be five dollars, this extraordinary document was signed, in a sudden access of modesty that it had nowhere earlier revealed (the previous page having listed seventeen names of TU national officers in addition to the nine already-mentioned locals) only as emanating from "The Dinner Committee." A pity, too, as there was plenty of space left at the bottom of the second page for a bold John Hancock flourish.

But for this, there is no other written entry for 1963 in the club's annals, as the next item is dated January 3, 1964. But going back of the written record, and relying on a compound of memory and legend, the first four members of the Theodore Gordon Flyfishers were, again alphabetically, Walt Kehm, Ted Rogowski, Lee Wulff, and Ed Zern. The last three, as already mentioned, had decided not to drop out of Midtown but to have another lunch away from lunch, so to speak, where they could, for one thing, hear themselves speak, and try to think of ways and means of doing something about the future of fishing. They were joined in these added lunches, by Walt Kehm, an ardent conservationist then as now, and off and on by others, but these four formed the nucleus. These lunches were first held Thursdays at the Roosevelt Tavern in the fall of 1962, and by the time the group had grown to the point where a baker's dozen could be counted upon to show up every week, Guy Jenkins found the group a home at the Williams Club. This was in early 1964, by which time the day had changed to Monday. Except for the change from Mondays to Tuesdays, which was determined, by voice vote in 1965, to be a more convenient day, this arrangement has remained in effect ever since.

The written record resumes on January 3, 1964, when Ted Rogowski, as secretary of the Theodore Gordon Chapter, circulated to all New York area members of Trout Unlimited a notice to reserve February fifteenth, a Saturday, for the annual meeting, at which the evening entertainment would feature Charles K. Fox, author of *This Wonderful World of Trout*.

This was followed by a much more detailed mailing, on January 24, 1964, outlining an all day meeting, from 3 P.M. to 9:15 P.M., for $6.25, or "a dollar an hour," to be held again at the Gramatan in Bronxville, enclosing a program, a raffle booklet, dinner reservations and return envelope, and the president's report.

In his president's report for 1963, Ed Zern spoke of the nine months of operation of "an infant organization," and said that progress had been hard to come by and slow. But he listed three major events held by the organization in its first year—the Charter Dinner, the Beaverkill Outing (the Flyfishers' Summer Outing at Antrim Lodge), and the Amawalk Stream Conservation Outing, and spoke of seven river projects that were already being considered for conservation and improvement efforts.

The fact that Trout Unlimited had refused the chapter affiliation under the name of "Flyfishers," but had insisted that it be changed to "Anglers," was touched upon by Zern with diplomatic restraint, limiting himself to the observation that "to our knowledge all of our members happen to be flyfishermen and it seems to us that few New York trout streams are of great enough size to tolerate spin fishing at all."

Zern reported that the directors had been meeting the fourth Tuesday of every month with all interested members to consider and act on New York stream conservation measures, and he urged attendance at these sessions as well as at the second annual meeting on February 15, 1964.

At that second meeting, according to a press release by Joe Pisarro, the Theodore Gordon Conservation Award was first established and presented to Harry Darbee and the first conservation raffle was held, featuring a rod made to the winner's order by Everett Garrison.

Officers elected at that time were Ted Rogowski, President; William F. Herrick, Vice President; Alan Schoening, Secretary; Herbert S. Skoultchi, Treasurer; and the board of directors was increased by the addition of Eugene C. Anderegg, David I. Kramer, Joe A. Pisarro, Richard E. Robinson, and Henry C. Schlichting.

At this time reminders were sent out that all members of the Theodore Gordon Chapter of Trout Unlimited were invited to its table at luncheon each Monday at the Williams Club, "by special arrangement of Guy R. Jenkins, long-time friend of Theodore Gordon," where conversations on angling and conservation were preferred.

Because of the continuing tension with Trout Unlimited the invitations for the second annual June outing at Antrim Lodge had to be couched in the name of the Theodore Gordon Anglers, but by the time of the outing the uneasy fifteen months of attempted consolidation of the relationship to TU had to be abandoned, and the members voted to withdraw the application for affiliation.

By mid-1964 the Theodore Gordon Flyfishers had a membership count of 180, which was 10 percent of the total TU national membership at that point, and the $1,800 that had already been paid in dues to the national headquarters in Michigan moved Ted Rogowski to comment on the situation with some sharpness, in a letter to Sparse Grey Hackle, which duly found its way into the next bulletin of The Anglers' Club of New York.

The nub of Ted's case was that "stripped of all its glamor, the mechanics of the local 'national' relationship of TU allow a group of residents of a region to fight their own stream conservation battles on their own, after having mailed their funds to a remote headquarters."

Pointing out that members were still free to give TU their individual support, Ted moved to a rousing peroration: "If the members want to work for the conservation efforts in the states in which they reside and fish, then we urge that they lend us their arms and typewriters, time and talents, energies and their dues."

All of these were abundantly forthcoming, and the no longer infant organization, free to raise its own colors again, was soon going great guns. The streamside educational posters, with their simple but eloquent message of "Limit your kill, don't kill your limit" were only the battle flags of a dozen or so campaigns of statewide and indeed regional scope. Special attention was focused on the Mahwah River, the Amawalk Outlet, and the Croton River as well as the Beaverkill-Willowemoc situation.

And right after this, like a declaration of independence came the next bulletin, at the end of June 1964, announcing that the petition for chapter status had been withdrawn, and on the organization's own new stationery, and beneath the heading "We're on our own," Ted said, "We are again the Theodore Gordon Flyfishers, with no strings attached, and devoted to trout stream conservation work."

He also announced that work had begun to get the members started on a book, to serve as a memorial to Gordon, to be published in a limited edition for members, and then later sold to the general public, with the royalties going to the Flyfishers.

At the same time, with the ties to TU severed, the directors began casting about for another means of reaching out to like-minded anglers everywhere, and Gene Anderegg was launched, like a guided missile, on the coast-to-coast search for other clubs. Gene, cheered on by the TGF general staff, and notably by Lee Wulff, went around the country spreading the gospel of fly fishing as a means and conservation as an end, and almost overnight the idea of federation caught on and the Federation of Flyfishermen was in being, with TGF not only one of the charter members, but what you could almost term the founding charter member.

The next year saw *The Gordon Garland*'s publication, on the fiftieth anniversary of Theodore Gordon's death, and the year after that the trade edition, *American Trout Fishing*, so the organization could feel at last that it was lengthening this frail little man's giant shadow across the land.

Thereafter, the annual TGF dinners moved into town from the outlands, and the effect was as electrifying as bringing a show to Broadway from the sticks, and some of them, as when the one in 1966 was combined with the annual meeting of the Atlantic Salmon Association, grew to really big-time proportions.

From then on the TGF membership ran on up into the hundreds, from the few score it had represented up to then, and the Theodore Gordon Flyfishers were solidly on the map of angling and conservation.

In the course of a scant decade, time wore off the sharp edges of the differences of attitude and outlook that brought about the early divorce of TGF from TU, and today the aims and objectives of the two organizations, in the area where the regional and the national overlap, are very nearly identical. Probably each still harbors some curmudgeons who would angrily deny it, but in their deeds, if still not altogether in their creeds, they are actually as alike as peas in a pod.

For that matter, you could say the same thing today of TU and FFF, with the same exceptions noted for a thin fringe of unreconstructed hotheads on both sides. But actually, between the water-testing kits and the Vibert boxes, for in-stream incubation of trout eggs, both outfits are today going about doing the Lord's work in the Devil's territory. It's as if they were saying the same prayer from different prayerbooks, with the variations between them very slight, as when one congregation says "forgive us our debts as we forgive our debtors" while the other intones "forgive us our trespasses as we forgive those who trespass against us."

Me, I'm a man of peace, perhaps because of a Mennonite background, but I for one never gave up my TU membership, even after it served as the original instrument of my getting into the Theodore Gordon Flyfishers and/or Anglers where I was for a time involved up to my eyelids, and similarly after the formation of the Federation of Fly Fishermen—as I kept on hoping, over the years, that the day might come when all these organizations might get a chance to put new proof to the old adage that in union there is strength.

There have, indeed, been some few tentative discussions between TU and FFF over the last couple of years, and there has even been one appearance which I would hope could be regarded as symptomatic, of a local chapter of Trout Unlimited on the roster of member clubs in the Federation of Fly Fishermen. Certainly, if that can be done without loss of identity, or even damage to it, then the way would seem to lie wide open for a form of rapprochement that would permit these two organizations, if not actually to unite, then at least to pull in some form of tandem harness. For that matter, the Izaak Walton League, which is older than TU and FFF put together, could even be invoked to make it a troika.

What little difference of credo they in their turn may manifest, like the tremendous trifle of "fly only" or "fly too" that kept FFF and TU growling at each other like strange bulldogs, I have no idea, but surely it can't be as great as the bond that exists, among these three groups, in being for life as against death, and for preservation and conservation versus the exploiters and despoilers.

All three, I should think, could afford to ponder the wisdom of that sage among the founding fathers who said something to the effect of: Be assured, gentlemen, if we don't all hang together, we shall all hang separately. And it may well come to that, if things don't start getting markedly better before they get even worse.

Today, if we hope to angle long, it's much more important that the angler be concerned than that he be well equipped, or well versed, or well skilled. For what matters all the tackle and techniques that we can get our hands on, or all the history and theory and lore that we can cram our heads with, if the fish are no longer there that are, after all, the object of the game?

In the less than ten years that my own doorstep has been on the

Saddle River I have watched that once redoubtable trout stream turn from deep to shallow and from blue to brown, as the silting has turned the pool above the dam, where a mill once stood, from over my head to below the tops of even my hip boots, as one after another the woods upstream from me have succumbed to developments.

Take no Wednesday nights off to weep for me, as I have more luck than I deserve, and in five minutes I can be at the club, casting over fish as long as my arm. But not everybody can, and this disappearance of recreational resources is occurring everywhere. What's happened to the stream that happens to pass my front yard is only a minor manifestation of a major misfortune that's befalling us all, as the countryside all around us gets wizened and shriveled by citification and all its attendant blights.

There are very few places that can be left to Mother Nature's care, and that's as true of the places where we live as well as where we work. Largely, of course, it's because Mother Nature has taken such a pushing around from man-made interference with her processes. Why, even the ponds where I fish at Joe Jefferson Club, though fed from springs that have been there since time out of mind, require constant care or they too could soon go to pot. That might not have been true back in 1874, when Joe Jefferson first acquired them, and perhaps not even in the nineties, when he let Charlie Ackerman fish there as a kid. But Charlie and some of the other older members have told me that by midsummer, a dozen years back, the ponds would be so gooked over with growth as to be no longer fishable, and they'd have to wait for fall to fish them again. That's how the habit began of holding opening festivities both on a weekend in April and on another in October. It took bulldozing and the judicious use of weed killers, before the ponds could be brought to their present pristine state, where they're fishable the year around. And if this could happen inside the fenced and locked grounds of a caretakered private area, it's easy to see how much more deterioration could occur even faster in the untended waters, the open streams and rivers, lakes and ponds, that dot and streak the landscape everywhere. Except where the direst kind of emergencies compels some measures of flood control, the care of public waters seems generally to be considered nobody's business, unless and until it suddenly becomes everybody's business. With relatively few and very honorable exceptions, stream improvement still generally takes a back seat to the more conspicuous activity of stocking the streams with even the tamest of fish.

If we want to fish, we have to realize that a free country is only free to go to rack and ruin, at least as far as natural fishing is concerned, under present population pressures and their consequences in suburban sprawl and the proliferation of industrial parks. Except for those few individuals and groups who "do something about it," the rest of us are content to sit around and grumble, while hoping that things will somehow get better, though knowing that if left to themselves they hardly ever do.

The least the rest of us can do is pay our dues, so to speak, to help insure the success of the efforts of those movers and shakers who show some willingness to let what should be everybody's business become their own. Joining and contributing to some of the national groups that are fighting our battles collectively should be as automatic a part of all but the most indigent of anglers' annual outfitting as the replacement of items of tackle needed individually. But while opening day exerts its own lure to turn on our springtime fancies in a way that precludes all need of reminders, we all still seem to need some sort of alarm to wake us up to the call on our attention of these other less glamorous aspects of our sport.

I have little natural aptitude for the role of Paul Revere, so in what follows I will devote as few pages to spreading alarm about fishing's dark underside as my conscience will allow. And I can only hope that they will be the few pages that your conscience won't let you skip. The theme song is as familiar to us both as "The Star Spangled Banner," even if we have to grope a little for the words. But we both know the sound of the music; it's "The Vandals Are Coming."

You may never have heard of a Long Island lawyer named Vic Yannacone, but your reading of the papers must have been casual indeed if it has escaped all mention of the Environmental Defense Fund. Well, that's his creation. In the last few years it has stalked the land like a little David, bringing corporate Goliaths to their knees. Its motto, though strictly a working one and not actually official, is the most inspiring I know: it is, quite simply, "Let's sue the bastards." The music he and his wife have made to it, in the courts, if not exactly sweet, is the most stirringly martial to be heard since the days of John Philip Sousa and "The Stars and Stripes Forever."

It's gadflies like this that it takes to arouse sleeping giants, and unless their tribe increases, the whole ecology movement may become what Mark Twain said of the weather, something that everybody talks about but that nobody does anything about.

I will hope, before we come to the end of this book and go our separate ways, to give you one or two more names like that, of people who though not directly concerned with fishing nevertheless merit every angler's applause and support. It is perhaps more to the point to say "especially" rather than "nevertheless," because in the vast hordes of people who must be moved before things of consequence, like needed new legislation, get accomplished, those who give a damn about trout constitute a minuscule minority. As anglers, we are apt to be classed, with bird watchers, as amiable but insignificant eccentrics, whose interests are to be discounted in any weighing of really important issues. Though a number of our presidents have fished, I have yet to hear of a politician being seriously concerned about the anglers' vote, as a bloc to be either particularly feared or especially courted. Much more typical is the arrogant assurance of that bureaucrat who asked the sportsmen's delegation from the Beaverkill, "What makes you believe a river is more important than a concrete highway?" As Admiral Hyman Rickover put it in his salty way, "The only voices raised in protest are of those who are personally hurt, and of a small minority of citizens who cannot sit idly by watching God's own country turned into God's own junkyard. Until this minority becomes a majority, the destruction will not cease."

Flyfishermen, God knows, are a minority's minority, so it's futile for us to protest what's being done to this country on the almost laughably naive basis that it's bad for the trout. Any hope of remedial action against the spoliation of the countryside must be cloaked with majority appeal, taking Admiral Rickover's cue, to disguise the fact that what we're seeking to protect is actually a minority interest, and our agitation should be not on a basis of what's good for trout is good for the country, but rather relying silently on the obvious fact that what's good for the country is good for the trout. If we can get to the engineers and the developers and the politicians and the bureaucrats, never as sportsmen, but only as humans, scared of threats to their own health, and that of their wives and kids, they'll listen if only because they'll be afraid not to. But we could shout at them until doomsday, on behalf of the trout, and never get a tumble out of them.

What the future of fishing may be, with or without our best efforts to assure it, is of course something we can never know. We can only hope that it is here for us to enjoy as long as we are here to enjoy it. Both our knowledge and our enjoyment of fishing to come is necessarily finite, so he who would aspire to getting as much of it as possible must turn the other way where, at least in terms of one man's capacity to absorb it, the availabilities are almost infinite. This is following the old Santayana line, to the effect that since no man can know how far he will live into the future, it behooves the wise man to live as long as possible into the past. It has been said that the past is the only thing we truly possess—that is, that we possess irrevocably.

Here the angler's luck is greater than that of any other sportsman, for no sport has been more widely or richly written about than fishing. Hunting enjoyed a slight head start, as the scholars date the first book on hunting about a hundred years ahead of the mid-fifteenth-century date now generally ascribed to the actual composition of the Dame Juliana Berners's treatise which was first published in 1496. But fishing soon caught up with hunting and passed it, and has never been headed. For three centuries, since the time of Walton and Cotton, there has been a spate of angling books, where there was only a trickle before, and while there is no current exact count (other than of the editions of *The Compleat Angler,* which alone number nearly four hundred), the number of fishing books long since passed the total of five thousand in English alone. And of these, the books devoted to the salmonids constitute a solid majority. (As for ichthyology, while the entries are generally shorter than complete fishing books, their number is at least ten times as great.) So one of the privileges of the fly fisherman is that he is partaking of the most written about of all sports, and not to know its literature is to miss half its fun.

I think of Bus Grove's felicitous title, *The Lure and Lore of Trout Fishing*, which I've always felt summed up the whole gamut of the sport better than any other. The lure of the sport is something we all feel intuitively, and don't have to be taught; the kid with the cut-off branch and a piece of string and a bent pin can feel it just as intensely as any of us—but the lore is something that is reserved for the thinking man.

For the rationale of fishermen's reading, I hark back to the first page of *A Book of Trout Flies*, where Preston Jennings wrote in 1935: "Anglers, and especially writers on the subject of angling, owe a debt of gratitude to all angling writers who have preceded them, for much that we know, or think we know, is the result of actual trial and error experiments which have been carried on by those who have gone before."

There is no more fruitful additive to any sport than the ability to think back, whenever the action lags, to the stored-up increment of lessons learned from "those who have gone before." Poor Preston is himself today among their blessed number, and every time I think of the night he saved me from utter and abject fishlessness, back in the old days on the Esopus, to say nothing of the many times since, I feel like saying a little grace of thanksgiving.

In the chapter of *The Well-Tempered Angler* called "The Angling Heritage," I gave a list of thirty books that I thought constituted a short but comprehensive outline of angling literature, and made the statement that any man who has read these thirty books could feel entitled to regard himself as a well-read angler. For purposes of easy identification, I labeled those thirty titles with a system of stars and crosses; the stars to indicate attraction, or literary value, and the crosses to indicate instruction, or technical value. (Just as you can divide all your flies into two basic categories, the attractors and the deceivers, so you can divide the literature of angling into two sharply defined classes, those books that attract and those that instruct.)

The thirty titles were divided into three groups of ten each, as Classic, Vintage, and Modern, ranging in point of time from Dame

Juliana Berners in 1496 to Helen Shaw in 1963, and I still say it wouldn't hurt any angler a bit to read, or reread, all thirty of those books. And for those who would aspire to postgraduate work, after that short course, I named just three of the many books there are "about books about fishing," Hills, Marston, and Robb, and said that among them they provided sufficient guidance for a truly scholarly knowledge of our sport.

Actually, that list is more useful now than it was then, because a lot of the books, that were pretty hard to come by in 1965, have since been reprinted, thanks to the commendable efforts in this direction of two editors who both happen to be college professors, Nick Lyons of Crown Publishers, and Mike Cohen of Freshet Press. Most of the titles can in any event be found in the library of any good-sized city, although many of them are the kind of books that, if your interest in fishing is more than casual, I should think you'd really want to own. For that matter, despite frequent assumptions and even occasional mentions to the contrary, *The Well-Tempered Angler* is itself still available; the publishers in fact celebrated its fifth birthday by raising the price of its second printing by a dollar.

The Classic and Vintage portions of my list were predominantly English, whereas the Modern section was all-American. This was justifiable, in my admittedly rather arbitrary simplification of the vast lore of angling into thirty books of three periods, on the ground that the English heritage accounts for all our fly-fishing techniques of today. As Charlie Ritz says, the language of fly fishing, the world around, is English. The English heritage was only exceeded, and amplified, on this side of the water when Theodore Gordon took the dry fly from its English high priest, Halford, and Americanized it. This, and the development of the split-cane rod, both of which were phenomena of the last quarter of the last century, signaled the actual departure, almost a hundred years later, of American fly fishing from its colonial dependence on the British. A quibble could be made, I suppose, on behalf of the mid-nineteenth century Kentucky development of the multiplying reel, but that has never had more than marginal importance to the flycaster. It isn't, really, until we come down to such relatively recent changes as the now universal use of

synthetics for both lines and leaders and the almost universal acceptance of glass for rods, to which even Lee Wulff and Charles Ritz now
lend their names, that American fly fishing can at last be said to be
standing squarely on its own two legs, with no more tendency to lean
on the British. The bandana has replaced the old school tie, and today
the American angler need feel beholden to nobody. Nowadays the
English are more interested in our tackle and techniques than we are
in theirs.

But the past is another kettle of fish, and no American angler can
begin to feel that he is at all well read unless and until he has first
done his homework, so to speak, and at least covered the high spots in
the traditional development of angling literature in the classic line
from Berners and Walton on down through Stewart and Francis and
Halford and Skues. Once that's out of the way, as an indispensable
prerequisite to the fullest comprehension and enjoyment of any other
angling literature, then there are any number of delights and surprises
to be encountered in poking about among the byways of American
fishing books, both present and past.

I'm all for shunpike traveling, but only after you know an area at
least well enough that any time you get lost you can find your way
back to the main highway that cuts through it from end to end, and
know that you can get home in a hurry if necessary. There are occasions when wasting time can be a delight, but they are confined to
those circumstances where you're doing it on purpose, and can stop it
any time you wish.

With that in mind, in the pages that follow, we can take time out
for some off-trail browsing, at least some of which I feel fairly sure
you'll wind up wanting to thank me for. But only on the first-settled
basis that we've both got the time to waste and that this isn't stuff I'd
open up for anybody I didn't think could handle it.

Call it part of the psychic gear you'll take with you next time you
fish, and don't blame me if you find, after you get back, that it didn't
add appreciably to your enjoyment. All I can say is that it has added to
mine.

If we fish, we know how things like that can be. You could be catching fish like crazy and hand me the very same fly, and I could watch every move you make and quite possibly not catch a thing.

I've had it happen more times than I can count, and I've had almost as many instances where it worked just the opposite way. Give it to me and I do great with it, and suddenly it stops working for you.

That happened to me with the Mrs. Simpson, for instance. Traver can take fish on it now, as if he had a license to steal, and so could I, until I gave it to Traver.

And just now, even worse than that happened with Ricky. If you fish you'll believe it, when a nonfisherman never would.

I was fishing just before it got light, as I always try to do at least every Saturday and Sunday, and since I can't tell one fly from another at that hour, I always take four or five rods down to the lean-to beside the little bridge that goes over the spillway between the first two ponds. They're all strung up, so if a fish breaks me off, or I louse up a leader casting in the near-darkness, I can just put that rod back in the rack on the shelter wall, and take another, and go on fishing without having to go back up to the cabin either to put on another fly or unsnarl the leader, as the case may be. I always start out with the *Isonychia,* since that always seems to have the best chance in poor light. I simply make it a point to remember, before I begin, which rod has the *Isonychia* on it, since once I'm down there I can't tell.

Well, bang, first cast to the left, even before I'm across the bridge, being careful to angle it so I know it will miss getting hung up in the down-hanging branches of the big tree, and a heavy fish is off with it and running.

"Praise Preston Jennings," I say, as I start to run with the fish. "Good old *Isonychia bicolor!*"

I judge him to be about eighteen inches, and I know he's a rainbow from the way he punctuates his runs with jumps, like a Spanish dancer using castanets, but I can't really make out the stripe, as he looks black and white in the net and as I gentle him in the water in the upper pond where I put him. I can't see well enough to know the exact moment to let go of his tail, to make sure he won't keel over after swimming a few feet beyond my reach, so I hang on until he literally explodes out of my grasp, before I go back to try another cast.

The same thing happens three more times, before it's light enough to see the fly clearly, and then I realize that it isn't the *Isonychia* at all, but a plain black nymph.

I'm puzzled, but not enough to want to argue with success, so I go right on using it, and take six more, culminating in a brown that I measure, because I can't believe he's as long as he looks to me. He is. A good twenty-two inches. The net with the scale in the throat is out being restrung, so I have to guess his weight, which I do conservatively, considering what a deep fish he is, at four-and-a-half pounds.

It is now six thirty and this is the tenth fish since five o'clock, but only the fourth I've put in the upper pond, as only two of them, after the first one, came anywhere near this size. The rest ran around fourteen and fifteen inches, and I put them back in the big pond, where they have the best chance to grow.

Ricky arrives, just after I've released the twenty-two incher into the upper pond, and at the sight of him I am triggered to remember what that black nymph is that I had supposed, in the dark, was the *Isonychia*, and then didn't want to change after there was enough light to distinguish the difference.

The other night, in trying to find a way out of the doldrums, I came across Ricky's Blue-Behinded Baboon, a fly that he had tied a couple of years ago, more or less as a joke, and certainly no more than an idle fancy, and had surprised himself by taking a couple of fish on it.

It was a simple black-dubbed body, on a number twelve hook, at the head of which, with no hackle, Ricky had fastened a single bright blue feather, so that it arched over the body of the fly like the plume on a Cavalier's hat. Very handsome, in the eye of the angler if not of the fish. After hours of trying everything the least bit logical, I decided to try something completely illogical, and in looking through my flies, spread out on the bench beneath the rod rack outside the lean-to, I picked this as looking least likely to succeed.

It was a good choice, on that basis, because after trying it on all three ponds for the better part of an hour, I hadn't succeeded in catching any more than a leaf or a twig on it, as once I hung it in the branches of a small tree and, in retrieving it with a rake, managed to knock its bright blue feather off. So, as it was beginning to get dark anyway, I retired that rod in favor of one carrying the *Isonychia*. With that, on the last disgusted cast, to the familiar tune of "Just this one more and then the hell with it," I finally caught a rainbow. Just a rainbow, a routine, run-of-the-mill, uninteresting, and undistinguished rainbow, of a scant twelve inches in length, that flip-flopped through three uninspired and almost dispirited jumps, before quitting cold and going belly up, and though I'd caught him in the big pond, I decided to penalize his performance by putting him in the spring pond, where if he didn't shape up and look lively enough, one of the cruising big old brown "battlewagons" might just possibly decide to eat him up. (Actually, I've never seen one of those brutes with a fish bigger than about nine inches in his mouth, but there's no telling what they do in the dark, when I can't see them.)

Well, seeing Ricky I remembered that I hadn't replaced his deplumed fly with an *Isonychia* as I had intended to do, but had picked up the other rod that already had the *Isonychia* on it, and then this morning, in the five o'clock gloom, I had simply failed to distinguish the difference between them. Of course, after the fourth or fifth fish, when I finally saw my mistake, I was glad of it, as the *Isonychia* very seldom produces after the dawn's early light has been succeeded by the clear light of morning.

I asked Rick if he recognized the black fly that I showed him on the end of my rod and he didn't.

"It's your Blue-Behinded Baboon," I said, "minus its blue backing which I left in that tree over there the other night. I've been fishing it this morning—by accident, actually, because I mistook it for an *Isonychia*—and I've caught ten fish on it, since five o'clock."

Rick was on his way to the steps, to go back up to his car, where he thought he remembered seeing a few of the blue-feathered flies, before I finished telling him that the four fish I had put into the upper pond ranged from eighteen to twenty-two inches, and then his pace redoubled.

As he was on his way back down I hooked another, on his same black fly, formerly blue, and as he was getting out his scissors to trim off the blue feather, we agreed to let the fish, a fifteen-inch rainbow, go back under the tree, where he had just come from.

"Yeah, let him go," said Ricky, indicating the corner toward which he now directed a cast, "because there's a monster over here that'll go six pounds if he'll go an ounce."

But the monster wasn't having any, nor indeed, as it developed, were any of his neighbors. For the next hour, while I caught three more, all on his fly, Rick couldn't raise one on it, and by that time he was fit to be tied.

"I think I'll take up tatting," said Ricky. "You may not like what you get, but at least you get something to look at for your pains."

There sounds, of course, the oldest cry of the angler. The golfer knows, when he comes to play a round, that the course won't have disappeared overnight, and the tennis player knows that, whether or not his serve is working well, he'll at least get a given number of chances to use it. But for the fisherman, all too often, he makes all the requisite motions, and the result is tantamount to the frustration a golfer or a tennis player would feel if he made all the moves of his game, with all his accustomed and long-acquired skill, without either a club or a racket in his hand.

There are the times when, as the cartoonist Webster used to put it, a feller needs a friend. But sometimes the angler needs more than that, because friends can sometimes, with the best will in the world, take fish when you don't. It's then the angler most feels the need of a well-furnished mind, into which to retreat as his one sure bastion of defense, lest he see and treat his friends as his enemies.

There are many mental devices, such as counting five hundred before you let yourself say a word, when you're afraid that whatever you start to say will turn into an explosion. But these are poor palliatives at best, because they provide nothing to lessen, or cushion, your mounting sense of frustration. So there really is no remedy, outside of philosophy, for the always potentially recurrent fits of fisherman's anger.

The only sure savior of sanity, I feel, is the possession of a rich enough mental store, or inventory, of thoughts or memories or associations with angling to see you through, no matter how soon or often or long the fish may be out on strike against you. You can never know when they will be. They can stop biting as suddenly and inexplicably as they begin, or even worse, they can simply refuse to start biting. When that happens, the odds are all theirs, because they have more time than you have, and they have no other calls upon it. They have no appointments to keep, no deadlines to meet, no urgent duties or obligations to worry about—when you stop to think about it, don't you marvel that we ever got into the habit of referring to them as "poor fish"?

One thing that does help maintain the angler's equilibrium, I feel sure, is the realization that the experts, for all their vaunted prowess, can get just as ingloriously skunked as you can. In this sense, we are indeed all equal. But unless you happen to be personally acquainted with some experts, I know you find this hard to believe. We all assume the other guy knows something we don't know, and are never content until we find it out. We can't believe that the answer is that there is no answer.

When Charlie Ritz lived over here as a young man, he fished a lot, and whenever anybody on a stream asked him what he was using he'd say "Coachman," whether he was or not. He never got over being surprised at how often it worked. People would come back and thank him for the tip, until sometimes he was even impelled to put one on himself, thus finding himself in the bizarre position of accepting his own advice, even if it was on the rebound.

He simply reasoned that more people know about the Coachman than any other fly and are thus more likely to have one, and that in the long run it doesn't matter much anyway, as the only fly that positively won't catch a fish is the fly that isn't in the water.

It's either this last consideration, or sheer fatalism, that impels some fishermen, every so often, to go through protracted phases of using only one fly. You get convinced that the one moment that a fish might take your fly is the one when you have it out of the water, to change it for another. And if enough of them in succession don't produce a strike, then you're sure that you must have missed a lot of strikes, in all that time you spent with your back turned, changing flies one after another.

I know one season on the Esopus, when I was religiously keeping exact track of how many fish were taken on which flies, and at what time on which date and under what weather conditions, etc., etc., etc., I finally got so infuriated at a prolonged spell of fishlessness after opening day that I decided to chuck the whole routine, and stick to the one fly I had on, which happened to be a Light Cahill size fourteen, and by the season's end I found I had taken just about as many fish as I had the year before, when I had consistently carried close to five hundred flies in my overstuffed fishing clothes and made a conscientious effort to use them all. Still another year, after a weekend of great success with the Cahill bivisible spider size sixteen, I stuck to it the rest of the season, and wound up doing just about the same as the other two seasons.

If you fish enough, you're going to take a certain number of fish, over a given amount of time, and while this is both hard to remember and fairly poor consolation, on those occasions when the fish are refusing to give you the time of day or night, it ought to be a sobering consideration in those moments of high elation, in a hot spot at a juncture when you can seemingly do no wrong—this is when we ought to remember, but somehow never do, that the time is surely coming when we can seemingly do no right.

Some form of rainy-day insurance against the gloom of those times is nice to have, and I've been gleaning my own, by little bits and pieces, for some time. In the next section, I've tried putting it together, with no more rhyme or reason than that orderly chaos caused by following the letters of the alphabet in their turn. Maybe you will find, somewhere in it, something that can serve you as a sort of lucky charm. There's nothing in it, I know, that will make you catch fish when they don't want to be caught, or at least to take a chance on being caught. Fish are our superiors, in that they seem to know, although they really know very little, that one sure way to stay out of trouble is by keeping your mouth shut. If other considerations didn't arise to make them forget it, there'd be no point in fishing for them.

You can still be skunked, after reading the next section, even if you were to follow all the possibilities for further study that it raises. You can, because anybody can. But maybe, after reading it, the next time you're skunked you won't mind it quite so much. It's a little like the story that ran around the Viennese coffeehouses about Freud's great success with the man who was a bedwetter. What, he cured him of that? Well, no, the man still wet the bed. But he stopped feeling guilty about it.

Or let's liken it to this. Some of us have the habit of carrying a pocket piece, for no better or other purpose than to have something to finger, or rub or twist or turn or touch. For all I know that could be where the word touchstone comes from, for more often than not a pocket piece is a small stone, with some gratifying aspect to the touch. It certainly can't keep us from being arrested, or mugged, and it's obviously of no use as a weapon, but just the same it feels good to touch, if only because it's there, and there are times of stress and exasperation when there's some reassurance in being able to satisfy ourselves of the continued existence of such an elementary circumstance as that.

There are things that have come to be to me more or less like that, when I'm out fishing and want something pleasant, or different, yet not utterly unrelated, to think about. Some of them are people, met in books or in life, and in some cases both, and some are things those people remind me of. I've already told you, for instance, of how often I find myself fishing with Preston Jennings these days, whenever the light is dim, because of recalling that first experience with the *Isonychia bicolor* now over a score of years ago on the Esopus. And Paul Young's Strawman nymph is another case in point. And some are things to think about, and on occasion do something about, not utterly unrelated to fishing, when I'm off the stream and away from the ponds, that I feel have some value in and of themselves, whether or not they ever aid me directly in catching another fish. And I hope that you may come to feel, for some of them, the same way.

If something you read, or something you do, after finishing this next section, gives you pleasure, then I will feel entitled to think of myself as sharing it with you, to some degree, and that's a thought I would enjoy.

So I will arise and go now, to meet you there early and, I hope, often.

Part Three

THE ANGLER'S BEST COMPANIONS

A Congeries of Aids, Authors,
Organizations and Purveyors,
Not Unworth the Attention
of Most Who Fish for
Trout and Other
Salmonids

*C*ANGLER'S ANGLER

The acknowledged dean of living American Anglers

Miller, Alfred W. (1892–). Sparse Grey Hackle, as everybody knows who can tell a fly rod from a buggy whip, is the dean of American fly fishermen, and the remaining link in the continuum that led, through Hewitt and LaBranche, back to Theodore Gordon himself. He is more than that, though, hard as it may be for a fisherman to believe that there could be anything more. He is the remaining link in the authentic chain of American literary humor that led, through Robert Benchley, back to Mark Twain himself.

Like Mark Twain, whose pseudonym became so famous as to

obscure his own name of Samuel Clemens, Sparse Grey Hackle has become so celebrated among anglers as to cast Alfred W. Miller into the shade.

If you look up Sparse Grey Hackle in the Manhattan telephone book you won't find him, but if you look among the many Millers you will find an office number for Alfred W. (or you could until recently, when the listing was changed to that of his firm). The onetime *Wall Street Journal* reporter is still active, at eighty, as a stockholders' relations counsel, and so devoted to his duties that he couldn't miss a client's annual meeting on November 28, 1972, to let the Theodore Gordon Flyfishers celebrate his birthday which had occurred the day before. So the celebration had to be put off for a week, to the next regular TGF meeting day at the Williams Club the following Tuesday. There his presence swelled the attendance to a new record for one of the club's weekly luncheons, breaking the old one hung up by Charlie Ritz some years before, as over fifty of his fans stood still to watch him blow out the candles on his cake; stout fellows all, under the circumstances, as he had just given them fair warning that after three martinis his breath might cause an explosion.

Even after the postponement, his attendance still represented something of a case of playing hookey, as on a normal weekday, from noon on, Sparse Grey Hackle is expected at the Long Table at The Anglers' Club, where he has been the *genius loci* for longer than any of the members can remember, and the club's historian, as well as editor of its bulletin since 1954, when his classic *Fishless Days* first appeared under its imprint.

That book's fame was largely legendary until the fall of 1971, when it was reissued, expanded to twice its original size and with the title appropriately broadened to *Fishless Days, Angling Nights,* in the Crown Sportsmen's Classics series. But even before that, no byline was more familiar to literate anglers of our time than that of Sparse Grey Hackle, as no angling writer has ever before been half as generous as Sparse in furnishing forewords, prefaces, and introductions to other people's fishing books. In fact more often than not his help has not stopped with writing such send-offs, but in many instances he has either directly inspired, rewritten, edited, or proofread some of the most important angling books published over the past thirty years. This was almost always without any sort of acknowledgment, and never any sort of pay—and it extends to some of the mightiest titles of the mid-century period.

As Sparse says, in the course of his commentary in another of the Crown Classics, the collection of memorabilia compiled by Sam Melner and Hermann Kessler under the title *Great Fishing Tackle Catalogs of the Golden Age,* "the best fishing is done not in water but in print."

As Sparse would be the last to point out, but I am surely far from first, some of the best of that best fishing in print has been his own.

ANGLER'S AND SHOOTER'S BOOKSHELF

Col. Henry A. Siegel
Goshen, Connecticut 06756
Out of print and rare fishing books. Good source.

Hank Siegel, one of the pillars of the Theodore Gordon Flyfishers and an accomplished trout and salmon fisherman, is undoubtedly one of the best-read anglers of our time. A longtime collector of angling books, after a career in the army and some experience in tackle retailing, Colonel Siegel became one of those fortunate few—high on my list of lucky dogs to be envied, like Al McClane—who have succeeded in making a vocation of an avocation.

From his home in Connecticut, which also houses his private collection, Siegel does a land-office business in angling books and art, and can usually be counted on to have, or know where to get, the fishing book you've lost or lent and never got back, or the one you've been looking for and never could find. In acquiring his initial stock, against which he first sent out simple mimeographed lists, Hank had the unofficial but very active help of Gene Anderegg, himself a book finder of near-professional expertise, and as Gene went around the country in the early sixties, calling on angling clubs to get the Federation of Fly Fishermen started, he was also keeping a weather eye out for books for Hank. Today the lists are formidable and so on occasion, for items of extreme scarcity, are some of the prices. The current list will set you back a dollar, although this can be deducted on any order from it of ten dollars or more. All items are subject to prior sale, so second choices should be indicated, where more than one edition or printing is listed for any title, and unless you order more than seventy-five dollars' worth at a crack, postage should be included, at the rate of a quarter a copy.

Books are certainly one of the most dependable sources of companionship an angler can have, and at the rate the prices of out-of-print volumes have been going up over the last decade, books can be on an investment basis almost what diamonds are to a girl, in the best friend category. In actual practice, you'd probably be about as likely to sell your books as she would her diamonds. But if you did, after you'd read them, you would at least have the satisfaction of knowing that as an angler your head would now be at least a little less empty than it was before.

Whether Hank Siegel is alone to blame for the way those prices have gone up is a different question. Probably not. But it would be nice to be able to cite some one instance of what he's done, à la the little Dutch boy with his finger in the dike, to stem the inflationary tide. I just can't think of any, and I don't know that Gene Anderegg can either. The last thing I'd call either Hank or Gene is stupid, which as collectors they'd have to be, to applaud a decline in angling-book prices.

So the best chance the rest of us poor fishermen have, if we want to read a book that's become an angling classic and is out of print, is either to go fishing for it in the public library or try to persuade Nick Lyons at Crown Publishers or Mike Cohen at Freshet Press or Sam Melner at Van Cortlandt Press (all of which see) to reissue it at something less than the price of an arm or leg.

Meanwhile, if you can't live without it, try Hank Siegel. After all it is a competitive business, though Colonel Siegel has raised its personal practice to the level of a sport. But if you want a book in

July, try Aldy Williams at The Sporting Book Service. In July, Hank's on the Miramichi, as you and I would be too if we were as smart as he is.

ANGLING IN ART

An appreciation of William J. Schaldach's
The Wind on Your Cheek

The art in angling is, I am afraid, a lot more important than angling in art. As everyone knows who has ever seen a copy of Sparrow's *Angling in British Art,* there have been a great many fine anglers who were artists, but very few fine artists who were anglers. Of course, there have been thousands of books spawned by the sport over the last five centuries, and most of them have been illustrated, but out of hundreds of angling artists, only a handful have attained master status as artist anglers.

Rowlandson and Turner yes. Both great artists and both frequently treated angling subjects. Landseer, Raeburn, Alma-Tadema . . . and in America, Winslow Homer and John Singer Sargent—it's hard to muster any very glittering galaxy of names. Also sad but true is the fact that the better the artist, the fewer the angling pictures by him.

But the paucity of fine artist-anglers is as nothing compared to the scarcity of angling artists who are also angling authors. Try to find the blend of artist-angler and author in anything like reasonable balance and you have a very rare specimen indeed.

In England there is Bernard Venables, and here we had—alas, not for long—John Atherton. There remains, praise be, William J. Schaldach.

On all three counts, as artist, author, and angler, Bill Schaldach passes anybody's test. But when you add the fourth dimension, which is artistry with the gun as well as the rod, then the man begins to stretch the corners of credulity, and you start to wonder, with the farmer at the first sight of a giraffe, whether there can indeed be any such creature.

There is and has been, as I can attest, over the span of very nearly forty years, to my own knowledge and great satisfaction.

William J. Schaldach began to glorify the pages of *Esquire* with words and pictures invoking rods and guns almost before the magazine was out of its swaddling clothes, and he remained one of the chief ornaments of its sporting side through its vintage years.

He warmed the cockles of this manic angler's heart as far back as May of 1936, by pointing out that "one has only to see a skillful performer casting a fly to appreciate that the sport has in it the elements of art. And an artist thinks seriously about his tools . . . the angler has much the same feeling for his rod as that possessed by a violinist for a rare Amati or Guarnerius."

But even more endearing, to me, because it's more enduring, is this tenet of the Schaldach dogma, as laid down away back in those days before we'd ever heard of glass rods or floating lines or nylon tippets: "One of the reasons that fly-fishing appeals to so many men, I think, is that the sport is non-competitive. There are occasional individuals, I know, who can't seem to be happy unless they go forth for the day's fishing laden with bets on the first fish, the largest fish, the heaviest creel, and so on. Such men miss the point. Angling is an aesthetic pleasure."

There speaks the kind of man who can give a sport a good name. And angling is indeed an aesthetic pleasure as practiced and preached and portrayed in such books as *Currents and Eddies* and *Coverts and Casts* and no less in this new one.

Here, in every line of the pictures as well as in every line of the prose, there is the inimitable authority and the sure hand of the veteran, who has kept his eyes and his mind open to every new experience and every sensation of ever-recurring wonder. The latter is the difference, between the days spent out of doors by the sensitive artist and the unthinking clod. Some men could go through the same motions, over the same grounds, and come back with nothing but some meat and a monosyllabic grunt. Others would talk your head off, without conveying the least idea of what it was like to be there. Some can make you feel what it was like. Of this gifted company is Schaldach. But better yet, with him, you can see it, too, not only once, but again and again.

He dates from the days of the untreated split-cane rods that you had to coddle constantly to keep from acquiring a "set," of the gut tippets that you had to soak between felt pads overnight, to avoid snapping your fly off on the first cast, of the silk lines that you had to take off the reel and wind around a line dryer (or a chairback) to avert the damp rot that would let a little fish become a tackle buster—he dates, indeed, from those good old days that we marvel now that we could ever have enjoyed.

But his art is ageless, and his viewpoint is as eternally fresh, with this book's many exemplifications of its recurrent motive of "you never can tell," as a tug on your line, or a sudden whirr of wings behind you, or, indeed, the wind on your cheek.

ATLANTIC SALMON ASSOCIATION

(Daniel O. C. Doheny, President) Shell Tower, Room 705
1255 University Street
Montreal 110, Quebec, Canada

International public nonprofit organization devoted to the conservation of the Atlantic salmon. Founded in 1948, ASA is the oldest of the various North American groups now concerned with the survival and restoration of this gravely threatened and severely depleted resource. Membership of twenty-five hundred, of whom approximately 67 percent are Americans, and the rest almost all Canadian, with half a percentile of members overseas. Membership includes subscription to Atlantic Salmon Journal, *normally a quarterly but latterly reduced to trimestral appearance by escalating costs and determination to retain its character as the authentic and complete journal of record throughout the period of the Atlantic salmon emergency. Contributions over the $5 annual membership fee are deductible for tax purposes.*

Under the pertinacious leadership of the late T. B. "Happy" Fraser, its onetime president and longtime manager, ASA was first to sound the alarm over the effect of the Greenland high seas fishery on North American salmon stocks and was largely instrumental in bringing about the Canadian government's curtailment of commercial salmon fishing in response to the disastrous decline in the 1971 run. As far back as 1966, when ASA held its annual meeting in New York jointly with the Theodore Gordon Flyfishers, it passed a resolution condemning the Danish fishing in the Davis Strait and in the open ocean off Greenland, and Happy Fraser was unremitting in his efforts to raise the hue and cry against the Danes thereafter. By the summer of 1972, when he died, he had at least lived long enough to see the Danes agree in principle to the phasing out of their Greenland high seas fishery and to see measures taken to end the offshore salmon fishing in Canada's territorial waters. Happy could die, as he had lived, in full consonance with his nickname, knowing that his early and constant warnings had not gone unheeded. The last words of his last public utterance were "there may be some prospect of curbing the Northern fishery in time to save our salmon."

But he knew, as does everyone who has made more than the most superficial study of the international Atlantic salmon emergency, that the mere ending of the high seas fishery, severe as its effects have been, will not be enough in itself to constitute a definitive answer to that anguished SOS of "save our salmon."

The deterioration of the habitat for the once-teeming runs of Atlantic salmon, which has been happening for a hundred and fifty years, can hardly be repaired overnight, no matter how much dedication and knowledge may be applied to the problem. There are undoubtedly decades of uphill struggle ahead, before anybody can say with any certainty that the future of the Atlantic salmon is assured. But it is heartening to see how many forces are being girded for the attempt. To the pioneer efforts of ASA, half-a-dozen new ones have been added, on the order of CASE and IASF, and one, the North Atlantic Salmon Council, which they have formed jointly, to correlate and organize all their separate actions. This is all to the good, for as ASA President Dan Doheny says, "While we as the oldest North

American salmon association welcome any new organization interested in conservation of Atlantic salmon stocks, there comes a point when the aim of all—the preservation of *Salmo salar*—may be less well served if our energies are too diversified."

Meanwhile, through ongoing studies and researches begun as far back as 1967, through the beneficence of such stalwarts on the ASA board as John Olin and the late Charles Engelhard, ASA has to a certain extent taken time by the forelock, and begun to uncover through some of its genetic investigations what may well serve, to the benefit of all, as shortcuts on the long hard road back for this mighty but beleaguered fish.

As Dan Doheny also says, with understandable pride, "We started the crusade, our banner is still in the forefront."

There's a limit, of course, to how many organizations even the most concerned of fishermen can support, but even ordinary membership is helpful to the Atlantic Salmon Association at this critical juncture in its long and useful life. And even the armchair angler, who may never set eyes on a salmon except in a Lee Wulff movie, can regard the ordinary membership in ASA as a good investment, because he'll certainly get his money's worth out of the pages of the *Atlantic Salmon Journal* alone, yea though its frequency should shrink again to twice a year. It's hard to put a price tag on anything you know you can't get anywhere else. Under the circumstances, I'd say it was cheap at twice the price.

$\mathcal{B}$ERGMAN

Bergman, Ray (1891–1967). The Dr. Spock to a whole generation of American fishermen who were literally brought up by the book—the most widely read book on trout, by a wide margin, is Ray Bergman's, first published in 1938, by Penn Publishing Company. It was reissued by Alfred A. Knopf, New York, in 1944, and unlike the vast majority of angling books of this century has been kept in print ever since. A revised and enlarged edition was published by Knopf in 1952, and has been reprinted at frequent intervals since then. Second in size only to the English Eric Taverner's *Trout Fishing from All Angles,* Bergman's *Trout* is the largest (451 pages) ever devoted to one fish in American publishing history. Many anglers, obviously feeling that there's nothing that you can learn from a book that you can't learn better from a fish, consider their libraries complete once they've bought their copy of Bergman's *Trout.* They don't expect or want a fishing book as a birthday or Father's Day present, on the perfectly logical grounds that they've already got a book. Nobody would ever argue, beginning with Bergman himself, that this is the best fishing book ever written, but its continuing sale seems to indicate that it must be the most satisfying. Many of the best fishing books are like Chinese food, in that they very quickly make you want to come back again for more, soon after you've read them, whereas Bergman's *Trout* must stimulate the appetite to go fishing for them, rather than wanting to read any more about them.

Bergman was for many years fishing editor of *Outdoor Life,* and his books reflect the professional's wide acquaintance with all aspects of the subject. In a lifetime of listening to, and appraising, the passionate advocacy of many specialists for their theories and techniques, Bergman's position can be likened to that of the old-fashioned general practitioner—he had some sympathy and understanding for all the many schools of modern angling, but largely felt that nature should be allowed to take its course, and that the element of luck might possibly be abetted, but never supplanted. His other books were *Just Fishing,* 1932, *Bass,* 1942, and *With Fly, Plug and Bait,* 1947. Since his death, his onetime associate Edward C. Janes has compiled a book of his magazine writings, *Fishing with Ray Bergman,* but it is as the author of *Trout* that Bergman will go on being read. And certainly worse things could be said of a fishing book than that it makes you want to stop reading and start fishing.

BETHUNE

Bethune, George Washington (1805–1862). A Doctor of Divinity, who styled himself only "The American Editor" out of deference to the feelings of parishioners who might be scandalized at the thought of an angling work by a minister, Dr. G. W. Bethune was America's foremost angling scholar and first angling book collector. In 1847 he edited, for publication both here and in London, the first American edition of Walton & Cotton's *Compleat Angler,* changing the spelling of the title word to *Complete* and old Izaak's spelling to Isaac. At a time when the English were still saying that nobody reads an American book, the impact of this scholarly work was sensational. Bethune not only provided copious notes of irrefutable authority, but also a "Bibliographical Preface" that was an account of fishing and fishing books from the earliest antiquity to the time of Walton, together with a notice of Cotton and his writings, and also an appendix that was monumental, including, as advertised on the title page, "illustrative ballads, music, papers on American fishing, and the most complete catalogue of books on angling, etc., ever printed." It was, and remains, one of the very best of the nearly four hundred editions of Walton and Cotton to date. Bethune's only previous publication was *A Plea for Study,* an oration before the Literary Societies of Yale College, in 1845, and his only subsequent works were *Lays of Love and Faith, with Other Fugitive Poems, The British Female Poets,* and *Orations and Occasional Discourses.* He was a minor literary figure, but of major stature to anglers, who have developed an affection for him reflecting his own for the *Compleat Angler* which he termed, "this darling book." Bethune's own love of books was too great to let him give his own six hundred angling volumes the "affront" of a bookplate or any other mark of his ownership, a detail that caused anguish to subsequent collectors, avid for his "association" with his books, when his collection was sold at Sotheby's after his death.

BROOKS

An Appreciation of Trout Fishing, *by Joe Brooks*

For an entire generation there was one book that gave point to the legendary Dumb Blonde's plaint of "Oh, I can't give him a book, he's already got a book." But if he was a trout fisherman, and just an ordinary guy who would rather fish than read, then dumb or not she was right, and the book was Ray Bergman's *Trout,* and it made him feel that if he read it through he'd never have to read another.

Today, at long last, we again have such a book. The new "one book to have, when you're not having more than one" is *Trout Fishing* by Joe Brooks. Read this, and you won't have to feel half-safe with a fly rod in your hand, no matter where you go, and unless you harbor designs on succeeding both Bergman and Brooks as fishing editor of *Outdoor Life* yourself, you can depend on this one book to tell you everything you really have to know.

For once the blurb on a book jacket could stop short of the whole truth, as this one does when it says "The trout, the tackle and techniques are all here in *Trout Fishing,* the expression of a lifetime of angling by the master fisherman, Joe Brooks." That's all true, as far as it goes (and Joe's death on the heels of publication gave poignant points to the use of the word "lifetime"), but it doesn't go far enough. As a character in a Broadway play once said, "That's not the truth—that's only the facts."

Well, the facts would be enough to characterize the previous nine books by Joe Brooks, which were all good straight workmanlike jobs of doing simply what he set out to do, and doing it without fuss or feathers. There's always been an irreducible reduction of every sort of ostentatious pretense down to an almost vacuumlike absence from every Joe Brooks book. Though the titles, like *Saltwater Game Fishing, Bass Bug Fishing,* and *Saltwater Fly Fishing,* were as straight as this one, you always felt they could have been preceded by such a phrase as *"The Common Sense of"* their various subjects. On the other hand, you'd as soon expect Sonny Tufts to play Hamlet as to look to Joe Brooks for any such fancy-pants trappings as *The Mystique of Trout Fishing.* But that's exactly what the old fooler tossed into his tenth and last book, along with all the factual stuff that the jacket promises and Joe duly delivers. Along with the facts, which are all here and admirably organized and presented, he gives you the truth, the bright blinding revelation of all that makes this one species rise above the status of a fish to achieve almost that of a religion. This is the part of the Brooks story that, in his foreword to this book,

Charles K. Fox characterizes as "the magic of trout fishing" and that the author himself, in his preface, terms "the universal charisma of the trout."

And beginning with the first chapter, a history of trout fishing that has to be the best job of condensation since H. G. Wells wrote *The Outline of History* in one volume, and continuing with the next, called "The Trout We Fish For," which is so good it makes you almost start feeling yourself for fins, the master fisherman puts you through the best short course of trout appreciation and understanding that our day affords.

The book's one flaw is that the mastery of the text and the overall "packaging" of pictures and format is marred by sloppy copy-editing, such as allowing Harry Darbee's name to go through spelled wrong twice and right once. But then, nothing's perfect, though in every other respect this book comes mighty close.

CASE*

Committee on the Atlantic Salmon Emergency
Box 164
Hancock, New Hampshire 03449
(Richard A. Buck, Chairman)

An ad hoc committee, formed for the immediate purpose of countering the depredation of Atlantic salmon stocks by high seas fisheries, but with long range aim of promoting the conservation and restoration of Atlantic salmon. Of crucial importance as a catalyst of otherwise disunited and uncoordinated forces.

Although CASE appeared to be nearing its goal in 1972, and was generally recognized as the single most responsible factor in bringing

---

* As of this printing the name of this organization is being changed to RASA, Restoration of Salmon in America, Inc.; all other aspects of the organization remain the same.

about the agreement for the phasing out over a four-year period of the Danish high seas salmon fishing off Greenland, which appeared to be threatening the ultimate extinction of Canadian salmon stocks, it is evident that the committee still has a lot of work cut out for it, and the date when it can in good conscience contemplate its own dissolution may well be a long way off.

Although the short-term fisheries agreement between Denmark and the United States for the phase-out of the high seas fishery was reached early in 1972, it was soon apparent that the war to save our salmon was far from won, even if the Danish-U.S. agreement should be later formalized by the International Commission for Northwest Atlantic Fisheries. For one thing, even if the open-ocean fishing for Atlantic salmon off Greenland should end, it would not remove the last threat to the future of what Anthony Netboy has termed "the vanishing species," but would merely eliminate the latest and most serious one. CASE quite properly concentrated its attention on the Danish fishing on the basis of first things first. After all, the Committee was formed on a footing of urgency, like the spontaneous organization of a bucket brigade at the scene of a spreading fire, when it became evident in the late sixties that the toll of the seagoing Atlantic salmon was rising at very nearly geometrical progression.

But the forces inimical to the survival of the Atlantic salmon have been gathering ever since the beginning of the Industrial Revolution, and the high seas fishery is only the newest of them. Much more difficult to isolate and extricate are the hydra-headed problems left in the wake of a century and a half of heedless exploitation and spoliation of the environment on this side of the ocean where the spawning runs occur, or used to occur, with resultant accretions of excessive pollution and thermal loads and insufficiencies of water levels and fishways. For Canadian salmon fishing, the problem is preservation, but for American salmon fishing it is still primarily one of restoration. The future possibilities are dazzlingly bright (there is hope of having as many salmon in the Connecticut River alone by the end of this decade as there are now, some forty-five thousand, in the mighty six-river complex of the entire Miramichi system in New Brunswick) but the actual accomplishment to date is meager. Federal funds have been assured, for instance, for the design of a hatchery that would assure salmon seed stocks patterned to return to the Connecticut and other Northeastern United States rivers, but the money for the bricks and mortar, to take the hatchery beyond the blueprint stage is still to be found.

CASE is growing, as its appeals reach out beyond the ranks of those with some immediate interest in salmon, and its mailing list, which is constantly pruned for effectiveness, now reaches some twenty-five hundred concerned persons, of whom close to five hundred contribute financially, and nearly eighty in a substantial way. Some large items, such as the cost of making the film *High Seas Fishing off Greenland,* and the original extensive public information program, were respectively met by Philip Morris, Inc., and the International Atlantic Salmon Foundation.

But CASE must also contend with complacency, because every news story about the imminence of an agreement to end the high seas fishery, or about the partial suspension of commercial fishing and netting in Canada, and indeed every fisherman's tale of better salmon fishing in Canada since the low point of the 1971 season, leads people to the false belief that the "emergency" aspect of the Atlantic salmon situation is over.

I'm something of a Johnny-come-lately to CASE myself, as I went onto the Committee only in 1972, after the agreement in principle to phase out the Danish high seas fishery had already been announced. But I've since come to realize that even if it were ended now, it could still mark only "the end of the beginning" in the long uphill struggle that still lies ahead before we can hope to see New England rivers once again adorned by the leaping of these noble fish.

Any angler who has any sense of wanting to "pay his dues," for the satisfaction he gets out of the pursuit of his sport, could look long and hard before finding a better place to put his money than CASE.

CATCH AND RELEASE CLUB

Bud Lilly is a trout's best friend

Fly-fishing's legion of honor decoration is the lapel recognition button devised by Bud Lilly, which reads "Released 20″ Trout" and carries the slogan "Support F.F.F.–T.U." The club's purpose is to get fishermen familiar with the idea of releasing trout. Anybody can join. All that's needed is a dollar, and the simple statement that a trout of a certain size was returned to the water. The statement and the dollar can be sent to Bud Lilly, from November to May, Sourdough Road, Bozeman, Montana 59715, or to Bud Lilly, from May to November, in care of The Trout Shop, West Yellowstone, Montana 59587. Bud's pragmatic philosophy on keeping the membership requirement this simple reflects the belief that all fly fishermen are naturally honest and that any who are not will at least be publicizing the principle.

The principle of trout release, first and best stated by Lee Wulff, has since had many genial variations, one of the nicest of which is the Klamath Country Fly Casters' motto, "Keep your lines tight and your creels empty." But however it's codified it couldn't be better propagandized than by the general adoption and use of the Bud Lilly Catch and Release Club lapel buttons. Bud Lilly donates the proceeds from the sale of the release recognition buttons to Trout Unlimited and the Federation of Fly Fishermen.

Bud Lilly's Trout Shop for the past twenty years has been a virtual gateway to paradise for fly fishermen. From May first to the end of October, Bud and his wife, Pat, and his children, Annette, Mike, Greg (and Greg's wife Bonnie), are all at the Trout Shop or out on the stream guiding fishermen. Guiding others out West began in Bud's family with his great-grandfather who, as wagonmaster, led wagon trains from St. Louis, Missouri, to Montana, and with his great-uncle Amos Hague, who guided various noblemen's parties on tours of Yellowstone Park in its very early days. His tackle catalog and handbook for western trout fishing is the best I know. But send for it at your own risk, as it's highly infectious. Don't say I didn't warn you, that you'd better be prepared, before you open its covers, to be lured into a trip to Montana. Few better fates, however, could befall a fly fisher.

CROWN'S SPORTSMEN'S CLASSICS

Crown Publishers, Inc.
419 Park Avenue South
New York, New York 10016
(Nick Lyons, Consulting Editor)

Certain books were sorely needed—and
Crown was first to bring them back alive

If the literacy of anglers as a whole and as a class has measurably increased in recent years, and it has, as one glance at the vaulting prices of collector's items in angling literature is enough to attest, then the one man more responsible for it than any other is Nick Lyons at Crown.

And what a difference it makes, when a fisherman takes charge of the angling titles issued by a general trade publisher. If Nick Lyons had done nothing else but restore to active circulation such legendarily scarce items as Vince Marinaro's *A Modern Dry-Fly Code* and Preston Jennings's *A Book of Trout Flies,* to say nothing of Sparse Grey Hackle's *Fishless Days,* anglers everywhere would already owe him a statue.

But these were only the harbingers of a steady flow of authentic sporting classics, both old and new, to come out under this one imprint over the last three years. As if to furnish further proof of the old adage that it takes one to know one, Nick Lyons is himself the author of a modern classic, *The Seasonable Angler,* which he characteristically brought out under the imprint of another publisher.

The farthest possible remove from the old rough and ready stereotype of a fisherman, as fostered by a whole generation of demotic rod-and-gun editors across the land, Nick Lyons is by vocation a professor of English literature, currently at Hunter College in New York, and only an editor by moonlight, so to speak, serving as a consulting editor at Crown without prejudice to either his tenure or his tenacity as a professor.

His avocation keeps him up nights, since the better part of both his days and evenings have to be subjected to the first call upon his time of his profession. But he has nevertheless managed to get out and around among the trade, and in concert with the sporting editors at other houses, such as Angus Cameron at Knopf, he has worked up a whole program of additional outlets for hunting and fishing titles, above and beyond the conventional channels through bookstores to which such books were almost exclusively confined in the past. This has resulted in a better than doubled sales expectancy for books in this category, with a consequent general grading up of production and manufacturing quality.

Anglers have never rated as heavy frequenters of bookstores, and Nick Lyons, in the pragmatic attitude of Mahomet to the mountain, made the first really energetic move in the direction of taking the bookstores to the anglers, so to speak, in compensation for the well-known reluctance of anglers to come to bookstores on their own. One result has been a greatly increased willingness, on the part of trade publishers generally, to take a chance on sporting titles that they might once have turned down out of hand as being too special in nature, and too limited in appeal, to warrant hard-cover distribution.

In consequence, both publishers and booksellers, as well as anglers themselves, have good reason to be grateful to Crown and the breakthrough brought about by its Sportsmen's Classics program.

BRIAN CURTIS

Ichthyology for everybody—a rare achievement

Curtis, Brian (1893–1960). The not very happy life of the author of *The Life Story of the Fish, His Manners and Morals* is a study in frustration, with a surprise ending, like an O. Henry plot. Born in New York, Harvard-educated, then settling on a ranch in northern

California, he had every advantage of breeding and money in his background, yet felt unable to achieve his one ambition, which was to be a writer. So he took up ichthyology instead, to give himself some occupation in place of the one for which he felt unfitted. He grew up to be a tall quiet man, anything but the life of the party, silent as the fish that became his life study, and even in his looks, though his bearing was distinguished, he came to resemble the objects of his attention, with his characteristic attributes of strong mouth and receding chin and brow. With a possessive mother and a younger brother on whom he doted, he was relatively late in getting around to any other living companionship than that of his work, but when he married it was to his opposite, a woman as witty and outgoing as he was taciturn and reserved. They were happy together, until one morning at breakfast he punctuated their laughter and chatter, quite simply, by dying. His wife sold the ranches, moved to a duplex in a big San Francisco hotel, seemed to be adjusting to a movemented existence involving a lot of people and travel, but one night went to bed full of pills and never woke up, leaving a note that thanked everybody and said she'd had a wonderful life.

With his own sudden death and his wife's suicide, the annals of Brian and Meta Curtis would have been as short and simple, despite their station, as those of the poor are poetically supposed to be. But Brian Curtis had put on paper all the wit that he had eschewed in social converse, talking shop to himself, in a manuscript, because he was too well bred to do so in small talk. First published in 1938, *The Life Story of the Fish* was published again in 1949 in a revised edition, and then reissued in 1961 in a Dover reprint. In it, Brian Curtis, the failed writer, achieved one of the rarest forms of writing success, the attainment of a scientifically sound, but still wittily and entertainingly comprehensible simplification of one of the most complicated of subjects. It is the story, not of fishing, but of fish, and although the average angler may think, looking at dealers' shelves, that there are a great many books about fishing, the card catalogs of the world's libraries contain ten entries under ichthyology for every one under angling. Most of the ichthyological items are intelligible only to other ichthyologists, but *The Life Story of the Fish* is a felicitous exception.

Any angler who can read without moving his lips can follow Brian Curtis through one of the most fascinating life stories ever told, and no angler can be so proficient that he doesn't need to know what this unique little book can tell him.

Most books on fishing seek to persuade the reader to think and act like other fishermen. This one, without presuming to tell the reader how to think like a fish, at least affords him some insight into how and why fish react to certain stimuli in a certain way. It can be debated, indeed, whether fish can really think at all, for thought in the human concept of the process of ratiocination is as alien to all animals as taxation, but fish like many other members of the animal kingdom can act as if they could think, and Curtis is brilliant at explaining these actions, and reactions, that to the human observer appear tantamount to thought. In fact, it is that higher strata of fishermen, who are concerned with what they regard as "educated" fish, who can read *The Life Story of the Fish* with the most enjoyment and profit.

As the Supervising Fisheries Biologist of the California State Division of Fish and Game, Curtis could track his way with ease through the intricate layers of scientifically established fact and the formidable clouds of learned terminology that make his specialty such an impenetrable thicket of detail. But his mastery of his subject was so consummate that he could, without losing his way or short-circuiting the complicated relationship of the essential facts, strip away all the obfuscations of detail with which scientific pedantry blindfolds the layman. Listening to two biologists talking to each other is about as rewarding to the ordinary angler as listening to two consulting physicians is to the average patient. But listening to Curtis is like hearing the sweet bird of truth through the orchestral din of a jungle of scholarly fact.

One case in point: he describes how "the eel's life-cycle is the reverse of the salmon's. The latter is born in fresh water, goes to sea to live, feed, and grow, returns to fresh water to spawn and die. The former is born in salt water, goes into fresh water to live, feed, and grow, and returns to salt water to spawn and die. It is difficult to conceive how the salmon finds its way back from the sea to its home tributary; but it is even more difficult to conceive how the eel finds its way back across the trackless ocean to the Sargasso Sea.

"A very different kind of spawning migration is that of a little smeltlike fish six inches long called the grunion. The grunion lives along the Sandy California beaches, and it has worked out an equation in timing in which the movements of the sun and the moon are the variables.

"The moon, as we all learned in school, is the principal cause of the tides of the sea, but the sun also plays a part . . .

"In plain words, for the benefit of those not astronomically minded, approximately every two weeks there is a period of two or three days when the high tides are higher than usual. These are called spring tides. At such times, the waves come up on the beaches further than they do at most high tides, and reach points on the sand which, after their subsidence, will remain above water until the next spring tide comes two weeks later to wash over them again . . . [and] the grunion has arranged its whole life-cycle in such a way as to take advantage of it.

"Every two weeks during the spawning season, which lasts from March until July, the grunion mature . . . At night, in great numbers, the fish congregate in the surf. There they wait, rising and falling in the long Pacific roll, until just after high tide. At the proper moment something gives them the signal, and they begin to come in. Like skillful surf-boarders, they ride the crests of the waves, and they bounce and tumble along with the foam until they land high up on the beach. There each female's tail drills a hole in the dripping sand; into it she pours her eggs, which are fertilized by the nearest male, and the fish, except for the unfortunate few who fail to extricate themselves and are found dead the next morning up to their armpits, so to speak, in sand, squirm their way back into the next wave and are sucked out to sea. The mating act, including the selection of partners, the digging of the nest, and the deposition of the sex products, takes no more than sixty seconds, and the whole spawning migration sets what must be an all-time record for speed, for from the moment an individual starts in on the crest of a wave until it is back again in deep water cannot be over three minutes.

"The parents, having done what is called their duty, but what in this case must be nothing but a pleasant and exciting excursion, go on their way. The spring tide recedes, next day's sun shines down upon the beach, and there, safely buried three or four inches deep in the warm, moist sand, the eggs develop. Two weeks later the next spring tide scours them from their nest, washes the ready fry out of the egg-membranes, and sweeps them out to sea . . .

"The eggs take only nine days to develop, but the fry do not emerge until the waves dig them out of the sand. They are thus ready for the appointment ahead of time, in case winds or other circumstances should bring the releasing tide earlier than usual, but they none the less suspend their progress and wait patiently within the egg until the water comes to set them free. If they did not, they would emerge into the almost dry sand, and would perish.

"The whole thing is an equation in timing even more complicated than that of the eel, and, to my mind, even prettier. I would rather be a grunion than an eel.

"There is one fish which has pushed the matter even further. It apparently appreciates the desirable features of the grunion's system, but being an inhabitant of tropical fresh waters it has no tide to help it, and has to take the parts played by the sun and the moon itself. It spawns out of water entirely. Through what feats of acrobatism can only be imagined, the female sticks her eggs to a rock a little above the surface, and the male then goes on duty to keep them wet by splashing water on them until the young hatch. Gilbert and Sullivan could not have thought of anything more nonsensical, nor Alice's White Knight with his

> . . . *plan*
> *To dye one's whiskers green*
> *And always use so large a fan*
> *That they could not be seen.*

"The little *Copeina* described above shows a commendable interest in the eggs after they are laid, but there are other fish which go even further. Most touching instance of post-natal care is the so-called 'mouth-breeder.'

"Here we have a fish—a cold, dull, selfish animal in the eyes of most people—going without food for weeks for the sake of its children. This occurs not only among the cichlids, which we mentioned in the preceding chapter as outstanding examples of parental solicitude, but also among the catfish. One of the parents—in some species the mother, in some the father—takes the eggs in the mouth after they are fertilized, and not only holds them there throughout development, but also holds a mouthful of squirming fry until the yolk-sac is absorbed. In spite of all temptations, no food is eaten. And in the case of the cichlids the young, even after they are free-swimming, return to the parental mouth each evening and spend the night there until they are literally too big to get in."

Among the cases of parental solicitude mentioned earlier by Curtis, he cited that of the male bass, with his providing and caring for the nest, out of which he chases the female as soon as she has served his purpose by laying eggs for him to fertilize, and then tends jealously. "His care continues until the yolk-sac is absorbed . . . but as soon as the fry begin to swim he deserts them. Up to this point they have been his joy and pride and the darlings of his heart, but from now on he ceases to recognize them. They are just little fish, and all little fish are good to eat. Parental instinct, at this stage in the evolutionary scale, has made a brave beginning, but it lacks endurance. It breaks down under temptation."

The Life Story of the Fish ends, like a Fourth of July fireworks display, in a bravura demonstration of the ultimate in oddities of adaptation of which fish are capable. After citing the seahorse, in which "it looks exactly as if the father were giving birth," Curtis trots out his penultimate "believe-it-or-not" exhibit:

"And in a very different species the father, incredible as it may sound, actually does give birth—or, to put it more correctly, the same fish which at one time in its life gives birth later becomes a father. For in one of the live-bearers, Xyphophorus, the sword-tail, authentic records are numerous of complete change of sex. An individual starts life as a female, becomes a mother, and gives birth to numerous offspring. After some years of this she gets tired of males, starts taking up with other females, and before long has fathered numerous offspring. As one ichthyologist described it, 'A mother becomes the father of her own granddaughter.' It seems a happy division of domestic labors," muses Curtis, quietly anticipating Women's Liberation by some three decades, "and one which human beings might well envy. After a youthful probationary period during which she underwent the trials, as well as the joys, of womanhood and motherhood, the individual, instead of becoming barren in middle life, would turn into a man, enjoying thenceforth masculine freedom from physical and domestic woes, and assuming masculine responsibilities. What wise old men we should have! For it is difficult for even the most sensitive of us fully to appreciate situations which we have not personally experienced; but an old man who had been in his earlier days maiden, wife, and mother would be capable of a boundless sympathy for and understanding of all mankind."

Then, with a ringmaster's zest for the spectacular, Brian Curtis introduces the last act in the extravaganza which *The Life Story of the Fish* has by then become: "And now we come to the climax, the ultimate height, the wildest flight of fancy, exemplified by a certain large and quite ugly deep-sea angler-fish. This animal is a perfect Christmas tree of adaptations. Being an angler, it has the dorsal fin modified into a dangling lure. Being a deep-sea fish, it has, as many deep-sea fish do, phosphorescent organs which light up the darkness in which it lives—whether to signal mates or to lure victims is undetermined. And then it goes a step further and stupefies the rest of the animal kingdom by taking unto itself a parasitic mate. Parasitic not in the manner of some human females: here the parasitism is physical, and is practiced by the male . . . The female is forty inches long, her devoted husband four inches long—only one one-thousandth of her weight.

"This species lives at great depths, in complete blackness. Its numbers are few. The chances of a male finding a female are poor, and of his losing her after he has once found her good. What he does, then, if he has the good luck to find a mate, is to make sure that he will never be separated from her. He takes her by the throat or the back, or some other portion of her anatomy. His jaws sink in. And he never lets go again. By and by his skin grows together with her skin. Her blood-vessels make connection with his blood vessels. His mouth degenerates and becomes functionless. He becomes literally one with her.

"In an earlier chapter it was said that no cases of monogamy in the fish world could be proved, and even here, in spite of first appearances to the contrary, true monogamy does not exist, for the female may attach onto herself several males. But of unswerving masculine devotion to a single spouse this is unquestionably the world's outstanding example. Here is conjugal faithfulness carried to the ultimate degree. Here are no puny words about 'till death do us part.' Not even death will part this little fish from his mate. If she dies, he at once dies also. Here is marital fidelity beyond the powers of the most virtuous of the human species.

"Poor fish, indeed!"

These words, with which Brian Curtis concluded *The Life Story of the Fish,* could well leave many readers in the mood for an encore. Their disappointment, in searching out the other writings of this man who thought he had flunked out on his self-imposed tests for authorship, would be as great as Queen Victoria's was when she sent for the other writings of Lewis Carroll after reading *Alice in Wonderland* and discovered that they all dealt with mathematics. The only other writings of Brian Curtis lie in the files of the *Bulletin of the American Museum of Natural History* (vol. LXXVI, art. 1, pp. 1–46, 1939) and the *Transactions of the American Fisheries Society* (vol. 64, pp. 259–265, 1934) where they would seem to be beyond what Walton termed "the perusal of most anglers."

(In fact, since Curtis is gone, the nearest approach to "more Curtis," in terms of similarly assimilable information if not of his inimitable wit, is the 1973 volume *Through the Fish's Eye,* by Mark Sosin and John Clark, who comes closer to Curtis than any other presently "popularizing" ichthyologist.)

But *The Life Story of the Fish, His Manners and Morals* should be read, if not as long as fish still swim, then at least as long as there are still people left who feel like fishing for them.

DEEP-FREEZE FISHING

"Don't use Vaseline—use measured casts"

Maybe you're so sensible that the problem of what to do when ice freezes your line fast to your rod's guides will never come up. But if you live in a state, as I do, where the only closed season for trout is a couple of weeks before opening day in the spring, you're a pretty dull fellow if in the months before that time you're never once tempted to get to some open water and try a few casts. Your excuse, lest your peers deem you ready for commitment, needn't even be that you're going fishing, but only to try out a new line or rod or reel that you got, say, for Christmas. But if you do that, in any state above the Mason-Dixon Line, any appreciable length of time after the end of daylight saving, you're going to find your line sticking to your rod tip and frozen more or less fast to all the other line guides, within a matter of minutes after you start casting. What to do about it?

"Use Vaseline—just smear it on each of the rod's guides," say the old-timers, returning to their papers before the cozy fire. They never offer to come along, to see just how foolish and futile their advice is.

The one thing you accomplish by taking their advice is to delay the freezing of the line to the guides by from two to three minutes, if the air temperature is appreciably below the thirty-two degree mark on the Fahrenheit thermometer. After that you're just as stuck as if you'd left the Vaseline tube or jar at home in the medicine closet.

Better than smearing the guides with petroleum jelly is to dip the rod in the water, to immerse it up to and including the large guide nearest the reel, being careful not to dunk the reel itself or you're really in trouble, and also trying to keep your hand out of the water. Your hand can get cold enough without this treatment, if you're fishing in really cold weather. But if you cast quickly after doing this, the chances are that you can make one fully normal retrieve of your line before the accumulations of ice on your rod guides forces you to repeat the process. And if you're lucky enough to hook a fish big enough to take line off your reel, the odds are all against your having to interrupt the play—unless or until he chooses to lie doggo—for the necessity of breaking the ice on the guides with your fingers.

But a much better alternative is to make measured casts, and refrain from retrieving any line through the guides until the moment a fish forces you to do so. In other words, start fishing by stripping just as much length of leader and line off your rod tip as you can comfortably keep in the air without recourse to any use of your left hand (assuming that you're right-handed). Start with only as much line as you would normally have out when you are dapping, which is hardly any line at all. In fact, start with dapping. You'd be surprised how often it works in extremely cold weather. Go along the shore or bank just flailing the water repeatedly, with a plain black or white fly, and see what happens. If nothing does, repeat the process, but letting the fly sink to a slow count of, first, ten, and then even twenty, before you lift it for the next cast. You can go on doing this until your parade runs out of marching ground. If you do that without getting so much as a touch, I'll be surprised. I've had trout rising to a dap like kernels of corn popping in a pan, when the air temperature was anywhere from two to twenty-two degrees. But I've also had them, after driving me and themselves wild one day, blandly ignore me the next day, in the same place and under the same conditions. That, as they say, is fishing.

So, after they've ignored your dapping as long as your patience can tolerate (theirs is endless, because unlike you they've got nowhere to go and nothing more pressing to do), then let out more line, to the limit of how far you can cast one-handed, that is, without touching the line with your left hand at all. This should be the length of cast that will let you draw the fly back toward you for a dozen feet or so simply by raising your casting arm and/or retreating a few steps while you make a normal retrieve of about that length. The line is coming back through the water, but not through your line guides. Now try fishing that way, casting as often as is necessary, with only about a dozen feet of retrieve at a time, to cover completely the fishable water within reach.

You can fish all day this way, and never have to give any more thought to your line guides than if it were the Fourth of July. You can even fish a streamer very satisfactorily this way. And it's for sure that your chances of hooking fish will be twice as great, whatever the length of time you keep at it, than they would be if you spent some half of your fishing time breaking the ice off your line guides before hurrying out another cast.

Many's the four-pounder I've caught when the thermometer stood at four above zero, or even two, on a dapped or very slowly retrieved (so slow as to be the next thing to a state of suspension just below the surface) white or black Strawman, or a Quack Royal Coachman, or even—just before daylight or just before dark—a Preston Jennings *Isonychia bicolor*.

November and December, for no good reason that I've ever been able to figure out, aren't as good as January and February for this kind of fishing. Between mid-January and mid-February I usually get my records for the year, with somewhere better than fifty trout in one of those two-day weekends, and seldom fewer than twenty-five on each of the others, whereas on other weekends around the year my score can dip to as low as two or three fish without my feeling that the matter calls for a federal investigation.

How long you can keep at this kind of fishing depends almost entirely on your tolerance to pain in your extremities. Hands are a problem, of course, but I've long ago learned that you are cold (or as hot, depending on the season) as your big toe is. For a long time I didn't have sense enough to realize this, and fished summer and winter wearing the same light loafers or espadrilles on my feet, though I might vary the swaddling of the rest of my body by as much as a dozen layers. I put down to the advance of age the spectacular decrease in my onetime long tolerance of extreme cold. Then I found out, simply by noticing other people's fleece-lined boots, that in very cold weather you are comfortable only as long as your feet are, no matter how much more you seem to be aware of your hands. The latter can always be rubbed, or blown on, or tucked, one at a time, inside pockets, but about the only thing to do with your feet is find a pail of hot water to soak them in. Now I wear boots from October to April, and fish happily at least every weekend in between. The other side of the calendar, between those two pivotal months, I fish every day, as the late Happy Fraser advised everybody to do "whenever you have the opportunity."

Of course I realize that all of this may be academic, if you don't live within five minutes of ice-clear spring ponds, as I do, but if getting to open water in the winter months is at all practicable for you, maybe you're in for the surprise of your life if, under the cover of any pretext at all, you make some time for some cold-weather fishing.

SEWELL N. DUNTON & SON, INC.

4 Fiske Avenue
Greenfield, Massachusetts 01301
(Sewell Dunton, Sr.)
Best rod repair service I know

More rods are broken by car doors, any year, than by fish or even by fishermen. But every so often I'll snap a bamboo rod, particularly of the ounce to ounce-and-three-quarters bantam and flea-to-midge sizes, from four-and-a-quarter to six-and-a-quarter-feet lengths, either just above or below the ferrule, or just above the grip. Sometimes it has been because of a careless movement in playing a fish, but more often it has been while making a cast, and it simply represented the cumulative effect of wood fatigue from overloading the little rod with a too-heavy sinking line, and getting too much of it in the air at a time. (See *Line Load,* for something to do about this problem.) Fatigue may not be cumulative in the human frame, as doctors and psychologists all agree, but it certainly is in bamboo, and I guess we're just lucky that we aren't made of it ourselves.

I used to kiss such rods good-bye, in the days when they ran from sixty-five to ninety-five or a hundred dollars apiece, but nowadays when they either don't make some of those extremely short sizes any more at all, or want a lot more money for them if you insist that they do, it's nice to know of a means of salvaging them.

Put the pieces of the broken rod in the aluminum tube it came in, and mail it to Sewell Dunton. Back will come the rod in from two to three weeks, somewhat shorter, but otherwise as good as new. And the bill will be somewhere between a quarter and a third of what it would cost you to get a new tip made.

I first heard of this marvel from Angus Cameron, my old editor at Knopf, and I thought at the time that it sounded too good to be true. But Angus does more salmon fishing than I do, at least of late, and is a lot fussier about his tackle than I am (I can't see Angus carrying a snarled mass of flies in a plastic pill tube, for instance), so I figured that if their work was good enough for him it would undoubtedly be too good for me. And it is—I don't deserve to be bailed out of some of the messes I've made of rods that they have fixed for me, promptly and without fuss or feathers and at fees that I found incredibly modest.

There may be other miracle workers in this line besides Sewell Dunton, and if you know of one, cherish him and keep the relationship cozy. But if you don't, as I don't, then let these happiness elves of Greenfield, Massachusetts, brighten the corner where you are, as they have, around a dozen times now, for me.

Chief among them is Sewell Dunton, Senior, now crowding eighty, but he has a half dozen helpers who share both his hobbyist attitude toward split bamboo, and his background of experience with the old Montague Rod and Reel Company, whose machinery he purchased in 1955. They regard the repair and rebuilding and reconditioning of split-bamboo rods as a challenge. In fact Dunton's avowed main purpose in setting up the company was to show that, despite the ascendancy of fiber glass, any American or European bamboo rod made within the past fifty years, regardless of make, is something to be cherished and well worth the cost of reconditioning. As he put it, "I didn't want to see them relegated to the dead past by the enthusiasm of the tackle industry for fiber glass."

With the prevalent resigned acceptance of the general assumption that the manufacture of handcrafted split-bamboo rods is a dying art, it's heartening to know that there's an outfit like this—pioneers of the past, so to speak—ready to help all of us remaining diehards fight a valiant rearguard action against the engulfment of this glorious artifact.

Not only is Sewell Dunton ready and willing to work on your old bamboo rods, however forlorn their state; he and his helping hands are also prepared to make you a new one. A fig for fiber glass, in other words.

With all due respect to the enormous general improvement in glass rods (and I regard Russ Peak as a genius in his field), I still can't help admiring and applauding the unreconstructed spirit of an old stager like Sewell Dunton.

On the back of the price list for Dunton's Angler's Choice rods there is this legend: "Take a Boy or Girl Fishing—Start Them Right With Split Bamboo. You'll Enjoy It, Too."

Personally, I warm more to the thought of split bamboo than to that of taking a boy or girl fishing. I always thought Milford Poltroon of *The Wretched Mess News* had a point, when he added to that favored cliché of the tackle industry his own zesty admonition "—and throw the little bastard in." But the rest of the sentiment is beyond reproach.

So praise Sewell Dunton, all ye who still cherish bamboo.

ℰNVIRONMENTAL DEFENSE FUND

527 Madison Avenue
New York, New York 10022
(Rod Cameron, Executive Director)

A nationwide coalition of lawyers and scientists (mostly young and largely volunteer and intensely dedicated), working through the courts to combat environmental spoliation, EDF was founded in 1967 on Long Island, where its main office still is, but now has three other offices in Washington, D.C., Berkeley, California, and New York City; a potent Board of Trustees (from Amyas Ames to Stewart Udall, just to give you an idea of their stature);

a staff of legal and scientific experts, with over seven hundred
on the Scientists Advisory Committee; and volunteer workers
and public supporters making a total membership of over thirty-
five thousand. "A veritable David among giants," it has scored
a dazzling record of legal victories, over titanic adversaries, in the
short time of its existence. Amazingly, contributions to EDF are
deductible for tax purposes.

Since ecology became chic, environmentalism has begun to run
patriotism a race as a refuge for scoundrels, but this environmentalist
group is one that is demonstrably on the up and up. A mere glance at
the lineup of its opponents in successful legal action (the U.S. Army,
the Corps of Engineers, government agencies, state governments and
polluting manufacturers) is enough to reassure anybody who might
wonder whether it is indeed above suspicion.

As Tom Paine remarked of patriots, there are a lot of fair weather
soldiers among them, and since the first fine frenzy of Earth Day put
the environment into the position of constituting a trinity with
Motherhood and God, there has been a distinct subsidence of the
initial enthusiasm, as with recruits who impulsively joined the colors
under the stimulation of the music of the band and the blandishments
of pretty girls' smiles, there is the sobering realization that "My God, a
guy could get *killed.*"

Inevitably a lot of the environmental evangelism of the sixties
has engendered a lot of backsliding in the seventies, as the enforce-
ment of air-and-water-pollution laws with teeth in them has resulted
in a lot of people's getting bit in that most sensitive of spots, their
pocketbook. Suddenly the environmentalists who were hailed only
yesterday as farsighted saviors, rescuing us from our own folly and sins
of omission, have turned into shortsighted obstructionists, muddle-
headedly gumming up the wheels of progress. At the same time, to
compound the confusion, a lot of the ravaging wolves of spoliation
have hastily donned the sheep's clothing of protectionists, running
expensive institutional advertising campaigns with which to congratu-
late themselves on all they're doing *for* the environment, to distract
attention from what they're doing *to* it.

When a game gets so confusing that you can't tell the players without a scorecard, it's good to have a scorecard like that of the Environmental Defense Fund, to know by their deeds that they are indeed the real thing, no matter how much they might be outshouted in the name-calling contest that has begun to obfuscate the rights and wrongs of so many environmental questions.

In its rough and tumble beginnings, as the outgrowth of a lawsuit filed on Long Island in 1966, which took the Suffolk County Mosquito Control Commission to court to stop the spraying of DDT, the Environmental Defense Fund was no mean name-caller itself. That original suit, as it happened, was finally dismissed, but it was the beginning of the implementation, across the country, of EDF's first battle cry, which was Victor Yannacone's motto: Sue the Bastards! Under the aegis of this quaint but hardly endearing device, Vic Yannacone (and when he couldn't make it, his wife) began popping up all over the place, with EDF litigation serving as the gadfly that finally resulted in the curbing of DDT in several states, and even in a court order compelling the federal government to regulate its use on the national level.

But after those early days of EDF the Yannacones went their own way, and in its subsequent development the organization has adopted a much more seemly motto. It is "The Care, The Work, and The Love," taken from this quote of Adlai Stevenson's: "We travel together on a little space ship, dependent upon its vulnerable reserves of air and soil, committed for our safety to its security and peace, preserved from annihilation only by the care, the work, and I will say, the love we give our fragile craft."

Working in concert with four other environmental groups, the National Audubon Society, the Sierra Club, the West Michigan Environmental Action Council, and the Izaak Walton League, EDF's lawyers finally carried their long fight against DDT to a victorious conclusion in June of 1972, with the ruling of the Environmental Protection Agency against all but a few minor registrations of DDT as of the year's end. Thus, though the rulings of governmental agencies are always subject to appeal, EDF largely won the battle begun a decade before by Rachel Carson's *Silent Spring*. This was a mighty upheaval that could hardly have been imagined when EDF, in its formative stage, loomed up on the horizon as a very tiny cloud, seemingly no bigger than one man's hand.

Appraising the DDT ban's "tremendous public impact," which he said "had come to epitomize the struggle over the environment," W. E. Kenworthy, writing in *The New York Times* on Sunday, June 18, 1972, said that "Most important was the sudden emergence of public concern for the environment in 1968–69, and with it the formation of public interest law firms, staffed with highly skilled and aggressive young lawyers, who knew how to assemble scientific findings and also how to thread their way through the labyrinth of administration law."

No better summation of EDF's astonishing success record could be compressed into one sentence. For it is indeed the combination of "scientific findings" with a highly skilled and aggressive use of the knowledge of "the labyrinth of administration law" that has enabled EDF to slice down both bureaucratic and industrial Goliaths to its own David-like stature. Some of EDF's accomplishments are indeed mighty, such as its stopping, at least temporarily, construction on two enormous projects undertaken by the Army Corps of Engineers, the Cross-Florida Barge Canal and the plan to link the Tennessee and Tombigbee rivers, and it has set its sights on even bigger targets, such as the massive Four Corners power project in Colorado, Utah, New Mexico, and Arizona, and the even bigger North Central Power Project in northeast Wyoming. The latter is so unimaginably vast that even the power *lost* in transmission would exceed the present peak and brownout-causing power demands of Manhattan, and it would emit more nitrogen oxides, sulfur dioxide, and particulate matter than all sources in New York City and the Los Angeles Air Basin combined. EDF's aim is not necessarily to halt or block this Four Corners construction, or any construction, really, but rather to diminish their scope, to minimize their environmental impact, to seek ways of making them prove that they really do need as much power and as many megawatts as they say they do.

No better statement of the importance of EDF's role has been made than that of Evelyn Ames, who joined her husband Amyas on its board: "All living things and their environment are inseparably connected. What we do to earth and to its other forms of life we do, inescapably, to ourselves and to our descendants. We must stop the senseless destruction of life on our planet, stop trespassing on the world of our children and start a responsible stewardship of the earth's community of being."

If, as a member of that community of being, such a statement stirs in you any sense of responsibility at all, then there could be no more appropriate response than some manifestation of support, whether in coin or in kind, of the gallantly continuing efforts, against constantly increasing odds, of the Environmental Defense Fund.

$\mathcal{F}$EDERATION OF FLY FISHERMEN

15513 Haas Avenue
Gardena, California 90249
(James Eriser, President)

International nonprofit public organization of fly fishermen and fly-fishing clubs, founded in Eugene, Oregon, in 1965, with first national conclave in Jackson Hole, Wyoming, in 1966. Dedicated to conservation and reclamation of natural habitat, and policy of fly fishing only, for all members of salmonid family, together with extension of fly rod use in marine fishery, and conservation and reclamation of wetlands. Roster of eighty-six member clubs in twenty-one states, two provinces, and two foreign countries, along with four thousand individual (associate) memberships. Subscription to quarterly publication, The Flyfisher, *included in annual dues of associate members. Associate membership $10 yearly.*

Although the concept of a federation of fly-fishing clubs was first spawned in the east, within the ranks of New York's Theodore Gordon Flyfishers—the first of its founding fathers were Gene

Anderegg and Lee Wulff—it was actually hatched in the west, with the McKenzie Flyfishers in Eugene, Oregon, providing the nest, where Gene Anderegg convened members of the first fly-fishing clubs to manifest interest in the idea. Formal incorporation followed the next year, with the first of the annual gatherings of representatives of member clubs held, like the next two, at Jackson Lake Lodge in Jackson Hole, Wyoming. The site of the annual conclave moved to Sun Valley, Idaho, for the next two meetings, then shifted for one year to Snowmass, near Aspen in Colorado, and returned in 1972 to Sun Valley.

The choice of conclave sites reflects the organization's predominantly western orientation, as the majority of the member clubs are located west of the Rockies. While the balance between Canadian clubs is equal, with British Columbia equated by Quebec, the roster of American clubs has a heavy westward tilt. Although ten of the twenty-one states represented in the membership lie east of the Rockies, only twenty-nine of the eighty-six member clubs are situated east of the Continental Divide, even counting in Quebec and Paris, France. Of the remaining fifty-seven clubs, only New Zealand lies outside the immediate neighborhood of the western United States.

In a pragmatic adaptation to these demographics, the editorial office of *The Flyfisher* was moved to Seattle, after its first four years in New York, and the editorship given to Seattle's Steve Raymond. Not that every effort hadn't been made, while it was edited in the east, to give an editorial balance to *The Flyfisher*'s contents that would reflect its preponderantly western readership. But it was assumed that Raymond, who had proved himself with an excellent book on the Kamloops trout, would be in a better position to establish and maintain contacts with western angling writers and correspondents. At the same time, the production and the advertising sales were turned over to Frank Amato, an established publisher of West Coast sporting publications, himself a fisherman and active in the councils of TU. There was the added consideration that Raymond and Amato were in much closer touch with the leadership of FFF to reflect their desires in policy matters, than Joe Pisarro and Hermann Kessler, who had been getting out *The Flyfisher* in New York, remote from the organization's officers, and working in a virtual vacuum.

For many of the associate members, the one sense of contact with FFF was through the pages of *The Flyfisher*, and it was somewhat off-putting, when turning to it eagerly for news of Federation activities, to find it too often devoted to general and scholarly articles on the English background of fly fishing and on its development into a colonial and early American pastime. What price abstract ruminations on the origin of the Parmachene Belle and the Pink Lady and the Quill Gordon, or early sporting magazines like *The Spirit of the Times,* when what you're itching for is where to go and what to do much nearer home?

Fortunately, the relevance of Federation's activities and programs has increased of late, and the newsletter has begun to fill the communications gap that many members must have felt. Also regional meetings have more and more begun to bridge the empty spaces that previously yawned between the annual conclaves, with the result that latterly FFF has come to have more year-round meaning and significance to its members.

Without this development, it could have become increasingly difficult to justify the continued existence of two such parallel organizations as TU and FFF, each really seeking the same aims of conservation and the development and restoration of quality fishing as opposed to hatchery truck chasing. They always had much more in common than not. But for the stubborn insistence of the TU diehards on the "democratic" necessity of permitting all shapes and forms of lures, and the evangelical determination of the fly fishers to hold out for Fishing for Fun and Fly Fishing Only policies, these doctrinal and dogmatic oppositions have kept both organizations from doing more good in concert than they have ever been able to do apart. Voices have been raised, within the ranks of both groups, to this effect both early and often, and many overtures have emanated from both camps, but so far they have always ended when some outraged elder, on either side, has suffered a sudden access of blood in the eye.

TU's "Not Only Fly Fishing" and FFF's "Fly Fishing Only" have become something of a tomaytoes-tomahtoes, potaytoes-potahtoes, eether-eyether wrangle, each time overtures have begun from either side, with a consequent quick progression to the point of "let's call the whole thing off."

And yet, ever since Martin Bovey attended the first conclaves out at Jackson Lake Lodge, the leadership of both organizations has always inclined toward working together, and Gene Anderegg, from the beginning and through Federation's first four years as founding president, always foresaw at least partnership with TU, if not actual merger. Yet, as with discussions between Yankee "imperialists" and Soviet "peoples' democracies," the semantics have often been bewildering. This is perhaps because, while the issue of fly fishing has always been the straining point between the two organizations, there are other differences that go back to their basic structure.

It is ironical, for instance, that it should be TU which holds out for the "democratic" permissiveness in the matter of bait fishing for trout, when at least in its original form TU was autocratic in its setup, with a vertical relationship from headquarters down to the chapter level, as opposed to the pure democracy of a horizontal grouping of member clubs of equal standing.

TU has changed, of course, and much more than FFF has, in the longer time-stretch since its beginnings. But to a certain extent it is still true, as the names of the two organizations suggest, that they have fundamentally different concerns. TU, taking its original cue quite openly from Ducks Unlimited, was chiefly concerned with the quarry and the assurance of its continued and continuing supply. The chief concern, in short, was trout in the one instance, as it was ducks in the other. And who ever heard of putting a duck back, except an artificial one used as a moving target in a shooting gallery?

TU's emphasis, from the beginning, was on the fish—trout and salmon—and their waters. Federation's emphasis, on the other hand, was always on method, and the extension of that method to as many forms of fishing as possible. That's why FFF was so quick to embrace the saltwater fly rodders, right from the start, and to make every effort to extend the fly rod's use to every possible application. The kind of fish was always less important to FFF than the kind of fishing, whereas exactly the reverse was the case with TU.

In Gene Anderegg's original Johnny Appleseed act, when he went around the country drumming up interest in the idea of federation, he used to say that he foresaw the day when there would be "a watchdog club on every stream," protecting the fish as well as the fishing. This is conservation at the local level and more truly a grass-roots democratic concept than the national action organization that TU has become today. In other words, TU is now more federal than the federation.

The play on words is not altogether fortuitous. Alvin R. Grove, Jr., as the editor of TU's official journal, *Trout*, is that organization's philosopher-in-residence. It is interesting, then, to recall that it was the essence of Bus Grove's classic title *The Lure and Lore of Trout Fishing* Gene Anderegg used in his original pitch that led to the banding together of the first member clubs to form FFF. He used to say that the lure of federation was the lore and the art of the sport—that this was the greatest common denominator of all fly-fishing clubs everywhere. And certainly this has been and remains the basic ingredient of the FFF programs, as circulated to member clubs—the fly-tying clinics, the casting games, the traveling exhibits of flies by famous flytiers, the audiovisual presentations, the casting instruction kits, and the youth program. Other programs have developed in which the stress is as much or more on conservation than on sport, like the water-surveillance systems and the Vibert box installations, and some, such as the saltwater techniques, have had aspects of both.

TU has leaned heavily, in fact, notably in New York and increasingly elsewhere, on some of the FFF programs, and would obviously do so everywhere if the working relationship of the two organizations could be tightened.

And TU, if still seen as a despotism in the jaundiced eyes of some of the most obdurate of the FFF adherents, has certainly become one of ever-increasing benevolence, as even they could probably be cornered into admitting, if ever pure logic could prevail over passion. But while TU refuses to abandon bait, just as stubbornly as the fly fishermen refuse to compromise their identity, which they equate with their integrity, the situation shows all the earmarks of an impasse—which is something that goes forward steadily backward.

Meanwhile TU has become, of late years, a great empire, with professional expertise and a proliferation of offices, while FFF remains a small republic, staffed and manned exclusively by volunteers, most of whom would appear to be descendants of Henry Clay, the man who would rather be right than president.

TU's philosophy is now as close to FFF's as the hands of the clock at five after one. They are even linked by the same TGF phrase about limiting your kill instead of killing your limit. Closer than that it's hard to see how you can get.

So what's the honest angler to make of all this, except to wish for a giant's strength so he could knock both their heads together?

Well, since they're both on the side of the angels, there's obviously only one thing to do. You've got to join them both, and keep your fingers crossed.

Maybe, if enough of us do, the problem might even solve itself.

FIRST LADY OF FLY-TYING

Helen Shaw
246 East 46th Street
New York, New York 10017

Helen Shaw was already a legendary figure in the tight little world of fly fishermen when she first came to New York some twenty years ago. Before that, most anglers had known of her fly-tying only through her astonishing feat of re-creating, from fifteenth century instructions, Dame Juliana Berners's original list of trout flies, for inclusion as a color plate in A. J. McClane's *The Practical Fly Fisherman*. But for years, in her native Sheboygan, Wisconsin, beginning as a mere child under the tutelage of the late Art Kade, artist turned flytier, she had tied flies for some of the country's distinguished anglers (including Herbert Hoover). Outdistancing her master, Helen Shaw could be called "flytier turned artist." She no longer ties flies commercially, but as of the last decade has confined her artistry to the creation of flies meant for presentation not to fish but to fishermen—special specimens intended for collectors, and for display rather than for everyday routine use.

In a sense, however, Helen Shaw's extraordinary virtuosity in fly-tying is now more widely available to anglers than it ever was in the old days, because she acted out, for the eye of husband Hermann Kessler's camera, her whole bag of tricks, performing all the motions of producing her entire repertory of different fly types. This was done almost ten years ago, in an unusual book, called quite simply *Fly-Tying*, published by The Ronald Press Company, New York, at the end of 1963. What makes it unusual is that while the hands performing each step of all these motions are Helen's, the angle of the posing is such that the camera's point of view is exactly your own—that is, the reader's—and as the camera's eye equates with your eye, the sensation you get, in looking at these hands performing the step-by-step process of manufacture of all these flies, streamers, nymphs, wets and dries, and even midges, is that the hands that are doing it are your own. In other words, in a *reductio ad perfectionem* of do-it-yourself-ism, Helen Shaw in *Fly-Tying* looks over your shoulder and guides your hands as she performs with her own, to let you see how you do it, step by step.

I wish I could in truth and honesty add that thanks to this humane provision, I became a demon flytier overnight. Well, I didn't, but that's not to say you couldn't, if you don't already tie flies and would like to learn. The mere fact that I couldn't do it is irrelevant, because I'm a charter member of the All Thumbs Club, who gave up all hope of ever becoming any sort of handyman back in 1926, when, in the process of trying to put up a towel rack, I damn near knocked a wall down. So I preen myself on such an elementary accomplishment as knotting together the lengths of monofilament that go to make up a tapered leader and don't even dream anymore of higher feats of manual dexterity than that.

A more recent demonstration of Helen Shaw's monkey-see–monkey-do method of fly-tying instruction is afforded by her section of Art Flick's *Master Fly-Tying Guide*, published by Crown in 1972, where her hands were again photographed by Hermann Kessler the same way.

It's worth the effort, to try to tie flies the way Helen Shaw does, and teaches, but this is one branch of the gentle art of fly fishing in which I am resigned to remaining a spectator sportsman. I have on my desk in my office, and have had for a decade, one of her Quill Gordons, mounted, under the protective encasement of a glass bell jar, and it's a sight I wouldn't exchange for that of any one of the seven wonders of the world.

FLY FISHERMAN MAGAZINE

Donald D. Zahner
Manchester, Vermont 05254
Only fly-fishing magazine
(other than club or organizational organs)

I feel about this much the way I felt about Trout Unlimited when it was first getting started. Sure, you could find fault with it, but what the hell, it's "the only wheel in town." Zahner got off to a rather wobbly start, a few years back, and the first issues showed a rather more elastic attitude toward what does or doesn't constitute fly fishing than its most fanatical practitioners were quite ready to applaud, but he straightened up fairly quickly and he's been flying right ever since. His material on Theodore Gordon alone would well have repaid any more than casual fly fishermen for the relatively modest price of a subscription.

The magazine's editorial board is now star-studded, and while that in itself doesn't mean very much (you can often get the big shots to lend you their names but very little more), it's at least reassuring in that it shows that Zahner knows the right people to respect. You know you can't be led very far astray from the true religion of fly fishing by anybody who surrounds himself with a galaxy of accredited saints like Charlie Ritz and Charlie Fox.

The magazine is bimonthly, coming out six times a year, and the yearly subscription price is five dollars, or nine dollars for two years. Fly fishermen have always seemed to me to be like people who smoke cigars; you know they would never have acquired the peculiar habit if they couldn't afford it. It "couldn't hurt" to pay this guy the five bucks, and it could help. It says something about the status of our sport, if it shows that it can support a magazine that's devoted to it exclusively. Golfers must have dozens of magazines at least. (I don't know because I played golf only three times in thirty-three years and then swore off, because I was getting to like it, and feared it would interfere with my fishing or my fiddling, and they interfere with each other enough as it is.)

Tell you what. I'll subscribe to *Fly Fisherman* if you will.

THE FLY FISHERMAN'S BOOKCASE, INC.

Sam Melner
138 Grand Street
Croton-on-Hudson, New York 10520
Discount lists on angling books and fishing tackle; also some reprints
(Van Cortlandt Press)

This guy must be, to other dealers in fishing books and tackle, what Icelandic Airlines is to the other transatlantic carriers, a pain in the neck to them, but a boon to the cost-conscious customer. He's unbelievable (so's Icelandic—the way those blonde Viking goddesses ply you with coffee and cognac, you don't care if you ever get to Reykjavik . . .), but I've tried him not once but often, and he's real. He carries all the best current angling books, including a lot they'd look blank at you for inquiring about at Abercrombie & Fitch, and he lists 'em all for less, and quite a lot less too. But he doubles—no, *triples*—in brass, having branched out, in addition to the ever-growing list of books, with the Fly Fisherman's Bookcase Tackle Service, selling rods, reels, lines, of premium quality at prices cut so deep they make you gasp (I swear, the prices he was asking for some of those rods, I couldn't afford not to buy four of them, to average out what I'd originally paid elsewhere for two of them), and now he has taken over, under the firm style of Van Cortlandt Press (same address as above) the line of reprint (facsimile) titles that began life as the Abercrombie & Fitch Library. These include those two classic volumes that are each a combination of other books by the same authors, E. R. Hewitt's *A*

Trout and Salmon Fisherman for Seventy-five Years and George LaBranche's *The Dry Fly and Fast Water* and *The Salmon and The Dry Fly.*

If he shows half the perspicacity in choosing future titles to reissue in facsimile that he has shown to date in the selection of tackle items to discount, then Sam Melner is the answer to the fly fisherman's prayers. What he'll do to the rest, or what they may feel like doing to him (I'd like to be a mouse and hear what they say about him at that annual tackle manufacturers' convention that Al McClane always used to go to every summer, leaving me in splendid isolation on our stretch of the Upper Beaverkill) is beyond my ken, but since you and I have only a consuming interest in the business, let's leave that trouble to those it troubles, and enjoy ourselves meanwhile. I figure we suffer enough, in fishless days and blank nights, to have earned an occasional break like this.

FLY-TACKLE SHOPS

A "for instance" directory, of the new breed of hobbyist-shopkeepers now springing up all over the country, to assuage the fly fisherman's anguish over the passing of a place like Wm. Mills & Son, New York's oldest tackle shop.

I mourn for Mills, as I mourn for the old Murray Hill Hotel, restaurants like the Cafe Chauveron, the old Ritz Grill, and indeed all the places that were once one of a kind. But the irony is that Mills closed down, in the fall of 1972, at a time when there was a more widespread resurgence of interest in fly fishing, both as regards books and tackle, than there has been in decades. New shops are springing up, literally by the dozen, that are obviously a labor of love, by fly-fishing nuts for people who are nuts about fly fishing.

Take, as typical, Len Codella's Anglers Den in Linden, New Jersey, which opened, almost to the day, as Mills was closing. In his catalog you'll find everything you could have found at Mills and more—the Leonard rods, the Walker reels, the flies and lines and leaders (down to 8X), the micrometer, and a dozen other little gimmicks that never existed in the old days, but today's more gadget-minded fly fisherman will swoon over.

Another, also typical, is Charlie Hirt's Orvis shop, on the Saddle River and in Saddle River, New Jersey. A few years back, such a place would have seemed, and probably been, virtually unique, but now its near counterpart is to be found across the land.

Not that all these places are new—some like Bud Lilly's in West Yellowstone, and Dan Bailey's in Livingston, Montana, are now beginning to be venerable—but the encouraging fact is that so many of them are.

No man can hope to provide a complete list, that won't be out of date almost overnight, of places like this where the wants and needs of the literate and sophisticated angler are either to be met or anticipated by his like-minded peers, but here, for a start, is a brief, selected list, as of early spring 1973:

Len Codella
Angler's Den
5 South Wood Avenue
Linden, New Jersey 07036

Anglers' Mail
6497 Pearl Road
Cleveland, Ohio 44130

James Deren
Anglers Roost
141 East 44th Street
New York, New York 10017

Dan Bailey's Fly Shop
Box 1019
Livingston, Montana 59047

Pat Barnes
West Yellowstone, Montana
  59758

Beckie's Sporting Goods
1336 Orange Street
Berwick, Pennsylvania 18603

Harold Whitman III
The Bedford Sportsman
Depot Plaza
Bedford Hills, New York 10507

Black's Custom Flies
Roseburg, Oregon 97470

Bodmer's Fly Shop
2404 E. Boulder Street
Colorado Springs, Colorado
  80909

Classic Flies
Box 192
Jackson Hole, Wyoming 83001

Jim Danskin Tackle Shop
Box 276
West Yellowstone, Montana
  59758

Harry A. Darbee
Livingston Manor, New York
  12758

Fireside Angler
P.O. Box 823
Melville, New York 11746

The Fly Fisher
8737 E. Jackrabbit Road
Scottsdale, Arizona 85253

Fly Fisherman's Bookcase
   Tackle Service
138 Grand Street
Croton-on-Hudson, New York
   10520

The Great Outdoors
Charles Hirt's Orvis Shop
Saddle River, New Jersey
   07458

E. Hille
Williamsport, Pennsylvania
   17701

Joe's Tackle Shop
Box 156
Warehouse Point, Connecticut
   06088

Bud Lilly's Trout Shop
West Yellowstone, Montana
   59758

Bill Mason's Angler's Mill
Sun Valley Co., Inc.
Sun Valley, Idaho 83353

Parks Fly Shop
Box 196
Gardiner, Montana 59030

Rangeley Region Sports
28 Main Street
Rangeley, Maine 04970

Reed Tackle Company
Box 390
Caldwell, New Jersey 07006

Dick Surrette Fly Fishing Shop
Box 200
North Conway, New Hampshire
   03860

Wanigas Rod Company
4855 Sheridan Road
Saginaw, Michigan 48601

FRESHET PRESS

Freshet Press Inc.
90 Hamilton Road
Rockville Centre, New York 11570
(Myron L. Cohen, editor)

Lightning strikes twice—another program, by another professor, resulting in some much-wanted reprints of scarce and hard-to-find fishing books, as well as a new source of original sporting titles.

It's ironical that after so many long years when only the well-heeled collector could come by a number of much-wanted but out-of-print items of angling literature, two sources of supply should spring up so nearly simultaneously. But the fact is, there were these two professors who both just happened to be fishing nuts, and each of whom was pursuing essentially the same idea without either of them being aware, when they began, of what the other was doing. One, of course, was Nick Lyons at Crown; the other was Dr. Myron L. Cohen, who had a publisher find him and make him turn his idea into a reality.

Mike Cohen is a professor in the Mechanical Engineering office at Stephens Institute, across the Hudson River in Hoboken. Unlike Nick, his subject is not literature—in fact, it's that farthest of removes from it, aerospace—but he has long been an avid collector of angling books. He found Armand Frasca out on Long Island, a retired executive of R. R. Bowker, who had cashed in his chips after their merger with Xerox. Bud Frasca, like his father before him, had served long enough as treasurer at Bowker to become thoroughly acquainted with publishing practice. But he was young enough to become restless soon after retirement. Learning of Mike Cohen's collection of angling books through his son, young Bud, who had worked as a clerk at Mills, Frasca sought Cohen out and asked to see his collection. Looking it over, he literally dared Mike to make a selection of ten angling classics that he thought deserved restoration to currency, so that ordinary anglers could obtain them without giving up the arm and leg that their scarcity commanded.

Some of these titles were such treasured but out-of-print items as *The Fly and the Fish,* by John Atherton, *The Lure and Lore of Trout Fishing,* by Alvin R. Grove, Jr., and *A History of Fly Fishing for Trout,* by John Waller Hills.

Others were the pre-Waltonian pastoral, *The Secrets of Angling,* by John Dennys, whom Walton incorrectly identified as Jo Davors, and such salmon classics as Jock Scott's *Greased Line Fishing for Salmon,* and Sir Humphry Davy's *Salmonia.* But the tenth on their original list, that they didn't manage to get, was *A Modern Dry-Fly Code,* by Vincent Marinaro. It was only in the course of trying for it that Mike Cohen learned of Nick Lyons's still-formative program of angling classics at Crown, when Vince said that Nick had already signed him up for it.

Again, as in the case of Nick Lyons at Crown, the success of a reprint program quickly led to the launching of some new titles as well, with the result that the Freshet Press list of classic reprints was soon augmented by such new titles as *The Wind on Your Cheek,* by the veteran William J. Schaldach, and *Fishing the Midge,* by the redoubtable Ed Koch, one of the Pennsylvanian masters of the minutae, like Fox, Grove, and Marinaro.

In this field, the more the merrier, and it is good news for fishermen that there is now more than one source for reissued classics, as well as additional outlets for original new titles. With Sam Melner's taking over of the Abercrombie & Fitch facsimile library, under the new firm style of Van Cortlandt Press, and the occasional reissue by even such a predominantly original house as Winchester Press, there was cast a sudden glow of sunny warmth over a previously dark and dour scene of scarcity, to the immense gratification of every angler.

Gaudeamus igitur, as the professors would say.

GILL

Gill, Emlyn M. (1862–1918). In 1912, when he wrote, in *Practical Dry-Fly Fishing,* the first cis-Atlantic book devoted to the dry fly, Gill ran for immortality as the American Halford, with LaBranche as his Marryat. But the aspiration ran afoul of actuality, because while the doughty Captain Marryat never double-crossed his Boswell by writing a book himself, George LaBranche within a couple of years did, with the 1914 volume *The Dry Fly and Fast Water,* and his fame soon surpassed that of his advance man. In football analogy, LaBranche outran his interference.

Gill's one rather tenuous claim to distinction might still have withstood the test of time, since his contemporary, Theodore Gordon, confined his own writing to letters and notes in *The Fishing Gazette* and *Forest & Stream,* and had these been allowed to languish in obscurity, then today it might be Gill, instead of Gordon, whom we would perforce be celebrating as the American Walton, or at least as the father of the dry fly. But Gill was twice unlucky, in that John McDonald in 1947 snatched from limbo the notes and letters of Theodore Gordon, and issued them with a scholarly introduction as *The Complete Fly Fisherman,* and the previously neglected Sage of the Neversink, whose hermitlike sojourn in the woods had gone completely unrhymed and unsung, attained instant sanctity and was enshrined overnight as one of nature's noblemen on the right hand of Thoreau himself, upstaging such venerated figures as Audubon and Agassiz in the process.

The luckless Gill, lacking either the matinee idol charisma of a LaBranche or the elfin wispy mystery of a Gordon, has been minimized rather than magnified by the passage of time and clings today to a sort of mini-eminence, a relatively pygmy position of puny stature among the stalwarts of American angling annals. If his book had been less slavishly devoted to Halford, and if he had at least made the attempt to provide, instead of merely deplore the lack of, an American entomology of stream insects, Gill might have carved out a larger niche for himself in the gallery of American fishing gods. But he shrugged off, as of undue immensity and complexity, the task of making a start toward a scientific entomological approach to the galaxy of American fly patterns, much as Louis Rhead did only a few years later, and both men missed greater subsequent stature as a result.

But Gill did recognize, more clearly than any American angling writer before him, the necessity for imitation not only of the natural fly upon which rising trout were feeding, but equally so for imitation of that fly's action upon the water, and it is this latter stress that makes him unique in his time.

Even more prophetic of latter-day practice is Gill's anticipation of the "fishing-for-fun" concept: "In these days of depleted streams it is most necessary that the doctrine should be spread broadcast that the one pleasure of trout fishing, apart from the joy of being close to nature, is the matching of one's wits against the cunning of the trout. He alone deserves the title of sportsman who returns carefully to the water all trout that he does not need for food; as soon as the fish is taken into the net, all sport to be had with that particular fish is over, and when killed and put into the creel it has become simply *meat.*"

The emphasis on the last word has not been added; it was placed there by Gill himself, as long ago as the spring of 1912. So Gill was not only the author of the first American book on dry-fly fishing, but the first American angler to express contempt for meat-fishermen as such. It would be a fair reward to have a local chapter, here and there, named for him, in the growing memberships of some of the national organizations devoted to conservation.

GREEN

Green, Seth (1817–1888). Outstanding flycaster and fish culturist, Seth Green is today best remembered as the first man ever to cast a fly one hundred feet. The accomplishment, in an 1864 tournament that was actually won by Robert Barnwell Roosevelt with a cast of sixty-eight feet, was disallowed at the time, but later officially confirmed, and Green's vindication was attested with a certificate. Anticipating later tournament practice, Green was the first to have a rod and line prepared specifically for distance casting. His more lasting contribution to today's angling, though overshadowed by his casting fame, was the introduction of California trout (*Salmo shasta*) to eastern waters, which occurred some twenty years later, and was a successful planting, leading directly to the subsequent widespread establishment of the rainbow trout throughout the east. Green's first book was *Trout Culture* in 1870, followed by other reports on fish and frog culture until the year of his death.

GROVE

An appreciation of The Lure and Lore of Trout Fishing,
by Alvin R. Grove, Jr.

For twenty years I thought, and often said, that Bus Grove had preempted the perfect title—that there were only leavings to be picked over, like a morning-after-the-holiday turkey carcass, among all the poor wights who had the luck to write books on trout and trouting behind his. The lure and the lore—after all, what else is there? It's like dividing flies into two categories—attractors and imitators. Do that and you find you've covered all the flies there ever were or will be. Or like fishing books—class them as instructional or inspirational, and you have no more classifying left to do. It's a mighty claim to stake out—the lure and lore of trout fishing—and better than three thousand books have been devoted, in English alone, to the one aspect of the subject or the other. But it remained for Alvin R. Grove to let loose with both barrels and wing them both with one sure shot.

That was in 1951, and the wonder was such that some of us have never stopped talking about it since. Not that this was a fallow time for good fishing books—it was the year of John Atherton's *The Fly and the Fish,* Lee Wulff's *New Handbook of Freshwater Fishing,* and the Scribner combined edition of LaBranche's *The Dry Fly and Fast Water* and *The Salmon and the Dry Fly,* and it was the year after E. R. Hewitt's *A Trout and Salmon Fisherman for Seventy-five Years,* J. Edson Leonard's *Flies, A Dictionary of 2,200 Patterns,* Harold Smedley's *Fly Patterns and Their Origins,* and Vincent Marinaro's classic *A Modern Dry-Fly Code*—in fact, there was a great flowering of good angling books just before and after the turn of the mid-century, from John McDonald's *The Complete Fly Fisherman: The Notes and Letters of Theodore Gordon* in 1947 to A. J. McClane's *The Practical Fly Fisherman* in 1953.

But good as all these books were, none of them essayed, as *The Lure and Lore* did, to balance a brimming bucket on both shoulders, so to speak. This was a book you could both learn from and dream on. That's as rare as an inspiring schoolmistress who is also a raving beauty. The difference is that books don't age, and this one is as fresh and inspiring to read, after twenty years, in the new Freshet Press edition, as it ever was, and with its handsome binding and slipcase it's even better looking.

I'm not saying it's perfect. No fishing book is, though Walton probably came closer than anybody could or would, or possibly should, ever again. Yet even he, without Cotton, would be like the appetizer without the dinner—long on the lure that entices, but short on the lore that endears and endures.

Grove gives you the works—the enticements *and* the endearments—and that's what makes this such a lastingly satisfying book, which you can read again and again.

Even its faults are somehow lovable, like the quirks of an absentminded professor. And since this is a facsimile edition, all the little sloppinesses of the first edition are still there. LaBranche is spelled with an "e" in Grove's bibliography and without in Charlie Fox's introduction. Grove gives the time of Walton's writing of *The Compleat Angler* on one page as 1648 and on another as 1655. Well, he could be right the first time, since Marriot's original edition of Walton came out in 1653, but there's no readily apparent rationale for having it both ways. Other niggling piggling little slips, of the kind that any literate copy editor should be competent to catch, give the volume a slightly raffish air, like a too hastily remade bed, and the facsimile, naturally, sedulously preserves them all. For instance, a note written by Theodore Gordon to Guy Jenkins in 1912 is referred to as being addressed to "Mr. Jennings." Oh well, Jenkins, Jennings, that's close, anyway.

And sometimes these editings, or failures to edit, are like having a planted stooge in the balcony. Here and there are bracketed queries, like a copyreader's questions, which they may well have been in the first place, which provide an almost comic obbligato to certain sentences, such as "No doubt lines have been made of many [any?] available materials," and "Oppian had described [all?] fishing methods some thirteen hundred years earlier," to cite just two.

So what? So nothing, if all you're writing for is the mindless fans of the "my reel screamed" sagas in the more fugitive print of the periodicals, but Grove is a professor, after all, and what he writes is literature, and deserves to be edited and proofread as such.

It isn't very sporting of me to point these things out now, since I failed to mention them when I lent my well-thumbed copy of *The Lure and Lore* for use as the prototype for the Freshet Press edition, but I suppose we all tend to expect, on looking at a new edition, that it will clear up the little imperfections we remember from before and are surprised when it doesn't.

One thing I wish somebody had taken the trouble to correct. Of all books, this is the one you'd least expect to make that common error of confusing *minutae*, which are the tiny terrestrials and "smidgens" that are so important to the fishing of the Pennsylvania limestone streams, with *minutiae*, which are trivial, unimportant, and often petty small details. That this solecism should be allowed to mar any page of the work of a botany professor, as accustomed to handling Latin tags as you and I are to counting small change, is bad enough, but when that professor happens also to occupy a position, in relation to the minutae, roughly analogous to that of the Pope to Catholicism, it verges on scandal.

Some years ago, in print, I used that term as follows: "He who would implement, by today's standards, the most refined application of Cotton's immortal exhortation to fish fine and far off must now sit at the feet of the three Pennsylvania masters of the *minutae*, Fox, Grove, and Marinaro, who will certainly some day seem as legendary to us all as Hewitt and LaBranche are already beginning to seem within a decade of their death." I'd have hunted down like a dog any proof-reader or copy editor who tried to sneak a second "i" into the minutae in that almost reverent context, and I still feel the same way about it.

There are only a handful of books that are as basic as freshman English—that is, absolute prerequisites to being anything like well read, by today's sophisticated angling standards. This is one of them. Its cost, if you have not yet read it, or even if you haven't read it lately, could well be more relevant, as an investment with direct bearing on your angling success next season, than that of a new line, or any one of a dozen gadgets that are likely to seem, next time you're at a tackle counter, less easy to get along without.

$\mathcal{H}$AIG-BROWN

Fly-fishing's ambassador to the world of belles lettres

Roderick Haig-Brown (1908–) is English by birth, Canadian by long residence, but American in the broadest sense of the term, since his name is one to conjure with in all the Americas, North, Central, and South.

Not in every generation, nor even in every century, does fly fishing enjoy the services of a writer whose work is universally negotiable as literature, quite apart from the happenstance that its subject is angling. But our time is lucky in this respect, because we have one in Haig-Brown. His writings are read, as Walton's are, as much in spite of as because of being about fishing.

This was brought home to me as far back as 1965 when I was first trying to arrange for a trade edition of the privately printed *Gordon Garland*, produced by and for Theodore Gordon Flyfishers as a commemorative volume marking the fiftieth anniversary of Gordon's death and I went to lunch with Alfred Knopf to discuss it.

I was armed with the table of contents of the limited edition, which had just gone to press up in Connecticut, and I was so proud of it that I was practically strutting sitting down. But as I began drooling over all the names, of the assorted McClanes and Wulffs and Schwieberts and Zerns and Soforths, I could see that I was making much less of an impression on my lunch companion than I was on myself.

It dawned on me then that, except gastronomically speaking, Alfred Knopf didn't know a fish from an oyster and cared rather less about both than either might care about the other. But about authors the venerable publisher of Borzoi books has a stored and cumulative memory and knowledge that is almost computerlike.

Taking the typed list that I was holding as an aide-mémoire, he looked it up and down with a bare stare until at one point he nodded as if greeting an old friend, and handed it back to me saying, "I've no doubt that to you fishers"—a word he pronounced like a man with mumps biting into a pickle—"every last one of these people is a household name, but I've never heard of any of 'em, except of course Haig-Brown."

It was like one Old Etonian picking out another from a lineup of aborigines. And it wasn't until I could show the list to Angus Cameron, who was then and still is the arbiter of sporting subjects at Knopf, that I was able to make the case for a trade edition of *The Gordon Garland*.

Fortunately for the state of knowledge of our sport, Haig-Brown isn't "only literary." For a long time he served his district in British

Columbia as a judge, and quite aside from being a superbly capable angler he has the breadth and depth of human understanding that makes his fishing writings intelligible to the commonalty of sportsmen. Witness this simple sample from *A River Never Sleeps.*

". . . I have never yet seen a river that I could not love. Moving water, even in a pipeline or a flume, has a fascinating vitality. It has power and grace and associations. It has a thousand colors and a thousand shapes, yet it follows laws so definite that the tiniest streamlet is an exact replica of a great river."

Haig-Brown's whole frame of mental reference lies some miles above that of the gee-whiz–oh-boy–sports-page level of too many of the perpetrators of what purports to be part and parcel of angling literature. He has the ability of the better novelists to make scenes and events "come alive"—what Joseph Conrad epitomized as "above all, to make you *see*"—that makes writing worthy to be considered literature. Things you read in Haig-Brown's books become so integral a part of your own memory and imagination that it is perfectly possible to become more than momentarily mixed up as you recall some fishing experience and can't be entirely sure whether it's something that actually happened to you or whether you only read about it in one of Haig-Brown's books.

Sparse Grey Hackle is of course perfectly willing and able to speak for himself, but I can't help thinking that he must have had at least some of Haig-Brown in mind when he made that memorable remark about the best fishing being done in print.

HALLOCK

Hallock, Charles (1834–1917). One of the more rewarding of the early American angling authors to read today, his first book, *The Fishing Tourist*, 1873, and his last, *An Angler's Reminiscences*, 1913, give the best account of nineteenth century American angling after Thaddeus Norris. In 1873 he founded *Forest and Stream*, enlisting the services of a distinguished roster of contributors, including Thaddeus Norris, Robert Barnwell Roosevelt, Seth Green, Reuben Wood, and the famous lady flytier Sara McBride. Soon tiring of the business side of publishing, he turned that aspect of the weekly publication over to William C. Harris (later to become editor of the *American Angler*), and sold out entirely by 1880, although the publication continued until 1930, when it was incorporated into *Field & Stream*. In 1877 his *Vacation Rambles in Northern Michigan* appeared, followed the next year by his compilation, *American Club List and Sportsman's Glossary*. Afterward, Hallock wrote *The Salmon Fisher*, 1890, and two books on Alaska, *Our New Alaska*, 1886, and *Peerless Alaska*, 1908, as well as his previously mentioned autobiography. He was outstanding in his time as angler, traveler, naturalist, and explorer, and through his magazine, one of the first voices to be heard throughout the land on the then almost unheard of subject of conservation.

HENSHALL

Henshall, James Alexander (1844–1925). Remembered today as the foremost champion of the black bass, about which he wrote the first complete treatise, the *Book of the Black Bass*, 1881, which reappeared in 1889, 1904, and 1923. Charles M. Wetzel, in *American Fishing Books* (1950), advanced the claim that Dr. Henshall "can also be regarded as the father of the present-day bait casting rods," saying that they were known in those times as "black bass minnow rods, and were manufactured as early as 1875 by C. F. Orvis of Manchester, Vermont, from specifications written by Henshall in a *Forest and Stream* article entitled 'The Coming Black Bass Rod.' These rods were three-jointed affairs, eight feet three inches long, weighing approximately nine ounces and designed for single-handed casting." With Henshall as the Pied Piper, American anglers went bass crazy in the eighties and nineties. On the assumption that the brighter the lure the better, trout flies too became increasingly gaudy, a tendency that was general until the turn of the century, after which Theodore Gordon turned the tide back toward more realistic imitation of natural insects. Henshall's was perhaps the most widely known angling name in the

The Angler's Best Companions 🖋 137

country in the nineties, but he never wrote anything else as colorful as his famous first pronouncement on the black bass ("I consider him, inch for inch and pound for pound, the gamest fish that swims"), and since most of his writings were as sparsely purposive as his prescriptions, they did not outlive him and he is today one of the most quoted and least read of American angling authors.

HEWITT

Hewitt, Edward Ringwood (1866–1957). One of the seminal figures of American angling, Hewitt was to the manor born, both figuratively and literally—he grew up in Ringwood Manor, a northern New Jersey demesne of positively feudal proportions and splendor, and combined the unusual advantages of a pampered background and upbringing (he was a direct descendant of Peter Cooper, the most lordly Mayor of New York since Stuyvesant's time) and the inquisitive nature of a mechanical genius with an inventive flair. With homes on Gramercy Park and on the Neversink, and the means and opportunities for frequent and extensive travels, Hewitt was familiar with the best fishing to be found everywhere throughout the last quarter of the nineteenth century and the first half of the twentieth. In *A Trout and Salmon Fisherman for Seventy-five Years,* published by Scribner's in 1950, he summed it up, and at the same time pretty well summarized the findings of his eight earlier books, *Secrets of the Salmon,* 1922, *Telling on the Trout,* 1926, his three Handbooks—*of Flyfishing,* 1933, *of Stream Improvement,* 1934, and *of Trout Raising and Stocking,* 1935—*Nymph Fly Fishing,* 1934, *Those Were the Days,* 1943, and *Ringwood Manor, The Home of the Hewitts,* 1946.

Hewitt must be credited, together with his fishing companions, George LaBranche and Col. Ambrose Monell, with the popularization of dry-fly fishing for salmon. He took a twenty-five-pound salmon on the Upsalquitch, before 1925, on his own size fourteen Neversink skater, and a twelve-pound salmon on a one-and-a-half-ounce rod, before 1922, both firsts and records that stood for decades until surpassed by Lee Wulff. At the same time he was more influential than any other single figure in the establishment of nymph fishing in America. The Hewitt nymph and the Neversink skater, an extremely long-hackled tailless spider, are still two of the most versatile and dependable attractors and takers of the salmonid species. But the fears, which he voiced in 1934, were groundless—that the general use of his nymphs might empty the country's streams of trout, and some of his dogmatic assertions, such as the attainment of "invisibility" for leaders, through use of his patented silver nitrate treatment, have proved to be of less than lasting significance. He was anticipated, notably by Mottram in *Fly Fishing, Some New Arts and Mysteries*, 1915, in some of the most perceptive of his pronouncements on the potentialities of light tackle, and despite his pertinacity in lifelong underwater photographic experiments to determine the taking propensities of the salmonid family, his actual findings never exceeded the dilettante level, and have since been surpassed by the observations of others, such as J. W. Jones in *The Salmon*, 1959.

But Hewitt and LaBranche will doubtless live on in angling legend, as two of the most colorful figures in the fishing of this century, such a large part of which they dominated, since both had the luck to fish in the limelight over a span of years as long as that of old Walton himself.

And Hewitt did formulate, as well as anyone ever did before or after him, the three stages in the development of an angler: we all begin as fishhogs at heart, with the attitude of little boys who will go to any lengths to get as many, and as big, fish as they possibly can; it's only later on that the angler learns, if indeed he ever does, to become selective and discriminating as to the means employed and, finally, to prize the means above the quarry. He could hardly have made any other finding less likely to be superseded than that.

HORNE

Horne, Bernard S. (1905–1970). Bibliophile and conservationist, compiler of the first comprehensive bibliography of Izaak Walton's *The Compleat Angler* to appear since the publication of *A New*

Chronicle of the Complete Angler by Peter Oliver in 1936. Horne's *The Complete Angler 1653–1967, A New Bibliography,* was published by The Pittsburgh Bibliophiles, of which he was cofounder and first president, and distributed by the University of Pittsburgh Press, Pittsburgh, Pennsylvania, in late 1970. Soon after completing its final typescript, the author was stricken with a cerebral hemorrhage and died at Hyannis Port, Massachusetts, on January 4, 1970.

Bernard Shea Horne was born in Keswick, Virginia, on September 6, 1905, and was graduated from Princeton in 1928. A student of angling literature for much of his life, he early became a collector of Walton's *Angler* and Waltoniana and over the years built from a wide variety of sources what was at the time of his death the most complete collection ever assembled, surpassing those of The New York Public Library, the Library of Congress, the Bodleian Library, and the British Museum. He was a fly fisherman of wide experience, and while studying his seventeenth century subject he fished the waters recorded by Walton and Cotton and made repeated pilgrimages to their haunts and habitats.

His original intention, in compiling his bibliographical notes, was simply to supplement the Oliver *Chronicle,* which he regarded as definitive. But when the simple annals of his own collecting activities caused him to draw ahead of Oliver—to note, for instance, that what Oliver recorded as the 100th edition turned out to be his own 136th, he began to realize that the pupil had, however unwittingly, surpassed the master. He recorded not only 106 editions and reprints published after Oliver, but twenty editions prior to, and not carried in, the earlier work. Ironically, he also proved, though his avowed admiration for the earlier work never wavered, that a few editions, which his predecessors had thought and reported to have existed, had never been published.

His bibliographic data infinitely more detailed than any that had been attempted by Oliver or indeed by Arnold Wood or Westwood and Satchel before him, he still stubbornly stood up for Oliver to the last, insisting that nobody could ever equal the original work that Oliver had done on the data of the five editions of Walton's lifetime. Even after allowing for the suppression of a number of disproved editions listed by Oliver, Horne's listing for the year 1935, which represented Oliver's ultimate total of 284 editions, still rose to 307, and Horne's last listing, including all the editions published after Oliver, a number of which were translations, surpassed Oliver's by over a hundred.

Bernard Shea Horne was also active as an ardent conservationist, serving for many years as a member of the Pennsylvania State Game Commission, culminating in its chairmanship in 1955. For more than a decade he was also responsible for the fish hatchery and streams of western Pennsylvania's Rolling Rock Club.

In his dual capacity of angler and scholar, Bernard Horne was a Fellow of the Pierpont Morgan Library in New York, a member of the Grolier Club, The Anglers' Club of New York, and The Fly-fishers' Club of London.

*J*NSTANT FLY FISHING—ALMOST

An appreciation of Simplified Fly Fishing, *by S. R. Slaymaker II, New York, Harper & Row, 1969*

At one of the annual conclaves of the Federation of Fly Fishermen, Roderick Haig-Brown made the pragmatic point that fly-fishing's future is imperiled by the awesomeness of its *mystique*—ordinary fishermen are kept from it by the belief that it is hard to learn, requires costly equipment, and is grudging in its rewards except after a formidable investment in both time and money. Haig-Brown said that what fly fishing in this country needs is a twenty-five-dollar beginner's outfit. That was back in 1967, and what with inflation . . .

But here's a book, for slightly less than five dollars, that may win even more converts to angling's most sporting and enjoyable form.

The title, *Simplified Fly Fishing,* is promising to the point of being catchy, and the first chapter's opening sentence is the best narrative hook this pursuer of the subject can recall in some hundreds of how-to volumes. It says: "You can become a fly angler in about thirty minutes." Wow. How simplified can you get?

The book is good. It does what it sets out to do, which is to demonstrate for the benefit of "non-fishermen who want to learn to fly fish, and for bait fishermen who have put off switching to flies because of the common but erroneous belief that they are for experts only, and for some-time fly anglers seeking simple but effective tips with which to improve their techniques," that fly fishing, thanks to the author's novel approach, can be made "one of the simplest of all pastimes to master."

The only word to quibble with there is the last one. For a quick analogy, it could be equally well argued that German is one of the simplest of all languages to master—in the sense that almost anybody can make himself understood in it in a matter of hardly more than minutes. If that constitutes mastery, then fair enough. But by the same token—that it is ridiculously easy to speak badly—it is diabolically difficult to master to any degree even approaching perfection.

The same applies to fly fishing, with or without this Slaymaker book. Still, I can't imagine anybody in his right mind wanting his money back after reading it.

The novel approach is to put first things first, and to put them very clearly, and—the one gimmick—to start the tyro off with pond fishing for panfish. Certainly there is no better kindergarten to show quick progress and provide almost certain and instant results, as a first step in the mastery of what the author himself characterizes, in a candid moment at the end of the introduction, as "the delightful art form that is fly angling." And when it comes to art forms, even delightful ones, the proverbial statement about the relative brevity of life and length of art still stands.

It might have been more accurate, if less compelling, to call this book *A Simplified Approach to Fly Fishing*, for that it is, beyond any possible quibble point. As such it can only be praised. But the fly fishing it covers, once past the rudimentary opening chapters, while very well clarified, is in no way simplified. In the last chapters the atmosphere is rarefied enough to satisfy the querulous requirements of any purist.

So the form of fly fishing both preached and practiced here, while it has a most inviting entrance, is no quickly thrown-up shirt-front structure. Once you get inside it's of cathedrallike solidity, and orthodoxy, too, for that matter.

Sam Slaymaker is as "compleat" a fly fisherman as we have, and despite his profession of simplification, he hasn't held back one iota of his own sophisticated practice of the art in the writing of this book.

So this isn't one of those half-baked brown-and-serve offerings of "instant cuisine" that are at worst a fraud and at best a contradiction in terms. What it is, and most welcome too, is a commonsense, no-nonsense coverage of the current state of the art of fly fishing. Added dividend, almost by way of warranty, it has a foreword by Sparse Grey Hackle, that angler's angler, that is alone worth much more than the modest price of admission.

INTERNATIONAL ATLANTIC SALMON FOUNDATION

425 Park Avenue
New York, New York 10022
P. O. Box 429, St. Andrews
New Brunswick, Canada
Wilfred M. Carter, Executive Director

Educational and scientific organization dedicated to the con-
servation and preservation of the Atlantic salmon. One of the last
best hopes of safeguarding the survival and restoration of this
depleted and threatened species. (Contributions are tax
deductible on U.S. tax returns only.)

There aren't many things these days to make you proud of being an American, but this is one. The sensible and rational but at the same time resourceful and farsighted attitude of this group toward the intricately tangled complex of problems endangering the continued existence of the Atlantic salmon is one of the few hopeful signs that a way may yet be found out of a dilemma that for the past few years has taxed tempers in high places on both sides of the ocean, worried and perplexed sportsmen everywhere, and engendered a lot more heat than enlightenment.

On its record so far, the International Atlantic Salmon Foundation deserves unqualified approbation. Getting the ball behind their own goal line, so to speak, in that they began at a time when the unchecked depredations of the high seas fishery appeared most alarming, they took a purely pragmatic approach and went at the salmon problem on a first-things-first basis, giving direct aid to CASE, and not until they could begin to see some "light at the end of the tunnel," in terms of the phasing out of the high seas Atlantic salmon fishery, did they begin to concern themselves with the long-term aspects of the problems of restoring American salmon resources. Here, too, their approach has so far been sensibly pragmatic, covering those bets on which the odds seemed best to effect some immediate remedial action on what had long seemed to be a lost cause, the spawning run of Atlantic salmon in New England rivers.

Along with the funding of feasibility studies, and hatchery designs, for the development of improved stocks for the restoration of natural salmon runs and for salmon farming in the Northeastern States and Canada, the Foundation has taken positive steps to coordinate the Atlantic salmon conservation programs of various volunteer organizations, to eliminate duplication of effort, and has embarked on an ambitious program to stimulate public involvement. Phase Two of its activity is best expressed in its policy statement that "there is no future for salmon if we succeed in controlling the offshore fishery but fail in efforts to eliminate other abusive practices nearer home."

The Foundation's sponsorship of the North Atlantic Salmon Council was a strategic move that led to its joining and helping the effective deployment of such an array of forces as the American Fisheries Society, Atlantic Salmon Association, Baie des Chaleurs Salmon Association, Conservation Foundation, Federation of Fly Fishermen, Miramichi Salmon Association, National Wildlife Federation, Nova Scotia Salmon Association, Sport Fishery Research Foundation, Sport Fishing Institute, and Trout Unlimited.

The mere act of mobilization is not in itself of course any certain assurance of victory, but every angler must applaud the aim, as expressed by Wilfred M. Carter: "The concern of our organization today is to assure that we preserve the Atlantic salmon for tomorrow."

If the job can still be done, then these are the men most likely to succeed in getting it done. But meanwhile they need all the help they can get.

IZAAK WALTON LEAGUE OF AMERICA

1800 North Kent Street
Arlington, Virginia 22209
(Founded 1922, by Will H. Dilg) Suite 806
National nonprofit organization, devoted to conservation

Over fifty years old and well over fifty thousand strong in its membership, the Izaak Walton League has been treating the Environment as a fighting cause since long before most people were aware of it as anything more than a not very interesting condition.

Its various classes of membership, and their annual dues, are: Regular, $10 (Student, $2); Supporting, $25; Master, $40. Life membership is $100. There is also a Legal Action Fund, to which contributions in any amount may be made, knowing that they will be put to good use.

The League has never tried to hog the credit for itself, but has rather shown really enlightened self-interest in joining forces with other conservation groups, both local and national, wherever there has been either the opportunity or the necessity for making common cause against an environmental threat, and has been in the forefront of every major engagement, from DDT to SST, and with countless cases of dams and damages to rivers and coastal wetlands in between.

If you feel any least twinge of a sense that you really ought to be "paying your dues" somewhere, to calm any qualms of conscience you may have over the inordinate enjoyment you get out of fishing, then this is one place to pay them.

Jennings

Jennings, Preston J. (1893–1962). Nineteen years after Louis Rhead, whom he dismissed as being both misguided and inept, Preston Jennings undertook to lay the foundation of an American angling entomology with *A Book of Trout Flies;* it was published in 1935 both as a Derrydale Press limited edition and in a trade edition, and then offered as a reprint by Crown Publishers. Within a very short time the Crown reprint was almost as scarce as the Derrydale first edition, and Jennings went into the same eclipse that he had helped to impose upon Rhead. Although Charles Wetzel, in 1943, offered a limited entomology in his *Practical Fly Fishing,* this, too, was of small circulation (1,395 copies), and it was not until the publication of Art Flick's *Streamside Guide to Naturals and Their Imitations,* in 1947, that anglers began to become generally aware of the scientific approach to imitation of American stream insects that Jennings had launched a dozen years before. Flick had fished with Jennings and along with a number of others had helped him in the preparation of *A Book of Trout Flies,* as Jennings had acknowledged in the book's preface. For that matter, Flick has also acknowledged Jennings in his own book. That still didn't keep Jennings from feeling, and saying, that Flick had stolen his thunder, and for the rest of his life Jennings went around saying that Flick had done him dirt. Actually, though Flick's *Streamside Guide* did make more of a stir than any of its three predecessors in the field of fly-fishing entomology, it too was something of a seven-day wonder and was soon allowed to go out of print. The same fate overtook the next brilliant contribution to this subject, Vincent Marinaro's *A Modern Dry-Fly Code,* one of the most innovative of American angling books, published in 1950 but within the decade as hard to come by as copies of either Rhead's *American Trout Stream Insects* or Jennings's *A Book of Trout Flies.* By 1955, when Ernest Schwiebert's *Matching the Hatch* came along, it was greeted as if it were a brand-new idea, and as if the trailblazing work of Rhead, Jennings, Wetzel, and even Marinaro had never existed. For their books were, if not out of mind, at least out of sight, and though Schwiebert took pains to point out that he was the last of a long parade, still he was received as if he were first, with a new field before him. He was, that is, until *Matching the Hatch,* too, became hard to find. So while Preston Jennings did feel unjustly neglected, and indeed was, he didn't lack excellent company in this respect.

With the exception of Ray Bergman's *Trout,* and McClane's *Standard Fishing Encyclopedia,* all the best American angling books of this century have had to become scarce before they were appreciated, a melancholy fate to which Jennings was simply no exception. Belated justice to Jennings came in 1970, with the issuance of the reprint; it is now in its seventh printing.

Jennings had the classic approach to exactness of imitation, which made him give short shrift to Rhead's attempts at impressionism, considering them simply badly tied. He wrote of him: "Mr. Rhead was an artist, and the plates in his book are finely drawn, but the flies depicted are not identified, and as Mr. Rhead named the flies himself, it is impossible to check the species, or even to determine whether the flies are actually different species or only different stages of the same species. Mr. Rhead apparently wanted to control the manufacture of what he called Nature Flies, which he designed, and for that reason no dressings of the artificial flies are given in his book. The writer has some of the Rhead flies in his possession and while they are nice to look at, they frankly do not come up to the standards set by the professional fly-tyer of the Catskill regions."

He went on to add that as of 1935, the moment at which he was writing: "Despite the drawbacks of the Rhead flies, the book *American Trout Stream Insects* has its place in the library of the fly-fisher. This is the only book which deals with the fly life of American trout streams."

Jennings had his blind spots and could be dogmatic in his insistence upon them. He was convinced, for instance, that salmon do feed in fresh water, not only before they leave it as smolts for their period of growth in the ocean, but also when they return to it to spawn, and he spent a great deal of time and trouble trying to prove it. He also was as convinced as E. R. Hewitt was that fish could be made to ignore a leader, if you treat it properly before presenting it to them. Hewitt's treatment was silver nitrate, while Jennings applied purple Tintex dye. He maintained that a 2X leader dyed purple would take as many trout as a 5X leader that was not similarly treated. Conclusive proof was never possible, as on every occasion when the experiment was tried, the trout confused the tests by either lunging headlong at flies presented on both leaders or, on other occasions, sniffily shying away from the flies affixed to both of them. He also attributed the success of the *Isonychia bicolor* nymph, when it was successful, to the fact that it represented "the nymph phase of a Royal Coachman" and when it was remonstrated that nobody had ever seen a Royal Coachman, except attached to a hook, he said that was because the fly itself emerged after dark. This argument he was even willing to dignify with print, which he did in a magazine article entitled "There IS a Royal Coachman." When taunted with the suggestion that quite possibly this fly constituted the diet of those upstream feeding salmon, he would only smile forbearingly, as if reminding himself that Columbus, too, was the butt of many jibes.

Deluded, or inspired, as he might have been in some of his personal convictions, Preston Jennings was resolutely disciplined in his scientific approach to the subject of stream entomology, and the result was that *A Book of Trout Flies* could stand, as Louis Rhead's *American Trout Stream Insects* whether rightly or wrongly did not, as the principal inspiration for all subsequent American books in this field. This has been acknowledged by Schwiebert, in the introduction to the 1970 reissue of *A Book of Trout Flies,* with the added comment, apropos of Art Flick's work, that "the stream studies that resulted in the *Streamside Guide* had both the book and Jennings himself—who often fished with Flick in the golden years of the Schoharie and its Westkill Tavern— as their wellspring and example."

Preston Jennings would have settled gladly for those two kind words from a peer, after three and a half decades of neglect, for they summarize all he ever wanted to be or seem to other anglers—a wellspring of inspiration and an example of perseverance.

*L*aBRANCHE

LaBranche, George Michel Lucien (1875–1961). Author of *The Dry Fly and Fast Water*, 1914, and *The Salmon and the Dry Fly*, 1924 (both books reissued as a single volume by Charles Scribner's Sons, New York, in 1951), LaBranche was the outstanding exponent and advocate of the dry fly at the height of its vogue in America. With his fishing partners E. R. Hewitt and Ambrose Monell, he established the possibility and popularized the practice of taking salmon on the dry fly, going on, almost by accident, to a further discovery that has since been put to use by many more anglers than the comparative handful who fish for salmon. One unique contribution was his invention of a deadly method for taking almost any fish that refuses to be taken by conventional offerings, the creation of "the artificial hatch" whereby repeated casts are floated over the same spot often enough to convince even the most skeptical fish that a hatch is on and that he'd better take before it's over. It was a demonstration of this method in England, where he was more widely acclaimed and feted than any American angler had ever been before, that elicited this encomium in Britain's oldest fishing weekly, the *Fishing Gazette*: "This remarkable caster cast the dry fly in places in which it would be extremely difficult to drop a worm, under overhanging alders and blackberry bushes, around trunks of trees, casting at will on to particular leaves that the fly might drop thence like a caterpillar from an oak leaf. His fishing is smooth and entirely effortless . . . his flies go where he wishes them to go and act as he directs them when they get there. Briefly, Mr. La-Branche is a very beautiful fisherman."

It may be a shock, by today's journalistic attitudes, to suggest that the last sentence of this tribute was intended to be taken both literally and figuratively, but George LaBranche was the Beau Brummel of angling annals, and the grace of his casting was matched by his garb, manner, and personal appearance. Slight and slender, but seeming taller than he was by his erect posture, LaBranche was a dandy both on and off stream, wearing vest, collar, and tie and the Sherlock Holmes-like helmet type of fishing hat. The delicacy and control of

FFF's founding father, Gene Anderegg, with a ten-pound brown on the Missouri River in Montana, 1962.

The real father figure of American angling literature, Walton's first American editor (1847) and still one of the best, Rev. George Washington Bethune.

>

Angler's angler, blithe spirit of The Anglers' Club of New York, acknowledged dean of American fly fishers, Alfred W. Miller, more widely known as Sparse Grey Hackle. Here he fishes the DeBruce Club water on the Willowemoc. *Photo by Hermann Kessler*

Pewter-haired, crag-faced Lee Wulff, the fly rod's most versatile exponent, and angling's most influential ambassador to the whole wide world of sport. *Photo by Peter Alport*

➤

Joan Salvato Wulff, the better half of angling's best-known "matched pair" and an exemplary sports figure in her own right. *Photo by Lee Wulff*

Historic step toward an American entomology; Preston Jennings gathering insects for *A Book of Trout Flies*.

Preston Jennings with some of his own collection of other anglers' flies, all catalogued with names of the flies and of their tiers.

Preston Jennings on the Neversink, the
hallowed water of Hewitt and LaBranche,
and of Theodore Gordon, its sage.

Adele (Tiny) Jennings on the Neversink
streamside in the time of bloom.

AG and Jane K. Gingrich on the Haffjördara in Iceland, 1956. *Photo by A. J. McClane*

AG and Jane K. Gingrich on the Stromfjördara with, respectively, Al McClane's rod and his fish. *Photo by A. J. McClane*

AG on the Nordura, Iceland, 1956.
Photo by A. J. McClane

Typical catch of salmon and trout
on the Big Laxa, Iceland. *Photo by
A. J. McClane*

Paul Young at play, somewhere up in Michigan, 1948.

Paul Young at work, in his Detroit rod shop, 1960.

Russ Peak, "who is to glass what Paul Young was to bamboo," doing his annual field work at Arcularius Ranch on the Owens River, 1970. *Photo by Herman V. Wall*

Russ Peak, doing one of the over two hundred hand operations on his glass rod (cementing cork rings on shaft), Pasadena, 1960. *Photo by Herman V. Wall*

This is—this has to be—the one and only Charlie Ritz. Doesn't a sight like that make you want to call him Mighty Mouse? He's only relaxing, at the casting pond in the Bois de Boulogne, site of his annual Fario Club exercises. *Photo Doisneau-Rapho*

Rare sight—a "still" picture of Charles Ritz, otherwise known as a man in perpetual motion. Past eighty, he maintains schedules that would daunt a dray horse, but here, for once, he's making like Walton, thinking long slow thoughts (though presumably about "high speed, high line"). *Photo by Peter Alport*

A. J. McClane, to whom a fish "long as your arm" is just par for the course. To say where or when he caught this one is like trying to count the teeth in a buzzsaw—he fishes more days of the year than most of us work. "He's the real McThing."

Roderick Haig-Brown, angling's emissary to the realm of belles lettres, at the 1967 FFF conclave in Jackson Hole, Wyoming, making a remarkably down-to-earth plea to free the ambiance of fly fishing from its phony frills and too rarefied mystique. *Photo by Gene Anderegg*

Last days of an old stager—Joe Brooks at a TGF luncheon in New York some months before his death in 1972. One of the best-loved angling figures of our time, he lived to see the publication of his best book, the truly perceptive and evocative *Trout Fishing*. *Photo by Gene Anderegg*

The boy grows older—Ernie Schwiebert (*right*), so long devoted to doing
high deeds on distant waters (like this record salmon in Norway) that
he began to seem perpetual student and perennial prodigy, suddenly
started in his fortieth year to cash in all his promissory prowess with a
vengeance, and with three books in a twelvemonth emerged as the major
angling writer he was so long in becoming.

The angler as artist: William J. Schaldach. Out of the hundreds of angling artists, only a handful have attained master status as artist-anglers. One of them is Bill Schaldach, artist and author of *Currents and Eddies, Coverts and Casts*, and, most recently, *The Wind on Your Cheek. Photo courtesy of Freshet Press*

The last word—and who should have it but Ed Zern? After all, it's his habit of long standing to leave you laughing, so we put him in here to help keep you from going away mad. Always kidding, as in his latest collection, *A Fine Kettle of Fish Stories*. But about conservation, his kidding is all on the square. See his parody on *America the Beautiful* on the last pages of this book. After that, if you want to go away mad, it's perfectly all right. You should. *Photo by Gene Anderegg*

his powerful casting was often likened to the mailed fist in the velvet glove. Convinced that accuracy and finesse in presentation were much more important than color or type of fly, he was known more than once to go through an entire season using for all his fishing, both for salmon and trout, only the single fly with which his name was most closely identified, the Pink Lady. Using tackle that was considered extremely light in the teens and twenties, an eight-foot, three-and-a-half-ounce rod, his sixty-foot casts in adverse winds astonished the English anglers with whom he fished on the Test, the Itchen, and the Kennet, where he leased some three miles of the stream at Ramsbury in Wiltshire.

A successful New York stockbroker, LaBranche never permitted business to cause more than minimal interference with his sporting activities. Almost as ardent for guns as for rods, he allotted a good deal of time to shooting, and to the raising of pheasants, and was also devoted to golf and yachting, his thirty-foot sloop the *Wee Betty* winning the championship in her class in 1927 and placing second the following year.

Asked in an interview by the feature writer Marguerite Ives whether he considered fishing an art or a science, and whether he thought of himself as what is termed a purist, LaBranche answered the first question with "Distinctly an art. Fly fishing is closely allied in my mind with music. I think that to cast a fly properly one must possess a sense of rhythm. The cast should be made in time to a rhythmic beat and the fly could easily be allowed to float on the water for the length of certain notes, withdrawn and the line straightened out and cast again all to musical measure and cadence."

And as to being a purist, he replied, "Not in the broad sense of the term. I consider that the real purist wastes countless joyous and active hours waiting, according to his theory, for the rise of the fish before he casts."

LINE LOAD

If you use a light short rod as I do, you'll probably have no trouble with it as long as you stick to a number four or five floating line, either weight forward or double taper. But if you want a sinking line for nymph fishing, unless you can remember to confine yourself to short casts, you're courting trouble if you put even the smallest size on any bamboo rod shorter than six-and-a-half feet and weighing appreciably under two ounces. Lines of current American manufacture, made of synthetics like Dacron, if they're heavy enough to sink are too heavy for even the impregnated bamboo rods in the bantam, flea, and midge lengths, from four-and-a-quarter to six-and-a-quarter feet. You can thumb the catalogues until your fingers blister, and you won't find a sinking line below size five. It's too heavy, and before long you'll find yourself snapping any small light bamboo rod on which you use it more than very occasionally.

Here's the solution. Buy the weight-forward sinking line and cut it off at the end of its forward taper. You can save that to use as a shooting head, tied with a nail knot to anywhere from a hundred feet to a hundred yards of twenty-pound-test monofilament line, depending on what amount of it can comfortably be accommodated on the core of your reel spool. You can use that safely on any other rod you've got. But now on the small rod use only the rest of the running line, which will be of about what we used to call the G or F diameter, in the days before line sizes were determined by weight, and put as much backing on it as you need to fill your reel spool comfortably. On the small light rod you will find that you have one of the sweetest casting setups you've ever had and, except for such continuing hazards as car doors, you won't find yourself snapping off any more small rods.

Even with this precaution against line overload, you may find it prudent to turn the rod over now and then, from the reel-up to the reel-down position, while engaged in playing really heavy fish, such as anything over three pounds. (Yes, I can hear you muttering "I should live so long," but still, you never can tell.) It's almost impossible to get a "set" in the contemporary impregnated bamboo rods, but on some of mine, such as the four-and-three-quarter-foot Midget Giant-Killer, and the five-foot-one-inch Mighty Mite, through carelessness in forgetting to rotate the rod's position as often as I should, I find I have acquired if not an actual "set" then at least a not altogether graceful "sway," from butt to tip, that I could easily have avoided.

Remember to turn the rod, when actually playing heavy fish, as Paul Young used to urge us to do with his first Midge rods, back in the early fifties, and you will find even your shortest and lightest rod staying arrow-straight through seasons of hard use.

*M*cCLANE

Angling's Brillat-Savarin, the peerless angler who can also cook

Everybody has to have a hero, to make his efforts in any chosen field of endeavor seem worth pursuing. In fiddling, for instance, mine was always Fritz Kreisler, and still is, though I've long known that there were others—Heifetz for one—who could outdistance him on sheer mechanical techniques. But for the unique magic of tone, just as there were no tenors beside Caruso, there were no fiddlers besides Kreisler. Somebody once likened the golden sheen of his tone to a glass of Gerwürztraminer seen through the romantic glow of candlelight—well, hell, I seem to be in the wrong book. But to get back to fishing . . .

. . . to me in my time, there are no anglers beside McClane. Oh, sure, there are other anglers that I've called complete, for no better or other reason than that they are. There's Lee Wulff, and Charlie Ritz, and Ernie Schwiebert, and Charlie Fox, and Sparse, and Robert Traver, to start to tick off a partial list. For that matter, there's Joan Salvato Wulff, and Patti Murphy McClane, and Helen Shaw Kessler, and Maxine Atherton Wyckoff, just to show you that I can be as broad-minded as the next guy. But talk to me of anglers and I have to tell you that in my book Al McClane is unique.

We could leave it at that, I suppose. It does sound like a conversation closer, doesn't it? After I've said that, what's left to say about him?

Well, I've known him since 1955, and fished with him, virtually to the extent of living with him, for five seasons from 1956 through 1960, up at Turnwood on the Upper Beaverkill. But I'd been reading him for eight years before that, beginning in 1947 when I was living in Europe, and used to get my copies of *Field & Stream* at the PX in Vienna or Munich or Paris. And all these years, as well as I've come to know him, I've felt that there is a lot more there to know.

I worked closely with him in the early sixties when he was first gathering material for his monumental *McClane's Standard Fishing Encyclopedia,* and in fact my own fishing book was an outgrowth of my efforts to serve as a sort of general handyman contributor to that gigantic volume. And ever since it appeared in 1965 I've been storing away, squirrellike, odd bits and pieces of angling lore, using him as a repository, with the next edition of the encyclopedia in mind. In between, meeting as often as his comings and goings to the far corners of the fishing world would bring him through New York, I've had frequent occasions to check with him on angling problems and questions that puzzled me, and I've never come away empty-handed. With other anglers, no matter what I ask them, I always have the feeling that I've just gathered one more opinion, whereas with Al McClane I feel, as Truman put it, that "the buck stops here." So often the rest think or guess or surmise, but Al always seems to know. I suppose it's because he did his groundwork thoroughly, with his training at Cornell, and subsequently out in the field, in fish culture and fisheries research, and has done his homework ever since, but with Al if you penetrate through the sportsman's rather permeable soft outer layers of opinion and experience, you come up hard against the bedrock of the scientist's store of exact knowledge and expertise, where there's no more room for guesswork.

But there's another side to this many-sided creature. The country boy from Margaretville, New York, has grown up to be not only the most knowledgeable of anglers, but also one of the most sophisticated and accomplished of gastronomes and chefs. As long as I've known him he has been working on a cookbook, in fact he started on it years before he even began his decade-long labors on the fishing encyclopedia, and when that finally comes out, then A. J. McClane will have a role in gastronomy and cuisine, if not as towering as his stature in the angling world, at least of real distinction.

When I look back in my mind's eye at those Turnwood years, the images I have of him are as often concerned with pots and pans as with rods and reels. Patti, his wife, and Susie, his then small daughter, knew that it was as important to keep out of his way when he was in the small pavilion that served as both kitchen and dining porch as it was when he was over in the cottage, closeted with his typewriter, working at his vocation. His work at his avocation, mixing bowl and measuring cup in hand, was every bit as important, and as unthinkable to interrupt or in any way impede.

The one place Al was always interruptible was on the stream, where he appeared to have all the time in the world. He seemed to feel that the fish would wait, and never begrudged the time it took to answer questions, or give suggestions and pointers. With most men it's just the opposite; where they might gladly suffer fools in their offices or on the street, back in the city, they would be driven half wild by the mere thought that they might have to brook any least interference with their precious fishing time. Perhaps one difference is that Al knows that he will be fishing about as many days in a given year as most men put in at their jobs. Hence he is freed from the pressure of that frantic sense of urgency that besets the rest of us, whenever we take any time away from the workaday world to go fishing. The great thing about being a fishing editor is that your work is the other guys' play, and vice versa. Just as a travel editor's job is to go traveling, so a fishing editor's work is to go fishing—lovely work if you can get it.

For twenty-five years Al McClane had an office, but it was one where, if he showed up there, he was likely to be asked, "Why the hell aren't you out fishing?" For common mortals who have an office, when they don't show up there, but have been out fishing instead, the question is, of course, "Where the hell have your been?" Obviously any man who can arrange to get that question reversed is just that much smarter than all the rest of us.

Of late, when it was announced that Al McClane would no longer be the fishing editor of *Field & Stream,* but would serve the magazine in some presumably more prestigious capacity, and with an

executive editorship—obviously meant to be considered more important than any departmental editor's title—some of us feared that a
good man had just succumbed to a fate worse than death. I for one
couldn't believe it. Al had managed to finesse his way around such
"improvements" in his working condition a half dozen times in the
course of a quarter century in the fishing editor's job, and I figured he
had become, like a wily old brown trout, much too canny to be caught
now. But when I learned that the new executive editor of a magazine
on Madison Avenue was going to continue to function from a Palm
Beach residence I canceled all plans to take Tuesday and Friday
nights off to weep for him.

And meanwhile the books continue to come out. The International Fishing Guides, like the encyclopedia, flourish and grow ever
bigger, and now are being joined by a volume on the game fishes of
the Americas, a project of the Gamefish Research Association, and
meanwhile three different publishers are disseminating paperbacks of
the fishing guide. Sometimes I get the impression that this is not just a
normal ordinary mortal with two hands and feet, like you and me, but
a one-man conglomerate.

Still, I'm consoled by the thought that it has taken him as long to
do his cookbook as it could possibly ever have taken anybody else to do
one, so that's a reassuring sign that even the great McClane may be
only human after all.

But awesome as all the new McClane books on fishing are, and
the evidences of his industry since the publication of the encyclopedia
are overwhelming, there's one that I wish a new generation could
grow up with, and that's his 1953 classic, *The Practical Fly Fisherman.* That's the book I cut my own angling eyeteeth on, and I pity
any other fisherman, young or old, who hasn't ever had a chance to
read it. It's long out of print, but up to now Al has refused to allow it
to be restored to currency by inclusion in any of the various reprint
series that have rescued so many other worthwhile fishing books from
oblivion.

Today's crop of anglers, agog over such modern heresies as
Leonard Wright's "sudden inch" and the radical concept of fishing the
dry fly downstream, would be bug-eyed to read, in the dry-fly chapter

of *The Practical Fly Fisherman,* a book now twenty years old, the prescription given, and the case histories cited, for the use of the "worked" dry fly, fished downstream. As a matter of fact, the title of that chapter is "The Dry Fly, Upstream and Down."

Thinking back over the book as a whole, and remembering that I turned down the corners of more pages in that book than in any other one fishing book I ever read, I venture the bet that there is still today, after twenty years, as much sound innovative practice left in the now long-neglected pages of *The Practical Fly Fisherman* as there is in any of the fishing books published in the last three years, not excluding Leonard Wright's *Fishing the Dry Fly as a Living Insect* nor even the vaunted Swisher-Richards volume, *Selective Trout.* The chief difference is that the new guys have made a religion of their "unorthodox methods," though actually they are no less orthodox and no more startlingly new departures than a number of the little wrinkles that McClane casually tossed off in stride, without pausing to posture or preen or chest-thump, two decades back.

In fact, remembering *The Practical Fly Fisherman* is to realize that recommending it today is about as venturesome as recommending twenty-year-old Scotch—this vintage McClane is the real McThing.

McDONALD

An Appreciation of Quill Gordon, *by John McDonald*

Here's a braw bonny bargain of a book, by the foremost angling scholar of our time. If there ever was any doubt of John McDonald's preeminence as America's most scholarly angler, there can't be after reading *Quill Gordon.* Here you have, in one volume, a distillate of all his angling writings, from the May 1946 and June 1948 issues of *Fortune*—two articles which remain to this day the best overall single statements on American trout and salmon fishing respectively—and all his writings on Theodore Gordon, from his monumental 1947 volume *The Complete Fly Fisherman: The Notes and Letters of*

Theodore Gordon, with which McDonald literally rescued Gordon from decades of obloquy as a shadowy figure of near-legend and restored him to his rightful place on top of the whole heap of hagiography as the patron figure of all our angling saints, up to and including the last word on Gordon which he contributed to *A. J. McClane's Standard Fishing Encyclopedia* in 1965. With a canny Scots instinct for hoarding treasure, he has also endowed this volume with all his own writings on Dame Juliana Berners, from his 1963 landmark *The Origins of Angling.*

Following an illustrious precedent, John McDonald has here done what E. R. Hewitt did in his retrospective volume, *A Trout and Salmon Fisherman for Seventy-five Years,* skimming the cream off his two previous books, *Telling on the Trout* and *Secrets of the Salmon,* and adding a highly personal overlay of anecdotage. In this latter element, McDonald goes Hewitt one better, because beyond the dimension of mere reminiscence he does hitherto undone justice to some of the great waters of the west. American fishing's last frontiers are still to be found in some of these western rivers that, while by no means unknown, are relatively unsung, as compared to the storied eastern streams that have become over the last century as much overwritten as overfished. Certainly the unique attractions of western fishing have long lacked (always excepting the inimitable Roderick Haig-Brown) the attentions of any laureate approaching McDonald's stature. So this volume includes, along with an essay both scholarly and personal on the Green Drake, a chapter on Yellowstone Park fishing, another on the salvation of Armstrong Creek, a wonderful one on the big fish on the wall of Dan Bailey's tackle shop in Montana, and one on steelhead fishing in the Salmon River Canyon in Idaho. These chapters will come as always human and sometimes comic relief to the book's more profound portions, serving the chapters on Gordon and Dame Juliana Berners the way seltzer serves a spritzer, lightening with the fizz and sparkle of personal recollection and observation the otherwise rather heady wine of scholarship.

The most endearing is the one called "All the Big Ones Got Away." To the question of what's a big fish? McDonald says, "Every angler has his private scale. On mine, thinking of good, not big, fish which I have actually caught, I can say roughly that a 14-inch trout in a Catskill creek equals a 2-pounder on the Yellowstone River equals a 17-pound salmon on the Restigouche. On the same scale, a 2-pounder in a stream equals a much larger one in a lake, and a 2-pounder caught on a fly representing an insect equals a much larger one caught on a streamer fly representing a minnow—all quite arbitrary according to one's own game rules and values. *Big* before fish is a peculiar word, suggesting, I imagine, for many anglers something outlandish in relation to the circumstances. I have seen Lee Wulff, who has taken the biggest fish in the world on the lightest tackle, catch a 10-inch trout on the Battenkill with sewing thread, to his evident pleasure. Joan Miller, who once caught a 900-pound swordfish off Cape Cod with spear and barrel, yelled, 'Oh my God!' when she hooked her first trout later in the Yellowstone—a 9-incher on a Tiny Gray Wulff dry."

As if McDonald's own words were not enough, *Quill Gordon* offers two smashing extra dividends, both in text and pictures. Included on the pictorial side are eight full-color pages of paintings of trout and salmon flies by John Atherton, and of the original twelve flies in Dame Juliana's fifteenth century treatise by John Langley Howard. Textually, the bonus section consists of a complete modernization of *The Treatise of Fishing with an Angle,* achieved by filling in the gaps in the 1450 manuscript with portions from the first printed edition of 1496; a "brazenly edited" version of Charles Cotton's contribution to *The Compleat Angler,* first incorporated into the Walton classic as Part Two of its fifth edition in 1676, and now ruthlessly stripped of all its extraneous matter—chiefly Cotton's imitations of "his father" Walton's matchless stylistic devices—to let it stand for what it is, the earliest still useful essay on the art of fly fishing; and last but hardly less novel, George Washington Bethune's essay on fly fishing in the United States, invariably overlooked by angling historians because he hid it in the form of a footnote to his first American edition of Walton in 1847.

Quill Gordon richly fulfills McDonald's avowed pattern of conveying the experience of fishing "in water and libraries," generously purveying "the old and new, the classic and modern, the two sides of the Atlantic, the traditional East and modern West in the United States."

It is hard to think of a single volume that would give the serious angler more thoughtful pleasure.

MOTTRAM

Mottram, James Cecil (1880–1945). The unsung genius of English Angling Literature, Mottram published in 1915 *Fly Fishing: Some New Arts and Mysteries,* an unusually forward-looking book, and one of its mysteries is why it has been so consistently overlooked. Major John Waller Hills in his classic *A History of Fly Fishing for Trout,* covered English fishing books up to his day with scholarly thoroughness and was conscientious about mentioning even those works, usually American, that lay outside his chosen theme of showing the development and the heritage of British fishing. But Hills had a rare talent and eloquence for advocacy of those writers whom he deemed in any way original in the advancement of the sport, and he was unstinting of his space and attention in dealing with otherwise undistinguished authors if he could but point out something in their pages that had some relevancy, however slight, to the subsequent development and refinement of the art. He might logically have been expected, then, to have jumped in joyously as chief drumbeater for Mottram as the most innovative talent of his time. But Hills dismissed Mottram with a sentence, saying in a mention of him among others: "Also there is much new and stimulating matter in Mr. J. C. Mottram's *Fly Fishing.*"

Even more mysterious is the faint praise with which Mottram is damned by James Robb in *Notable Angling Literature,* published in 1945 or 1946 (it is undated but interior evidence indicates its approximate date of appearance). Robb lists Mottram's book, and like Hills before him, praises it with minimal mention: "J. C. Mottram's *Fly Fishing* is broad-minded and challenging." He gives equally short shrift to Mottram's next work, the 1923 volume *Sea Trout and Other Fishing Studies,* saying simply: "He has much to say about worm fishing, and the use of fly, wet, dry and blow line. It is useful and practical."

Hills published before Hewitt's first book appeared, so he is not mentioned by Hills, although LaBranche is, but Robb lists both of Hewitt's first two books, published in 1922 and 1926, and the fact that Robb gives this much indication of being acquainted with Hewitt's work takes on additional interest when it is realized how startlingly Mottram anticipated by from seven to twenty-one years some of Hewitt's most important experiments and conclusions. Comparison of Hewitt's *A Trout and Salmon Fisherman for Seventy-five Years,* which appeared in 1950 and represented all Hewitt's theories and diagrams of the previous thirty years, from *Telling on the Trout* in 1922 through the 1934 *Manuals on Nymph Fishing and Stream Improvement,* shows that with the sole exception of the reporting of Hewitt's and LaBranche's experiences with the Neversink skater, the astonishing thing is that there is virtually nothing substantive in Hewitt in 1950 that wasn't anticipated by Mottram in 1915, including the diagram of the study of the stress and strain on a six-foot rod.

This comparison is not cited to take anything away from Hewitt, whose exploits are remarkable (and are the subject of another entry under his name), but rather to emphasize how extraordinarily prophetic Mottram was with his anticipation, as far back as 1915, of what anglers generally considered news, decades later, not only in respect to light tackle and short rods, and nymph fishing, and stream improvement, but even in some of Mottram's anticipations of the use of tiny terrestrials in the case of smutting fish, a phenomenon that also had to wait to appear otherwise in print until 1950 and the publication of Vincent Marinaro's *A Modern Dry-Fly Code.*

Mottram's subsequent books, *Trout Fisheries: Their Care and Preservation,* 1928, and the previously mentioned 1923 volume, are much less outstanding than his amazing debut in 1915 might have given every reason to expect. In the sweepstakes of angling, Mottram showed "early foot," to an astonishing degree, but without the stamina to maintain it over the distance. He did, however, make something of a comeback to his early form with his undated but post-World War II

Thoughts on Angling, a small but very thought-provoking book. His first book, *Fly Fishing: Some New Arts and Mysteries,* was reissued in 1921, but both editions are extremely hard to come by, and Mottram's turn has not yet come in the current scheduling of reprints of the various angling classics by Crown and Freshet Press. When his day does come, there will be a new star in the fisherman's heavens, and Mottram after half a century of scandalous neglect will be recognized for what he is, the most remarkable "sleeper" in at least seven decades of angling annals. When the currency of Mottram's classic is restored, and he receives the same belated justice that is now serving to bolster the reputations of Preston Jennings, Vincent Marinaro, John Atherton, and other innovative figures threatened with neglect, he will at last take his place, right next to G. E. M. Skues, in the gallery of great English angling figures. Until then, angling has the paradoxical irony of knowing who its Unknown Soldier is, as well as where the body is buried.

MUSEUM OF AMERICAN FLY FISHING

River Road
Manchester, Vermont 05254
(G. Dick Finlay, Treasurer)

Public nonprofit foundation. Yearly membership $10. Donations both of funds and of accepted tackle items of historical interest are tax deductible.

The Museum of American Fly Fishing at Manchester, Vermont, though originally launched by the Orvis Company and still housed in a wing of the Orvis building, was from the beginning intended to become a self-supporting and independent organization, open to public membership, and dedicated to the preservation of fly-fishing memorabilia of all kinds.

The nucleus of the collection was first recognized by Hermann

Kessler, then the art director of *Field & Stream,* on a visit to Orvis in the course of a Battenkill vacation in 1963. Intrigued by the fact that the Orvis files retained such rarities as the displays of flies and fishing photographs exhibited by the company at the Chicago World's Fair of 1893, and other items dating back almost to its founding in 1856, Kessler suggested the transformation of the company's collection into a museum. The idea was not activated until 1965, when the company reorganized and Leigh Perkins became president. Not wanting a company museum, but willing to see the Orvis items contributed to a more general collection, Perkins made an appeal through the Orvis periodical, *The Record Catch News,* for the preservation of fly-fishing antiquities, and was so encouraged by the response that he earmarked the profits from the company's sale of sporting prints as a stake for a museum's establishment. In 1968, a trusteeship was formed, with Hermann Kessler as president, Austin S. Hogan as vice president and curator, and G. Dick Finlay, who was then still in the Orvis employ as treasurer. The first incorporation was a private tax-exempt non-profit foundation, but this was changed to public at the end of 1971. The board of trustees has been enlarged, a professional staff of consultant has been organized, and over a thousand rods, reels, fly collections, works of art, and books have been contributed. Since Kessler's retirement, Ray Kotrla of Washington has served as president, and Charles Olin of the Smithsonian Institution has become the conservator.

To date the limitations of exhibit space have kept the showings largely representational, with the bulk of the museum's acquisitions kept in protective storage, but such displays as tackle belonging to Presidents Hoover and Eisenhower, the actor Joe Jefferson, and the painter Winslow Homer give a foretaste of future treasure, and traveling exhibits are being prepared, pending the ultimate housing of the collection in a permanent home of its own.

The fact that the museum is completely separated from the Orvis Company, with a governing body and membership drawn from the general public, has been hard to get across during the formative period when the Orvis Company has perforce done more for it, in getting it started, than anybody else. But the Orvis Company has made it clear, from the outset, that the ultimate aim is a completely self-sufficient organization.

In this the Museum of American Fly Fishing is unique, as the only other fly-fishing museums, to date, are completely dependent upon their parent institutions. They are Michigan State University's collection at East Lansing, and the Gladding Company's Museum, recently opened in the Octagon House in Otselic, New York.

I naturally favor the Museum of American Fly Fishing, since I have been interested in it from its inception, but I regard it nevertheless as a good sign of the vitality and importance of fly fishing as a sport that other collections have been formed, and beyond a doubt still others will be. The sport dates back over two centuries, in the New World alone, and well over five hundred in the Old, so its memorabilia, if collected soon enough to escape oblivion, can richly fill many mansions.

Two of the items I know they're going to get from me are a reel that Edward R. Hewitt made and engraved for presentation to Ellis Newman, and the 1847 first American edition of *The Compleat Angler,* that "darling book" that George Washington Bethune edited so anonymously and so well.

These are both good items, though neither is unique. Maybe a search of your attic or basement might unearth some grandfatherly item that is. There would be great rejoicing in Manchester (and here also) if that should be the case. And the appraisal, and consequent tax deduction, might make you pretty happy too.

𝒩ORRIS

Norris, Thaddeus (1811–1877). The cornerstone of American angling literature. There is no American counterpart to Walton, for none of our fishing books has ever achieved world stature as literature. For that matter, neither has any other English fishing book, as Walton is unique. But as a figure of influence upon anglers and those disposed to take up angling, then Uncle Thad was as meaningful to his countrymen as Old Izaak was to his.

The American Angler's Book, which was published in Norris's native Philadelphia in 1864, became all that its title staked out for it. It was the book for the fisherman of its time, and it is one of the few early American fishing books that can still be read with pleasure and profit today. Uncle Thad had all of Walton's zestful enthusiasm for the sport and just as lively an appreciation of the concomitant meat and drink, and he was as ready as Izaak himself to talk about other things than fishing, in the course of writing a fishing book. Indeed in this respect Walton is for once outdone. Thaddeus Norris's book, even in its first edition, ran over six hundred pages, a lot of it set in type so small that it taxes even today's readers' lighting facilities, and must have constituted a really arduous test of patience and endurance to readers by the coal oil lamps that afforded the best light for most of his contemporaries, and yet within the year he was back with another edition to which he added pages to make it run over seven hundred. But if Norris was more than Walton's match for garrulity, he was far from it in piety. In this, he was outdone by W. C. Prime, author of *I Go A-Fishing,* 1873, although the delightful chapter devoted by Uncle Thad to "The Angler's Sabbath" would more than satisfy even the most devout in our more permissive age. But Norris was far ahead of his time in his perception of the inevitability of conservation measures, and remarkably so in a period when most of America was still wilderness. Theodore Roosevelt's uncle, Robert B. Roosevelt, who wrote under the pseudonym of Barnwell, showed a more modern attitude than Norris, in anticipation of the angler-entomologists of this century, dismissing as old-fashioned the palmered flies that Uncle Thad still swore by, although the Norris book was two years later than Barnwell's *Game Fish of the Northern States of America and British Provinces.*

Thad Norris was in fact inclined to scoff at those who were beginning to entertain any notions of exactness in imitation, though he was the first to point out in print, by many years, the desirability of keeping the fly dry and the line and leader wet. But he was impatient of newfangled ideas, whether expressed in what he considered needless gadgetry or in overtheorized approaches to what was to him essentially a simple sport, and he was openly contemptuous of the tendencies to either overintellectualize it or overromanticize it. He poked sly fun at "Mr. Barnwell," both for his "fancy in high feather" and for "the Anglomania which has seized him."

In this latter respect he was the very prototype of the purely American breed of dry-fly men, in contrast to the purists of Anglophile persuasion, believing in fishing the water, not the rise, and concentrating on the broken water rather than the smooth, feeling that what fly you use matters much less than how you use it.

Typically American in his dry wit, as opposed to the more gentle humor of English writers, there is a great sense of gusto in everything Norris writes, and particularly in the casual side remarks he keeps dropping like pebbles along the wayside as he pursues the main theme of his thesis in each chapter: "My neighbor asked me once if trout fishing was not a very unhealthy amusement—he thought a man must frequently have damp feet. Well, it is, I answered; but if he gets wet up to his middle at the outset, and has reasonable luck, there is no healthier recreation." At another point, speaking of the pipe, and saying that it "must have been instituted expressly for the fisherman," he cannot refrain from interjecting, a few phrases farther on, "What a pity it is that infants are not taught to smoke!"

Though nobody ever paid greater respect to the place of potables in fishing parties, nor surpassed Norris in conveying the sights and sounds and smells and tastes in streamside eating of the quarry, still the fellowship aspect of angling has hardly lacked celebrants, from Dame Juliana's day to ours. But Uncle Thad was the first on this side of the water, and among the first anywhere, to emphasize the solo role of the angler, as opposed to all the partying and partnering with which angling's annals have always been replete. In his chapter "Fly Fishing Alone," Thad Norris gave the definitive description of the unique pleasures of solitary fishing, in a way that has never been equaled, and if only for this *The American Angler's Book* would be worth going back to, for any man who today either professes or aspires to be well read as an angler.

Although the portion of his book devoted to rod making was confined to giving the reader pointers on "homemade" rods and repairs, Norris himself went on to become one of the really skilled rod makers of his day, and the extraordinary quality of Norris rods is extolled by Prime and others in the angling writings of the post–Civil War decade.

Norris died at sixty-six, which is hardly premature against the actuarial averages of a century ago, but far short of his own expectations as an angler, as voiced in many different places in *The American Angler's Book*. With Reverend G. W. Bethune, the first American editor of Walton in 1847, and W. C. Prime, he stands as one of the three major American angling figures of his century which was, as concerns the recorded history of the sport, virtually the first. And while enthusiasts could make individual cases for Barnwell and George Dawson (*The Pleasures of Angling*, 1876), Genio Scott (*Fishing in American Waters*, 1869), Charles Hallock (*The Fishing Tourist*, 1873), James Henshall (*Book of the Black Bass*, 1881), for a place in any such proposed triumvirate (votes for Frank Forester would have to be disallowed on the ground that the author of *Fish and Fishing*, 1849, was actually the Englishman William Henry Herbert), still it is inconceivable that Uncle Thad would not be the last to be dislodged, for it is hard to cite any fishing book, Walton's not excepted, that constitutes a more engaging self-portrait of a sportsman. A case could indeed be made that a century hence Thad Norris might well stand alone.

Orvis

The Orvis Company, Inc.
Manchester, Vermont 05254
(Leigh Perkins, President)
Once and Again, The First Name in Fishing Tackle

Orvis dates from 1856, and has always been outstanding, but its present preeminence dates from the time, still less than a decade back, when Leigh Perkins came on from Cleveland, where he had already had enough success to suit most people for a lifetime, to give the old Orvis Company and himself a fresh start all over again. Since then, the refinement and extension and improvement of the whole range of Orvis goods and services has been spectacular, and nobody has enjoyed the change more than Leigh Perkins himself. His own best customer, he and his wife Romy are the living embodiments of the Orvis catalog, and they fish the world around.

To go through the current Orvis catalogs, with such embarrassments of choice as fifty-five different rod options, and a dazzling galaxy of flies and gadgets and gimmicks is to be reminded of the late Oscar Levant's classic crack—"shows you what God could do if he had the money." Add the casting clinics, and the travel club activities and such ingenious schemes as the trade-in of old tackle for a discount on new, and the goings-on that are periodically reported in the Orvis Record-Catch Club News, and the impression is inescapable that an enthusiastic fly fisherman could literally live in the arms of Orvis and die happy. The conclusion is equally self-evident that not to be on the Orvis mailing list is to miss half the fun of what's happening today in fly fishing.

My one quibble: gone but not forgotten is that glory, that Orvis pioneered, the one-piece, six-foot Superfine rod, that obviates both the "feel of" and the possible nuisance in the adjusting a ferrule midway of the stick's length. For anybody who can keep a rod set up, in camp or even in the car, the one-piece outfit is a boon and a number of other makers now feature it. Odd that the leader should quit the parade.

PEAK RODS

Russ Peak
182 S. Berkeley Avenue
Pasadena, California 91107

The Stradivari of the glass rod, Russ Peak is to glass as Paul Young was to bamboo, a complete master, both knowing and caring

Glass was still a dirty word to me, something I associated with bait fishing and spinning rods, when I wrote *The Well-Tempered Angler,* so the only mention of Russ Peak in that book is a passing reference to him as somebody I'd only heard of through Charles Kerlee, my old sponsor in the Big Bend Club on Mr. Hewitt's Neversink water. He was raving about the performance of Russ Peak's rods in fishing for tarpon with Frankie Albright at Islamorada, and since I half tune out any talk I hear about boat fishing of any kind, I barely noticed the name.

I should have remembered that it was Charlie Kerlee who first introduced me to Paul Young and the Midge rod that transformed my fishing life overnight, and realized that when Charlie Kerlee raves about anything it behooves the wise angler to shut up and listen. If I had acted as promptly as I had done the time before, I'd have had a battery of Russ Peak rods to put beside my full range of Paul Young featherweights. But as it was, a couple of years were to go by before I ever heard the name again.

Then I met Russ Peak in Jackson Hole, at the first FFF conclave, where he and his wife Edna broke their annual trip to Montana, an occasion when Russ tests his latest ideas in rod design in that best of ways, fishing with them for a month. His trailer, equipped for the Montana sojourn, was a veritable traveling tackle store, and he was able to fit me out from head to foot, to take me to the Firehole for my first taste of western fishing, after the conclave's last session.

Russ put me into the river at what he'd always found a pretty good spot, handing me one of his two-piece six-and-a-half-foot Zenith rods, with a buggy-looking black Martinez nymph selected as a suitable warhead to try while he went back to the car to suit up in waders so he could join me later.

On my first cast, before he'd had time to take more than the first steps up the incline from the stream's edge, I was obliged with visitor's luck by a fat and sassy fifteen-inch brown, which cooperated so beautifully that I had time to release him and get another cast off before Russ had reached the top of the little incline. This cast produced, quite evidently, the first brown's mate, about an inch longer and better than an inch deeper-bodied than her consort, and Russ, turning again at the commotion, said, "My gracious."

Two fish on the first two casts would have moved me to employ a more vigorous expression, but Russ Peak, a preacher by avocation, is anything but profane. He did add, however, that he'd have to get a hump on to get back before I'd hooked every blamed fish in the river.

So this is western fishing, I thought, as I lengthened my casts beyond the short lobs that had taken the first two fish. Because I have a low threshold of boredom when fish bite too readily I was really more concerned, for the moment at least, to get acquainted with the rod than with any more of the fish. With each cast I was more impressed, as the little rod seemed to possess the power to project a cast far beyond my ability to test it. And even though I was now making nonpurposive casts, to get the feel of the rod, fish kept adulterating the purity of my researches.

"So this is flying," I said to myself one blustery day in 1928, as a little Lockheed took me from Boston to New York on my first flight. It was buffeted by six kinds of weather, with frequent air pockets causing dizzying drops, scaring the daylights out of the other three passengers and, for all I know, the pilot, too. But never having flown before, I had no way of knowing that flights can be smooth as well as rough, and simply assumed it must always be that way. I made the same assumption now about western fishing, and had to have my first impression corrected later, as indeed I had with flying. Subsequent experience made me realize that both these "firsts" had been unusual in the extreme.

By the time Russ rejoined me I had worked my way downriver to the vicinity of the geysers which turn one section of the Firehole into, quite literally, hot and cold running water. I was amazed to see how the trout have sense enough to avoid the currents, right beside which they swim, that would poach them if they made the slightest navigation error. With the steamy smoke hanging over the river, the whole scene looks like a Doré drawing for Dante's *Inferno*, and fishing there is an eerie experience that must be unique in the whole wide world of sport.

Other times as well as other rivers made me later aware that it isn't only in the effete East that an angler can get skunked, but this first time my attention was concentrated more on Russ Peak and his rods than on any of the other wonders of the West.

I wondered, for instance, whether he could make me a six-foot one-piece rod, like the Orvis Superfine but a little more limber in the tip, because while I hugely enjoyed the Superfine for grilse I found its upper extremity a bit "thick ankled" for trout.

While we fished Russ took me on a verbal tour of the more than two hundred hand operations that go into the making of his rods after his initial selection of the blanks at the Conolon factory. Having seen something of the machine use that is involved in even the custom-made handcrafted bamboo rods, I was astonished that split cane could possibly be outcustomized by glass.

With something over thirty fly rods in my upstairs storeroom at home at the time, I had thought the day would never come when I'd hear myself asking for a glass one, but after a day with it on the Firehole, I knew I couldn't live without a Zenith. So I took the one I'd been using, and some months later Russ came through with the one-piece job I'd asked him about, that first day, finishing it in time to inscribe it with the notation that it was a Christmas present to me from Janie.

Of course, nothing involving that much hard work can be cheap, in this day and age, and there's a lot of bamboo around for less than Russ Peak has to get for one of his glass rods. But this is one case where the medium is far from constituting the whole message, and the fact that Russ Peak happens to embody his ideas in glass is as coincidental, say, as the circumstance that Benvenuto Cellini chose to work his artistry in a cup of gold. It would have been no less a marvel in silver or pewter or brass or even lead.

The big difference between a Russ Peak rod and one of comparable workmanship in split cane is that it can be used harder, over a longer period, with an extra margin of performance that only glass affords, and without any sign of that fatigue that even treated cane is heir to in time. And that's why, as an investment, a Russ Peak rod is an even better buy, despite its relatively high price.

I use a Russ Peak rod wherever I have occasion to need about 10 percent longer casts than I can get, with the same expenditure of propulsive energy, out of bamboo. Conversely, I use bamboo where I want about 10 percent more tip delicacy than even Russ Peak can wheedle out of glass. With these compensating differences, I regard his glass rods, and the best makers' bamboos, as fully equal examples of the rod maker's craft.

Despite the elegance of their mahogany finish, the extraordinary worth of the Peak rods is not immediately apparent to those who simply assume that any bamboo rod ranks any glass one. Fortunately this includes thieves. I've had relatively inferior bamboo rods stolen off the rod racks at the Joe Jeff Club, while my precious Peaks, hanging right beside them, were passed over.

The original most favored customer relationship that Russ Peak enjoyed at the Conolon plant has since developed, with the merger, into a consulting role with Garcia, and that's one of the best things that has happened in the continuing evolution of the glass rod. For Russ Peak is fortuitously well named; in the whole galaxy of tackle, his rods do represent one peak of perfection.

PIN, COMMON OR SAFETY

Of course you don't have to have a pin of some kind in or on your fishing clothes, to poke the lacquer or varnish or gook out of the eye of the fly you're trying to shove your tippet through, but there's nothing better for the purpose.

The hook point of another fly, through the eye of the recalcitrant one, will do the job just as well.

But if you're half as clumsy as I am, you will either drop one or the other of the two flies, before you succeed in fracturing the film over the eye of the fly causing the trouble, and spend from four to forty minutes vainly trying to find it in the grass, or between the pebbles and stones, or in the sand or mud. This is a minor catastrophe.

A major catastrophe, which the odds seem to favor in my case, is to drop the opened fly box, from which one fly has been extracted to try to free the eyehole of the fly that undoubtedly isn't, but only seems, bewitched. Then you can spend an even longer time on your knees, retrieving flies from the outer pale of a circle with a radius of some four feet.

A possible alternative would be to find a machinist somewhere, to put a real point on that extra dingus, looking like a blunted awl, that swings to no apparent purpose out of the nether end of those wayward nail clippers that are sold to fly fishermen under the infuriating trademark of Angler's Pal. What that thing is there for nobody has ever explained, as its point is not fine enough to go through the eye of anything smaller than a cruise ship's anchor.

So unless your brother-in-law is a machinist, or you are yourself classifiable, without jeers and hollow laughter, as a handyman, it's probably easier to remember to carry a pin.

PRIME

Prime, William Cowper (1825–1905). An acknowledged angling classic, *I Go A-Fishing* was first published, both here and in England, in 1873, with additional editions in 1901 and 1905. Few American fishing books have been more affectionately referred to in subsequent angling literature, here and abroad, and Prime's is one of the frequently quoted voices out of America's sporting past.

But *I Go A-Fishing* qualifies increasingly to that definition of a classic as a book that everybody talks about and hardly anybody reads. So much more of it is not about fishing than is, that trying to get to the fishing in Prime is like the proverbial attempt to pick flyspecks out of pepper with boxing gloves on.

While a few of the plethora of nonfishing stories in Prime are exotic enough or amusing enough to be rewarding, most of the non-pertinent matter is, in his own phrase, "garnished with abundance of rhetorical figure, loaded with imagery and sonorous with words." And since the wordy part of Prime is so largely religious, the average reading angler will find wading through it as tedious as sitting in prayer meeting during the one time he could be out fishing.

Prime's incessant God-hopping could perhaps be indulged, since anglers are noted for patience, if only the fishing parts were more pertinent than they now seem. Walton himself was pious, and discursiveness has always been pardoned in angling literature from his

day to ours. But by today's standards of decency, as concerns conservation, Prime's unabashed accounts of the weight of his baskets now
verges on the pornographic. His constant tallying of the size and
number of the trout that he and Dupont, his constant fishing partner,
and "P———" and even "———" and other guests took from this
pool of that river soon begin to pile up a cumulative sense of angling
guilt and shame that would make a Casanova's account of his con-
quests sound demure. Thad Norris, by contrast, and for all his enjoyment of trout roasts by the riverside, always seems much more aware
than Prime of the necessity of leaving some fishing in the stream for
us to enjoy a hundred years later.

Between his loquacity as a moralizer and his rapacity as a fisherman, Prime would seem on reappraisal to be one of the shakier titans
in our gallery of great angling figures of the past, and like some of our
statesmen, better to be admired from a distance than examined too
closely. Like Audubon's hunting, Prime's fishing tends to give the lie
to some of the veneration that over the years has enhanced his name.
That he enjoyed angling, and possessed the capacity for communicat-
ing that enjoyment, there can be no question, nor can either of those
certainties be taken away from him.

But between his prim mentions of dressing for dinner after the
day's fishing, and his noting that the room in the baskets taken by the
wine bottles would soon be needed for trout, it is like opening the
windows and letting a gust of good fresh air in to turn to Uncle Thad
Norris and his rollicking expatiations, when counting up the angling
parties' supplies, on the importance of gin.

Prime suffers from some of the snobbery that keeps Robert
Barnwell Roosevelt from being as endearing a figure to us, the readers
of today, as his importance in the evolution of American angling
would warrant. And as for the piety, Henry Van Dyke was a minister,
but it never kept him from imparting in *Little Rivers* and *Fisherman's
Luck,* as keen a sense of the uniqueness of the angler's mania as was
ever put on paper. He too was essentially a man of the nineteenth
century (1852–1933) but to an angler the Reverend Mr. Van Dyke
can never seem dated as Prime is beginning to do.

Quick-Grown Trout

"five inches in five months"

If you have a pond with a very active spring at one end, as we have at the Joe Jefferson Club in New Jersey, then you can grow your own trout as we have for the past few seasons.

Somebody seemed to remember, but couldn't find, a piece he'd read in one of the outdoor magazines—he thought it was by Al Mc-Clane—about force-feeding baby trout, in dense concentration, in a wire cage, and getting fantastic growth out of them. So we all said great, bring it in and we'll try it.

You know how that goes. The guy forgets, and so do you, and that's the end of it. But in this case, the idea seemed so simple we thought we'd try it, whether he ever found the piece about it or not.

All you do is construct a coffin-size cage of fine wire mesh—say six feet by three feet by three feet and anchor it at the inlet where the maximum oxygenation from the spring occurs. Be sure to have a hinged top, for putting in the live fish, and for taking out the occasional dead one, and be sure to have some kind of stile or catwalk arrangement, so you can stand directly over the cage, in order to drop pellets in, or to fish dead ones out with a dip net whenever necessary.

Put in from three hundred to five hundred baby trout (five-to-six-inch size) and feed them a quart can of Purina Trout Chow twice a day for five months. If you put them in, say, in April, you'll take them out, for release into the main pond or ponds or stream, at ten- and eleven-inch size in October. The casualties will run around 4 or 5 percent for rainbows and browns; 8 to 10 percent for brookies. The latter seem to support the crowding less well, and particularly in the fall, are prone to a fungus affliction that will knock off as many as three or four of them a day for about as many weeks, after which it will disappear as suddenly and mysteriously as it appeared in the first place.

The quick-grown trout will be as fat and sassy as you could wish, and will meld in with the rest of the population of your ponds or stream so well that after a few weeks you won't be able to distinguish them from their older neighbors.

But several cautions are in order. Be sure you get the Purina Trout Chow in the floating variety. It has been available for the last few years. The earlier form, which sank to the bottom, would be useless for this purpose. Also be sure you line the cage with very fine wire mesh—as fine as a screen door or finer—all around for a foot or so above your water level, to keep the pellets from floating out of the cage and beyond the reach of your captive congregation. Unless you do this you'll find that your water babies are getting very few of the pellets, and that the rest are fattening the big fish and all the visiting waterfowl, at the expense of your protégés. And also be sure that the wire mesh of your cage itself is new and sturdy. One season we forgot to check against rust and erosion and plain wear and tear, and within three days all the baby trout had fled their coop—you could hardly blame them, because they look like so many sardines in a can, crowded as they are in the cage, particularly after they've been growing a couple of months. We guesstimated that of the three hundred we had put in there the week before, possibly thirty survived the ordeal of running the gantlet of nineteen-to-twenty-two-inch browns and rainbows in that spring pond. We couldn't figure out the cause of the carnage for a couple of days, until it occurred to somebody to check the wire mesh of the cage. He found a gaping tear that had afforded an escape hatch of about six-inch breadth all along one side of the cage. We've been careful not to let that happen again.

As for the provenance of this idea, nobody has as yet remembered, or found out, where it came from. I asked Al McClane at the first opportunity whether he had written it, or whether he had come across it, either in *Field & Stream* or elsewhere, and he not only had never heard of it but doubted very much that it would work. He thought it sounded about as sensible as using the Black Hole of Calcutta as a nursery. Well, it may not be scientific, but it works. We have grown three fine crops of these crowded incarcerated little trout, before and since the massacre, and by the time we put them in the ponds as ten- and eleven-inch fish, they proved well able to fend for themselves and no more nor less eager than the regular residents to fall for the less artfully presented flies of the club members. This latter consideration is important, as it affords a strong contrast to the almost suicidal behavior, in the first few days after their arrival in our ponds, of full-grown fish brought fresh from the hatchery. Those innocents will strike so readily at anything that moves that, for a couple of days after their introduction to our ponds, they will even beguile the older and more settled denizens into making fools of themselves over flies—and particularly streamer flies—that they would ordinarily have disdained.

For the first few weeks of their captivity in the cage, the little fish may prove unable to cope with the regular-size Purina pellets. In that case, all you do is soak the pound can of pellets—hold your hand over it and dip it quickly in and out of the water and let it stand fifteen or twenty minutes, then knead the pellets into a soft mash. The stuff will still float, and the small fish will devour it avidly, until such time as they have reached the size (eight or nine inches) when they no longer need the provision of nibble-size provender. The pellets are so crammed, along with their basic cereal, with therapeutic additives that these quick-grown trout are probably fed, for the duration of their imprisonment in the cage, a lot more wisely than you are.

$\mathcal{R}$ETRIEVERS

(for flies hung up in trees)

I always blame Al McClane. You may have somebody or something else to blame, but I'm sure you agree with me that it would be wonderful if only we could catch fish as readily as we can catch branches, twigs, and leaves, on our back casts.

I blame Al McClane because, when he was re-forming my casting style (or maybe it would be more accurate to say my lack of style in casting) he used to ding away at me, "Up, up, up, with that back cast! The fish are 'way up in the trees behind you; come on now, get it up there! You'll always be a sloppy caster, if you don't get the habit of a high back cast." He used to drive me nuts over this, back there almost twenty years ago, but the repeated advice sank in so well that my fly has ever since spent a disproportionate amount of time in the trees.

There is, of course, only one really complete cure for this, and that is to move to Iceland, where there are no trees. Short of that, there are a few minor tactics that sometimes work. One is to get a rake, hook it over the branch to pull it down to where, with luck, you can get a grip on it with one hand, then reach up, far enough to free the fly, with the other. Lacking the availability of a rake, you can sometimes hook over the branch with your reel, by upending your rod, but that's a surer way to break rod tips than it is to retrieve snagged flies. Rather than risk that, and failing the availability of anything else, such as a gaff or wading staff or long-handled net or even a rod case, to use to bend the branch down to where you can grasp it, the one remaining ploy I always try is to take a spool of twenty-pound-test leader material, strip off enough from the spool, without cutting it off, to reach over the branch and back down to me, and tie it to any small, tossable object that I find in my fishing clothes. It can be, and in fact has been, a knife, a pen, a nail clipper, or even an apple core—anything I can toss over the branch, to pull it down to where I can get one hand on it. Along with a few spools of 4X to 7X, that I carry anyway, to replace tippets as they shorten, I always try to remember to include one spool of really stout monofilament, 2/5 or even stronger. You can almost always find some small object to tie it to, and toss it over the branch. And more often than not, it works.

But if at first you don't succeed, give up. Life's too short, and rod tips too precious, to fool around over one lousy fly long enough to risk reaching that point of exasperation where you're likely to break your rod or, just as bad, get a severe set in it. Follow the old retailing principle of "take your first loss," and break off before you lose more than your temper.

RHEAD

Rhead, Louis (1857–1926). This great contemporary of Theodore Gordon was a successful commercial artist who turned tackle dealer in order to devote his talent full time to what had originally been his avocation, the design of lures in imitation of natural bait fish. In the process he only very narrowly missed, by one basic error of judgment, the hagiographic stature of being enshrined today as the American Ronalds, and the father of our angling entomology. His aim, at the outset, was unerring and it has been best appreciated to date by the Boston flytier and angling historian Austin Hogan: "By going directly to the minnow Rhead took the old non-imitative streamers and reshaped them to what he looked upon as imitative smelts and shiners. His bugs were copied from the crawling things on the bottom, and his terrestrials actually looked like crickets, grasshoppers and beetles."

But the artist's eye and perception that led him to this impressionistic approach was also linked with the artistic temperament that made him impatient with the tedium of the scientific discipline involved in conforming to the accepted and established Latin terminological pattern of entomology, and his approach to the nomenclature of his insect patterns was also impressionistic, Rhead contenting himself either with following the colloquial folk designations, or bestowing fanciful names, such as Brown Buzz, Longhorn, and Pinktail, instead of the more exact and readily identifiable traditional and scientific names of flies.

The result has been that Rhead's remarkably original work, perceptive almost to the point of divination and augury, was too generally shrugged off as the amateurish fancy of a dilettante, or dismissed as a sales gimmick for specific flies of his own creation, and from 1916, when he brought out the first American book on insects of the stream, *American Trout Stream Insects: A Guide to Angling Flies and Other Aquatic Insects Alluring to Trout,* until his death a decade later, Rhead's pioneering work received insufficient recognition.

It had to wait until 1935, with the publication of *A Book of Trout Flies* by Preston Jennings, before American fly fishermen felt that a step had at last been taken on that proper track that had been laid out for the English a century before, when Alfred Ronalds in 1836 gave angling a new scientific dimension with *The Fly-Fisher's Entomology.*

The irony is that while Preston Jennings has been accorded the honor he·deserved, even though posthumously, with revival of his influence through reprinting after more than three decades, Rhead still awaits his due.

As Hogan points out, "In retrospect it seems strange to find that the finger pointed by Louis Rhead, the off-beat designer of curious imitations, was the finger of a prophet. Nymph, streamer and bucktail have kicked the old-fashioned wet fly into the curio cabinet. And the dry fly, so ably presented by the gentle Theodore Gordon, and so full of promise, has become just a status symbol."

Rhead's other work, both as editor and author, is representative of its time, but of no extraordinary pertinence today. It is his one blinding flash of revelation, the 1916 work, *American Trout Stream Insects,* that has so unfortunately been suffered to become the light that failed and that should ultimately illumine his name far into the future.

RITZ

Ritz, Charles C. (1891–). The first time I ever fished with Charles Ritz was on the Risle in Normandy in the spring of 1959. He was then nearing his sixty-eighth birthday, and his movements were graceful, but deliberate, as befits a person of a certain age. I don't say he was an adagio dancer, but let's settle for an andante walker. We had driven out from the Ritz in his mother's Cadillac—his own little Lancia was left in the semicircular cobblestone entrance of the Hotel on the Place Vendôme, as being too small for the three of us and the chauffeur and our picnic stuff and all our gear—and I noticed as we were getting in and out of the car that all his gestures and postures and stoopings and bendings were—well, not ponderous, because Charles is slight, lean, and lithe, but suitable to a senior citizen. His mother, in her nineties, was still living in the hotel, and checking up on his whereabouts as if he were a teen-ager, and by all objective accounts she seemed a lot livelier in those days than he did.

While we were fishing I kept noticing how measured his every motion was. He flicked his rod exactly as if it were a tack hammer, and he was just lightly nailing something to the wall, so he could step back and see how it looked and still change its position if he didn't like it. The very lightest forward motion of his thumb, as he held the rod up as you'd hold an umbrella while waiting for a tardy bus, and—whish—the line shot forward like something launched from a crossbow, and traveled a country mile in the blink of an eye, and at a difficult angle, to a spot near the other bank where he had apparently detected a dimple that nobody else had noticed. The dimple exploded into a little geyser as a fat brown trout began chinning himself on Charlie's fly and splashing water for a yard in all directions at once.

I watched this happen five more times before I'd had so much as a touch myself, and I came to the conclusion that nobody, to my knowledge and recollection, had ever exercised such economy of motion in relation to results, not only in fishing but in any other purposeful activity I had ever observed.

His example was infectious. Within minutes he had my wife imparting that same little tack-hammer flick to her rod, and the line going out with an impetus and distance that I wouldn't have dreamed she could have attained without shooting it from a gun.

Wow, I thought to myself as I looked across from the other bank, this is not merely the most efficient fisher I've ever seen, but also the best teacher, by far. I decided to profit from the opportunity and try a little of this tack-hammering myself. It looked completely effortless, as I stood there seeing them doing it, but all I managed to impart to my line was an unholy tangle, and a bird's nest of my leader.

Well, that was a dozen years ago, and I must have seen Charles Ritz at least an average of once a year since. He has gone from andante to allegretto to vivace to presto, in the interim, and I marvel at the man's seemingly infinite capacity for acceleration.

A few weeks back, as this is written, we were together in the Poconos, when Charles was taking in a Federation of Fly Fishermen's meeting by way of winding up a three-week cross-continent tour with a schedule that would have taxed the endurance of a horse, and he was bounding around under a broiling sun out on the casting green, for hours on end, with all the agility of a mountain goat from his ancestral Valais.

Along toward the mid-sixties, which were of course his own mid-seventies, Charles Ritz embraced a new religion, so to speak, and changed his casting style overnight. From Jon Tarantino, a man twice his size and half his age, and several times a world champion, Charles got the inspiration for a wholly new casting stance, which he proceeded to systematize into a technique called High Speed/High Line. With Charles to think is to act, and in no time he had spread the new gospel of HS/HL in the pages of angling publications in France, England, Switzerland, and the United States. Then, to make it official, as it were, he got his friend Max Reinhardt to put out another edition of *A Fly Fisher's Life,* with a new first chapter devoted to High Speed/High Line. He got his old *copain* Pierre Creusevaut, the Professional World Champion, to take up the new technique and Pierre obligingly set a new salmon-fly distance-cast record with it at Scarborough in 1963. Not content with that, Charles decided that Pierre might do still better with a rod more suited to the new technique and out of their consultations there emerged that strange device—strange coming from Charles, the classicist of the split-cane rod—a new rod called *Vario-Power,* with a bamboo tip section and a glass butt section.

Those of us who had thought of Charles Ritz as Baron Bamboo of Amboise, from his long years of research and development of the Pezon et Michel rods at the factory where he was the acknowledged *genius loci,* were a bit startled by this. Not that it is so unusual for Charles to invent something—after all, he invented the *après-ski* boot when he had a shoe shop on the rue St. Honoré, behind which he maintained a more or less clandestine tackle shop for the diversion of Pierre and some other cronies—but for Charles to do anything with glass seemed about like Toscanini taking up jazz. Still, it was only a foretaste of what was to come.

For now, Charles has once again come up with something new. It supplements HS/HL without supplanting it, and again it can be expressed in four initials, LL/LF, but this time Charles goes all the way with glass. This is the Long Lift/Long Flex rod, as conceived by Charles Ritz and embodied by Garcia, the colossus of the American tackle-making industry, and it was the object of the recent breakneck cross-country tour. There's no need for me to go into it further here, because, in a new first chapter in the latest edition of *A Fly Fisher's Life,* Charles tells about it as only he can.

But I would like to take a shot at trying to fathom what makes Charlie run today, when a dozen years back he had already slowed down to a walk. I have several notions, none of which he may like, but all of which I'm sure he is open-minded enough to entertain.

In that last sentence is my first clue. Open-minded Charles certainly is, and it may be the simple common denominator of his many successes. The rest of us make up our minds, or have them made up for us, and it takes something practically earthshaking to change them. Not Charles. He's as ready as a gypsy to move on to something new.

In fact, Charles *is* a gypsy. His mother couldn't nurse him, so she got a gypsy wet nurse to do it for her. And if that alone wasn't enough to instill a good deal of the gypsy into him, then the family's travel habits of the first few years of his life were enough to do the rest. The nineties were the period of César Ritz's most frenzied activity, as he doubled back and forth between hotels in England and on the Continent, which he was in effect managing to supervise and help direct all at once. Though the Savoy, where he installed Escoffier, was then his main post, he was like a juggler keeping others in the air without dropping any, and his wife Marie-Louise and the infant Charles found themselves almost living in *wagon-lits.* The hammocklike mesh hanger alongside the berth, meant for the passenger's belongings, became the swinging cradle for Charles on these frequent travels, so it is small wonder that he grew up to be a man in motion. These almost constant travels away from their then home in London persisted until 1898, when Charles was seven, and César Ritz at last had, in the Place Vendôme, a hotel of his own, the Paris Ritz of today, in which Charles literally grew up.

Add the fact that he spent the decade between his twenty-fifth and thirty-fifth birthdays in America to the circumstance that his first at least nominal home was London, and it is easy to see why Charles is the perfect cosmopolite that he is, and why he seems so much more at home and at ease with the English and the Americans than the average Frenchman or Swiss. He is both child and man of the big cities, London and Paris, New York and Boston—the one time he was ever married before was to a girl on Long Island—and yet he has had a lifelong itchy foot, to be out of doors and in the woods and at least near if not on the waters. Truly a gypsy restlessness.

Another paradox is that nobody could be either more Swiss or less Swiss than he is. The average traveler thinks of him as practically synonymous with Paris, yet the only citizenships he has ever held were Swiss and American (he got the latter after serving in the American army during World War I and gave it up when it would have occasioned his being interned, after the German occupation of Paris, in World War II) and though his birthday, August first, is the Swiss equivalent of our Fourth of July, being the date that celebrates the independence of the first three cantons of the Confederation, and though he is almost fiercely proud of being Swiss, and thus at liberty to make cracks about Frenchmen, he has spent relatively little of his long life in Switzerland.

Oddly, too, though his father's family since time out of mind were from the Valais, that mountainous canton lying between Lake Geneva and the Alps, he wasn't even born there, but in Molsheim, near Strasbourg, where his mother happened to be visiting her aunt and uncle. Certainly he never acquired that homing Swiss attitude that made his mother run back to Niederwald every chance she had to get away from Paris.

He hates to be called Charlie, and will always correct any such reference to him in print if he has the chance. Joseph Wechsberg wrote a piece about him in *Esquire* which he started to call "The One and Only Charlie Ritz," and Charles made no other objection to it than to insist that the "ie" be changed to "es," though Wechsberg quite logically pointed out both that he had never heard him referred to, by any of his friends, any other way, and that it made it doubly hard to avoid confusing his name with that of Charles of the Ritz, the trademarked firm style of a cosmetics manufacturer.

His mother, in her superb book about his father, frequently referred to her son as "Charly," but Monique, whom you will meet in the pages of his newest edition, never calls him anything but Charles. Neither do his friends, after the third or fourth time they forget, but speaking of him among themselves they never call him anything else.

Monique is another clue in the mystery of what makes Charles Ritz so much more dynamic today than he was a dozen years ago. A Genevoise named Ramseir, she was once married to a man called Foy, and it is as Madame Foy that she was listed (until their marriage in the summer of 1971) on the Board of Directors of the Paris Ritz. Though not born on their Independence Day, she is if anything and if possible an even more independent Swiss than Charles himself, and if the term "whim of iron" were not already in established usage it would have to be coined just for her.

Since the new edition of *A Fly Fisher's Life* has an added chapter on health, there is no point in second-guessing the author on this subject. But I would like to go back and .niggle a little more on this matter of open-mindedness that I threw out as the first clue.

In Charles I think it's not merely the mind that's open, but the entire essence of the man. He can change his mind faster and oftener than you or I can change our socks. He can and does rethink things through that you or I would consider as settled as the sum of twice two, and I believe this explains the phenomenon that is Charles Ritz as nothing else could.

About the only thing I haven't forgotten from four years of college more than four decades back is what they told us in a psychology class about those little dinguses we all have but aren't aware of that are called synapses, those little nerve endings that are distributed throughout our frames about as widely as our very marrow. In children the synapses are wide open, but they start very gradually closing from childhood on, and we are all as old or as young as this closing tendency of our synapses lets us be.

In Charles Ritz, somewhere along about his sixty-eighth birthday, for reasons quite possibly not clear to anybody including himself, the damn things must have started opening up again, and wondrous is the result to behold ever since.

Look at the change in the Paris Ritz itself, over the past dozen years, if you choose not to take at face value my appraisal of the change that has come over Charles. That, too, is a paradox. To all outward seeming, the Ritz is more fully the Ritz today than it has been at any time since the opening in 1898, when the future Edward VII told César Ritz that he seemed to have a better understanding of what royalty would like than they seemed to have themselves. Yet behind all that "instant elegance" that today seems tantamount to a veritable embalming of the past is an undetected subsurface of modernity, in the use of quick-cleanable and synthetic materials and a host of behind-the-facade, laborsaving devices and gadgets that could make a Hilton blink.

Charles is a gadgeteer, beyond any other that I know, and it shows in the Paris Ritz, but only if you know where to look for it, because otherwise it would escape your notice, or anybody's. He is a tinker, as becomes a gypsy, and has been all his life. Surprising in one seemingly so impetuous and so prone to what appear to be snap judgments, he has the patience, along with the ingenuity, of the born tinker. He was tinkering with fishing tackle in a room in New York, as far back as 1916, when his father first entrusted him to come over and make a deal for the use of the name Ritz-Carlton, and he transformed apparent junk into splendid rods, with nothing but a knack for patient and protracted experimentation.

It was not long after that, on the Jersey shore, that he was making movies of people on the beaches, as a come-on to get them to see themselves on the screen in his theatre that night—and if you see the name Ritz in a listing of New Jersey motion picture schedules, it's not because somebody in the ensuing more than half a century decided that it would be a ritzy name on a marquee, but quite simply because Charles Ritz started it, that long ago, in his restless youth.

He started other things, too, like couplings for toy trains, which are still being made over here, decades after Charles went back to Europe, and some of them he seems actually to have forgotten.

To the annual gathering of as many as four score friends he has fished with from all over the world, who gather for dinner on a mid-to-late November night, he has often said that without his American years he couldn't have had half the success he has enjoyed in Europe. These dinners constitute the only activity, except for casting the next morning in the ponds of the Bois de Boulogne, of an extremely democratic organization known as the International Fario Club, whose members preempt the dining room and the tea salon of the Paris Ritz for the occasion. Two drinks are followed by at least two fishing movies, in an adjoining downstairs room on the Vendôme side of the hotel, and the members' dinner is followed by a tombola, featuring prizes of tackle and flies, an event at which no member has as yet failed to win something, while Monique presides at a table in the Espadon grill, on the rue Cambon side, for the delectation and degustation of their nonfishing consorts, and Monique sees to it that their prizes are much prettier than anything that is drawn in the dining room lottery.

There are princesses as well as princes among the membership, and personages of every size and sort, and the only thing they have in common is that they have all, at one time or another, fished with Charles Ritz. Membership is facultative, as the Swiss say of some of their railway stops. You are a member as soon as, and indeed as long as, Charles says you are, and the membership though growing, over the past decade of the organization's existence, has obvious limitations. Membership is signified by a lapel button and an emblazoned embroidered patch for the blazer pocket, and in the streets of Paris the week of the dinner peers of the realm have been seen proudly sporting both.

What do you make of a man who has all this going for him? Charles C. Ritz, 15 Place Vendôme, is all his stationery says, along with the arondissement and the phone number. The "C" is for César, of course, and it is from him that he has his name and his innate elegance, for César Ritz was one of the dandies of his time. But his abounding health he must have from his mother, and more than a little of the spark besides. Marie-Louise Ritz was very much her own woman, in the long years after 1918, when her husband died, and indeed from the century's turn onward, for she had to carry on after her brilliant mate had literally spent himself, rocketlike, doing too much too soon, in too many places, at a burning pace. In her book about him she tells it all, eschewing both false modesty and any complaint, and the account is one that does them both proud. No man ever had a more affectionate memorial, and no woman ever did a man's job better, when it was beyond him to do.

Foolish to speculate what Charles would have been without them, for he is their sum. But there will be other books, about him and about them, for they brought out of Switzerland what is sure to be a lasting contribution to an important branch of the arts. An applied art, surely, but basic none the less, the art of making people both happier and more comfortable than they would otherwise be, and it is not for nothing that their name has invaded every language as an adjective standing for unique distinction.

Meanwhile, there is his book, about which I wrote, some years ago, that "he who would try today to lead a flyfisher's life will surely miss a few tricks if he doesn't, somewhere along the way, take time out to study the one now near sundown led by Charles Ritz, one of the most gracious as well as most graceful of its modern practitioners."

Silly of me, that was 1965, and it's an odds-on bet that a lot of us are nearer sundown now than Charles was then, but the rest of it still stands. I picked it then as one of the thirty outstanding fishing books out of all the thousands published since 1496, and I was interested to notice, in 1970, that the same choice had been made by the compilers of *The Contemplative Man's Recreation,* a Bibliography of Books on Angling and Game Fish in the Library of the University of British Columbia, listing *A Fly Fisher's Life* as one of the thirty-nine Landmarks in the Evolution of the Literature of Angling: 1496–1969.

Like his master Izaak Walton before him, Charles Ritz brought out the first edition of his book in a much smaller size than subsequent editions. First published, exactly three centuries after Old Izaak's first edition in 1953, under the French title *Pris sur le Vif,* his book has been reissued with added material in 1959, 1969, and again in England 1971, and America 1973. This compares with the various editions of *The Compleat Angler* in Walton's lifetime between 1653 and 1676. There were five of them, so that undoubtedly means that Charles Ritz has still another one coming after this. Don't bet against it. For that matter, though there is no now-known way of collecting, don't bet that they won't both be read three hundred years hence.

ROOSEVELT

Roosevelt, Robert Barnwell (1829–1906). The uncle of President Theodore Roosevelt, he wrote under the abbreviated by-line Barnwell and was a key figure in the early development of both the entomological approach to fly-tying and the modernization of tackle. He was also a pioneer of North American fly fishing for Atlantic salmon. His first book, *Game Fish of the Northern States of America and British Provinces*, appeared in 1862 and was a landmark in that it was this country's first introduction to angling entomology. Heavily derivative from Ronalds, his approach was dilettantish and slight, but it was a significant start. It was also the first American book to treat of salmon fishing, although anticipated by *Salmon Fishing in Canada*, by a Resident (Reverend W. A. Adamson), which was published in London in 1860. A perfectionist, rather pompously opinionated, insistent on the newest and best and remarkably gadget-minded for his time, he drew the sallies of Uncle Thad Norris for his fuss-and-feathers attitude, including dressing for dinner (Prime would have caught the same jibes, except that he wrote after Uncle Thad). As his subsequent books showed, he was not entirely untrammeled by traces of vainglory. His other books were *Superior Fishing, or, Striped Bass, Trout and Black Bass of the Northern States*, 1865, *Fish Culture Compared in Importance with Agriculture*, the pamphlet of a speech he made in Congress as a Representative of New York in 1872, *Fish Hatching and Fish Catching* (with Seth Green), 1879, and *Love and Luck . . .* 1886.

RUBBER BANDS

Form the habit of slipping rubber bands into your hip pockets, instead of throwing them away when you remove them from small packages, and at the first opportunity transfer them to the pockets of your fishing pants, or shirt, or vest, or jacket. There's nothing better, if you can remember to do it every so often, to keep kinks out of your leader than to rub its entire length with a rubber band. The bigger the piece of rubber the better the rub, of course, but you can do it effectively, taking just a bit more time and patience, with even the smallest rubber band. In fact, unless the look of it annoys you, the best thing to do with a good-sized rubber band is loop it a few times over itself, around your rod just above the grip. Do it enough times that the rubber band will more or less hug the rod, not just hang there like a noose. You can still pull the rubber band away from the rod with your finger, enough to rub the entire length of the leader with it, and then just let it snap back into its resting place above the rod grip. Seeing it there will serve to remind you to do it oftener than you would be likely to think of doing it if you have to fumble in a pocket for it every time. Time spent doing this will prove to help your fishing score more than comparable time devoted to changing your fly, because a well-rubbed leader will improve your presentation (I also find that it helps the leader sink). Often that in itself makes more difference than a change in either size or pattern of the fly itself.

Dave Cook Sporting Goods Co., in Denver, used to feature a marvelous gadget, called the Zip Leader Straightener, which was nothing but a piece of India rubber, cut in the shape of an arrow, with a small hole in it at the butt, or tail-feather as opposed to arrowhead end. (That was to tie a lanyard through, to keep the thing banging right beside your snippers or scissors, or angler's clip. But the hole would invariably break out to the end of the rubber, after a few rubbings of the leader, so that feature wasn't so marvelous.)

I used to think up vast orders to send to Dave Cook, just to keep up my inventory of Zip Leader Straighteners—they were something like six for a quarter, so you'd feel foolish ordering them by themselves—but in the last few years this item has disappeared from their catalog, with the natural result that I have disappeared from their customer rolls. They have so far borne this loss stoically, but I wish they would put the Zip Leader Straightener back in their catalog.

Meanwhile, I do fine with the rubber band wrapped around the base of my rod, above the grip, though admittedly with some lessening of chic. But I wasn't doing so great, after I first ran out of the Zip Leader Straighteners, and couldn't get any more, and found I was fishing more but enjoying it less, with the catches fewer and farther between. It took me a long time to figure out what I was doing differently (or not doing), to account for my diminished success, until the rubber bands came to the rescue.

SAGE

". . . the most valuable of all American angling works,"
Dean Sage's The Ristigouche and Its Salmon Fishing, *1888,*
now newly reissued in a limited edition . . . by Angler's and
Shooter's Press, Goshen, Connecticut.

The Ristigouche and Its Salmon Fishing (subtitle: Fishing in Canadian Waters), by Dean Sage, David Douglas, Edinburgh, 1888. (Printed by T & A Constable). The Douglas edition consisted of 105 copies, of which twenty-five were for sale in the United States; twenty-five copies for sale in Great Britain, fifty copies for private presentation and five for public libraries. All copies were numbered, the preface was dated Albany, N.Y., December 1887, and the author made a special point of the date, saying that "since the text of this Book was completed in 1886, some additions have been made to our knowledge of the habits of the salmon, and certain facts which then had the merit of newness have now assumed the respectability of age."

The volume, a large folio bound in green buckram, gold stamped, numbered 275 pages, of which the last forty-two were devoted to a chapter on angling literature.

On January 28, 1902 the sale of a copy at auction was reported as follows:

"A Douglas edition of 1888 of Dean Sage's *The Ristigouche and Its Salmon Fishing, with a Chapter on Angling Literature,* produced a vigorous bidding and was finally disposed of at $135. This volume was the most beautiful product of the bookmaker's art, as it was produced regardless of all expense, and is the most valuable of all American angling works. Only 105 copies were printed, of which only fifty were offered to the public. This was the first copy ever put up at auction in the United States, and as the work is constantly enhancing in value, yesterday's price was considered moderately cheap."

Dean Sage died at sixty-one, in his camp on the Restigouche, in

June of that same year 1902, and from then on the price of copies of his almost legendarily scarce book has risen steadily, and it's a long time since even five hundred dollars could be considered "moderately cheap." In the last decade, along with the rising prices of all antiques, copies of the Dean Sage book have set new records for nineteenth century angling literature whenever they have come on the market, and now a price of twenty-five hundred dollars would be considered realistic "for openers," should one come up at auction.

At the time of his death, Dean Sage's own collection of fishing books was beyond a doubt the best in the country, if not numerically as great as some later collections, such as The Wagstaff, which became the foundation of the present rich collection at Yale. A knowledgeable bibliophile, Sage did not confine his collecting to angling subjects, but garnered many other first editions and manuscripts, including a first folio of Shakespeare. But salmon fishing was his chief interest, outside of business, and it was the one subject on which he wrote extensively, contributing articles on it to *The Atlantic Monthly, Century Magazine, The Nation,* and a number of other publications, as well as the section on Atlantic salmon in the Salmon and Trout volume of the American Sportsman's Library.

That he was born with the proverbial silver spoon in his mouth is implicit from the first page of *The Ristigouche and Its Salmon Fishing,* with its dedication to his father for providing the leisure with which to write it. But although he did enjoy ample time to practice his favorite sport, and to write about it, as well as sufficient opportunity to pursue his interest in trotting horses, he was anything but an idler. After preliminary education under private tutors, he earned his LLB degree at the Albany Law School, just after his twentieth birthday in 1861. He went to work in his father's lumber business, H. W. Sage & Co., familiarizing himself with its mills in Michigan and Canada, as well as its distributing yards in Toledo, Ohio, and Albany, New York, and spent time in its main office in Manhattan. By 1893 the firm was succeeded by the Sage Land and Improvement Company, Inc., and he had succeeded his father as president, engaging in the acquisition and sale of timberlands in Michigan, Wisconsin, Alabama, Mississippi, and California. At the time of the formation of the successor company the H. W. Sage mill operations were discontinued and the mills sold. He had also followed early in his father's footsteps in carrying on, with his brother William Henry Sage, the liberal benefactions to Cornell University. His father, Henry Williams Sage, had donated Sage College and the university chapel and library at Cornell, and as early as 1875 he and his brother set up an endowment of which the income was to be used in paying the salary of a university pastor or the expenses of university preachers. In 1899 he and his brother set up another endowment, for the maintenance of their father's former residence as an infirmary, and later, to supplement the work of the infirmary, Dean Sage provided funds for the erection of another building for the medical department, bearing the name of Dr. Lewis A. Stimson, professor of surgery at the university. After his death, as if these recent deeds were not enough to keep his memory green at Cornell, a pulpit in the university chapel was presented by his family as a memorial to him. Two decades later his son and namesake, Dean Sage, Jr., was to surpass his achievements both as lawyer and philanthropist, playing the dominant role, as president of the board of managers of the Presbyterian Hospital in New York, in the creation of the Columbia-Presbyterian Medical Center, the world's largest. This son most nearly emulated Dean Sage himself in devotion to fishing, and indeed was to die, like his father some four decades before him, at their camp on the Restigouche. By the time of his death in 1943, the junior Dean Sage's collection of angling books was deemed one of the three best in the country. But no other member of his family ever approached Dean Sage's dedication, enthusiasm, and authority on the subject of salmon.

His book was the product of ten summers on the Restigouche, and years of study and observation of the river and its denizens, and for its time it was the definitive work on the subject. Its influence would have been greater, but for the paucity of its distribution, but it nevertheless became and remained a recognized landmark in salmon literature between the writings of Scrope four decades earlier and Lee Wulff six decades later.

He clung to the belief that salmon feed in fresh water, but empty their stomachs as an immediate preliminary to their struggles to disengage the angler's hook, and while this assumption is no longer widely shared it has persisted into our own time. The late Preston Jennings still argued it strongly, as late as the nineteen fifties, but later authorities, such as J. W. Jones in England and Anthony Netboy over here, now agree unequivocally that bright salmon do not actually feed once they have returned to their native rivers for the spawning run.

Be that as it may, there is certainly nothing else to be faulted, these more than eighty years later, in the basic tenets of the Dean Sage doctrine for the successful pursuit and conquest of this noble quarry. The one essential, now as then, is a willingness to persist, long after reason dictates giving up, in the endless attempt to engage the utterly unpredictable fancy of this lordly and disdainful creature, and an equal willingness to follow, at no matter what cost to your dignity and equilibrium, wherever his fancy forces you to go, once you have succeeded in engaging it. Tackle has improved since his day, to a point where it would be hard to imagine making do with his rods and reels, but it has never yet improved, and it is to be hoped never will, to the degree of eliminating either the need for his extent of patience, or his amount of fortitude, in the whole tricky chancey process of hooking, playing, and landing an Atlantic salmon. Read, for instance, his account of the salmon of the Matapédia Bridge, and ask yourself if there could be, anywhere in salmon literature, a better "final exam," to separate the men from the boys, in the pursuit of salmon. He who cannot look himself in the mirror and say with a perfectly straight face that he would have done everything that Dean Sage did, when confronted with such a situation, does not deserve to call himself a salmon fisher, whatever his friends and associates, guides, toadies, flunkies, and assorted yesmen may call him.

For that matter, forgetting the finals, how many of us today could even pass the entrance exam, to go fishing with Dean Sage? It involved, for a start, sleeping out in a tent, leaving the comforts of the lodge to the less ardently dedicated. And it often meant long hard canoe passages in rough weather, getting "nearly as wet as the Indians, and much more uncomfortable."

Even his lodge, Camp Harmony, which he found sumptuous, in contrast to his habitual tent, would seem Spartan beyond endurance to

most of us today. Arriving after a thirty-mile canoe trip from Pata-
pédia, through weather most inordinately foul, and breaking the back
door to get in, because his "help" had not showed up, he spent the day
in "putting things to right," and then permitted himself a session of
contentment:

"It was not until evening, when the storm had ceased and the
clear sunset and soft south wind gave an entirely different aspect to
nature, that I sat on the piazza with a meditative pipe and began to
appreciate that I was at last where for months I had longed to be. The
swallows were twittering and building their accustomed nest at the
point inside the house where the rafters meet at the peak of the roof;
the rounded top of Squaw's Cap Mountain was boldly defined against
the deep blue of the sky; the robins were singing joyfully, as if to
express their content at the change from the cold and dismalness
which had prevailed all day; and the crystalline Upsalquitch was leaping along to fall in the bosom of its stronger sister, and be by her
carried to the sea. Directly in front the Camp Pool, beneath whose
stream, and behind the rocks whose whereabouts is denoted by many
a swirl and break of the water, I know are now lying the great salmon
fresh from the boisterous North Atlantic, where they have for months
been voyaging beyond the ken of man, happily unconscious of the
perils before them. One leaps high from the water just where the two
rivers meet, another a few minutes later comes up at a fly further out;
and, after an interval of quiet, just as the sun is disappearing behind
the hill in front of me, a big one almost at my feet startles me by
coming straight up out of the water and falling back broadside with a
splash that, in the absence of another sound, could be heard a quarter
of a mile. I began to feel that this might be the eve of such another
happy day on the pool as the one on which it yielded to two of us
seventeen salmon on a still and burning afternoon, all taken in the
same place, as many lost as killed, and plenty more ready for the fly
when we stopped from a sense of shame. I was quite ready to go to my
tent at the end of the long twilight, though after getting there I lay
awake for hours listening to the noises which one hears in the most
solitary places the first nights he is alone."

The operative phrase in that passage, remembering that the time is the eighteen-eighties, when ecology and environment had not become headline words, is "a sense of shame." In a related passage, elsewhere in the book, he says:

"It doubtless seems to a great many an anomaly that there should exist a love in the breast of the destroyer for the creature he destroys; but it is a fact that the preservation of fish and game, which is due almost entirely to the efforts of sportsmen, is not by any means owing to a selfish desire for increasing their own amusement, nor to the more important economic reasons they urge, but very largely to a genuine love for the wild creatures of the woods and waters as a necessary element in the whole scheme of nature, the absence of which bereaves her, to them, of an essential part of her charm.

"The slaughter of fish is by no means the highest pleasure of the angler. The muscular exertion alone, under the soothing influences which generally surround him, is a delight; the thousand indescribable attractions offered, and indeed pressed upon him, by the sparkling waters, the sweetness of the air, the rock-bound shores, and evergreen hills, all insensibly add themselves to the joys of his pursuit, and perhaps without his suspecting it, form the chief part of them."

In other places, he poses as the great satisfaction of the angler's life, the ability of any man, "to whom the thing is not habitual," to prove "that he could, if he had to, get along agreeably on the most meagre comforts, or create them by his own ingenuity from the materials offered by nature, throwing aside as superfluous and effeminate the mass of the customs of civilization. It is the unconscious delight of a sound mind in the reversion to an aboriginal mode of life."

Note that his emphasis there is on the mind. He was far from being a mere chest thumper, in his advocacy of the strenuous life and its manly exertions. He was a thinking fisherman if ever there was one, and almost every other page of his book could serve as an example of what Walton must have meant when he called this a contemplative pastime. Dean Sage notes again and again the perplexities, anomalies, and vagaries of the behavior of salmon in the river, and he does his best to illumine them in the light of his experience, but he is not always intent on trying to solve them—sometimes he is content just to marvel at them and, rather than attempt to push his ratiocinations about them to the point of Q.E.D., is content to shrug them off with the philosophical comment of his favorite guide: "Salmon do as he dam please." That he became extraordinarily skilled, as well as extremely ardent and pertinacious, in the pursuit of salmon is evident in many passages of his book. But what is equally evident is that he would never have wanted to see that skill raised to the level of a science rather than a sport. He had the true amateur's love of the game for its own sake, instead of for the sake of whatever material benefits could be derived from success at it. There is some sense of that spirit in his attitude of not seeking, or expecting, an answer to every mystery of salmon fishing, but of being content to note many of its anomalies as being "the way things are, and not as we might wish them to be."

Probably cat lovers can appreciate this spirit, more readily than most other people. Cats, too, "do as they dam please," and in fact won't do anything until they have satisfied themselves that it is their idea to do it and not yours. They don't fawn and truckle, as dogs do. If cat lovers didn't esteem this characteristic attribute—this evidence that their pets are unready and unwilling to become their slaves— then they'd simply be dog lovers instead. Similarly with salmon fishing. If it ever becomes too easy, salmon fishers wouldn't like it anymore.

(I am reminded of the man who finally reached his turn at the teller's window in the course of a run on a bank, and said, "I want my money!" "Certainly, sir, and what denominations of bills would you prefer?" "You mean I can have it? Oh, if I can have it, of course I don't want it.")

In the entire range of salmon literature it is hard to think of another book that gives a more vivid appreciation of this aspect of salmon fishing than Dean Sage's, and it is the more remarkable in that it dates from a time that we tend to think of now as the good old days, when salmon were as abundant as they are today scarce. The answer lies in that elementary arithmetical truth that a thousand times nothing is still nothing, and there undoubtedly never has been a time when a salmon fisher couldn't have blank days. (It is this sense of feeling a continuum with the past that makes salmon literature so therapeutic for the angler who has come back to camp after a day, and perhaps not even the first day, of fishlessness.)

In his own chapter on angling literature Dean Sage shows a great appreciation of the lore, as well as the lure, of salmon fishing. As an angler he was extremely well read, and of the writers on salmon he was particularly fond of Scrope. Others of his favorites among angling authors were George Washington Bethune and Thad Norris. Could anyone ask three better companions, to go a-fishing with in the library?

He especially sought to emulate Scrope, in the lavishness of illustrations of his own volume, remembering how enamored he had been of the lithographs and wood engravings of the first Murray 1843 edition of *Days and Nights of Salmon Fishing in the Tweed*. Indeed, apart from the first Scrope, it is hard to find another fishing book anywhere nearly as well illustrated as *The Ristigouche and Its Salmon Fishing*.

As for Bethune, Sage suggested separate publication for the notes that made the first American edition of Walton in 1847 one of the very best of the ninety that had been issued up to the time of writing his own chapter on angling literature forty years later. It is interesting that the only thing done about this in the ensuing eighty-five years was John McDonald's rescue of Bethune's essay on fly fishing in America from the burial it had suffered as an anonymous footnote in the first American Walton, by inclusion of it as a separate chapter in his 1972 volume, *Quill Gordon*. But the rest of Dean Sage's 1887 suggestion remains open to the option of some enterprising reprinter even today. A complete Bethune volume by itself would make what the spritely parson called the Walton, "a darling book." An alternate proposal of equal validity would be to have a really worthy reissue of the Bethune edition of Walton, with all the editor's notes and essays played up with the proper display their importance warrants, instead of tucked away in footnotes set in minuscule type.

Speaking of worthy reprints, the progenitors of the current reissue of the Dean Sage volume deserve full marks for preserving the original edition's general air of sumptuousness. Since salmon fishing is itself, at least for Americans, an anything but demotic pastime, being the equivalent of caviar and champagne in contrast to the beer and hotdogs of such a blue collar sport as, say, bait casting for bass, it is altogether fitting that such an already special item as a rarity of salmon literature should receive pretty special treatment, and especially one that concerns such a very special place as the lordly Restigouche. For this river is certainly, in North American terms, what would be a royal river in Scandinavian ones. As concerns this consideration, it was a really inspired touch to crown the opus with an original Ogden Pleissner composition, created for and confined to the new issue of *The Ristigouche and Its Salmon Fishing,* for this alone would be enough to assure the reissue of a large portion in its own right of that scarcity value which was one of the great distinctions of the 1888 Douglas edition.

Add the factor that even the new edition of the Dean Sage classic is very strictly limited—there will be just about as many copies, even of the reissue, as there are authenticated genuine examples of Stradivarius violins at large in the world today—and what emerges is a scarcity of a scarcity, in line with the Waltonian dictum of "a recreation of a recreation."

To try to hazard a guess as to the probable future value of copies of the Dean Sage work, either in the original 1888 edition or the new reissue, is tantamount to attempting to chart the response to the proverbial question of how high is up. To go back less than a decade, some of the prices that have already been paid for copies of the Douglas edition would only that recently have seemed certifiable lunacy, and reducing the "moderately cheap" 1902 auction price of $135 to the fringe level of a sales tax.

But who can say what anything tangible is worth, in an era of worldwide devaluation and revaluation of currencies, and deficit financing on all governmental levels, from municipal to national, to totals so unimaginably high as to be beyond the comprehension of the ordinary individual citizen and taxpayer? It's no wonder, against such a frenzied backdrop, that recent auctions have seen single pieces of French furniture, a commode or a desk, for instance, bringing what used to be the price tag—and undoubtedly still is, with taxes going up like everything else—of an entire castle or palace. And for that matter, in this as in many other fields of artistry and craftsmanship, the prices of reproductions today are soaring high above what were the prices of originals only yesterday.

Probably the only true reason for the sudden spate of crazily record-shattering prices in every field of antique buying is one that seems too simplistic to credit—nothing more than a belated realization that the past is the only thing that any of us can possess irrevocably.

On this basis, and dismissing all other considerations, the Dean Sage work has its own unique value as an authentic and otherwise unobtainable slice of a great river's past—and that's a thing that's literally priceless. Like the mountain, the Restigouche is *there*, and the book is like a plaque attesting to its uniqueness.

Over the years, good and bad, the mighty Miramichi river system has produced salmon averaging just four ounces under a round figure of ten pounds. The Restigouche, by exactly the same few ounces, has just missed doubling the Miramichi's average.

The nearest I've ever come to fishing it is the pool it shares with the Matapédia, whose crown waters at that joint I fished one year when I thought (mistakenly, as it turned out) that I was a week too early for the first summer run on the Miramichi. The best I can say is that I partly caught one of those big Restigouche salmon in that pool. Since partly catching a salmon might seem to equate with being partly pregnant, I'd better explain.

I was there for that week with a film producer who has a place on the Miramichi, fairly near the one where I was going, and when he got the same misinformation about it that I had, and we compared notes, he lucked into these two Matapédia rods that had become available through a cancellation at the last minute and suggested that we take them, so we could both avoid losing a week's salmon fishing.

He was every bit as accustomed to getting fish on the Miramichi as I was, so we made a sorry pair as we went fishless for a week on the Matapédia. Each time we'd come back in from our different beats, we'd check to see how the other rods were doing, and with one exception their experience was the same as ours. The exception was a man who got a twenty-pounder in each of the first two beats he fished. His wife, who was fishing too, was skunked like the rest of us. He was a nice guy, as well as a very good fisherman, and he was most diffident about his exceptional luck. But we hated him nonetheless, and kept rooting all week for his wife to get a bigger fish than either of his. This looked less and less likely as the week wore on, and we were really downcast to learn that she had to leave a day early, to represent the family on some duty occasion that he could thus be excused from attending. So now we hated him double.

The beats were rotated, and I had the Restigouche junction pool Thursday morning. She was getting it that afternoon, after which she couldn't fish again, but had to leave on the evening train. He was staying on, keeping their car, and could fish again the next day.

I finally hooked a good fish in the junction pool that morning, had him on for two jumps, after the first of which I judged him to be twenty-five pounds, and after the second raised my estimate to thirty, with a concomitant rise in my spirits as I'd never had a fish on the Miramichi above fourteen. Then suddenly and sickeningly I felt the line go limp and he was gone, with half my leader. It was the one strike I'd had, or was to have, all week.

That afternoon, in that same pool, there didn't seem to be anything doing at all. It was as if I'd muffed the one chance there was to be that day. After a while she got both bored and sleepy and decided to take forty winks. On about the thirty-eighth or -ninth of them, the guide wakened her, telling her to grab her rod, and she did, to bring to his waiting net a salmon that went just under twenty-eight pounds.

We were as pleased at dinner that night as if we'd each landed one just like it. Toasts all round and jubilation rampant. Her husband said he'd always thought she was the better fisherman and now he knew it. Gala send-off on the evening train. And the next day neither of us minded, somehow, half as much to get skunked again, for virtue had triumphed and we felt good about it.

What about the salmon I partly caught? Well, that was it, only I didn't know it until much later. Guides confide in each other, if not always in their "sports," and hers told mine, one night when they'd had enough to drink and he thought enough time had passed that it didn't matter all that much anymore, that while the lady slept, he just happened to notice a funny gleam in the water beside the canoe, that ran like a pale thin streak through some grass. Very carefully he fished it out of the water, saw that it was monofilament, and very slowly indeed, with great care not to put any strain on it, knotted it to her leader, snipping off the terminal third of her leader with its fly, only as he was satisfied that the new connection with it was soundly knotted. Then he woke the lady and told her to pick up her rod. When she did, and he saw what happened, he was almost more surprised than she, because he'd tied the stray end of monofilament on as a crazy hunch, thinking there might, at most, be a trout on the other end. Such a thing had never happened to him before, and he was obviously bursting to tell somebody about it, to see if the like of it had ever been heard tell of before.

I can't say I've heard the exact like of it before myself, though I was glad to learn that my week of fishlessness on the Matapédia had not been as total a blank as I had thought. In baseball scoring, my share in partly catching that salmon would have been credited as "an assist," but I don't think salmon fishing has a name for it.

Still, nothing about salmon fishing should ever surprise anybody. Dean Sage has several stories in *The Ristigouche and Its Salmon Fishing* that are stranger than that, including "The Salmon of the Matapédia Bridge," now that I come to think of it. But more important than its stories is the book's sense of place, and the enthusiasm with which he conveys the feeling he had for it, and makes you feel why it was the place he always "longed to be."

For in all fairness it could almost equally be said of his, that which he said of Scrope's, that it is "one of the choicest volumes in text, illustrations, and rarity, that adorns angling literature."

SCALE NET

For years I wondered why somebody didn't invent a landing net with a scale in its throat (that spot between the head and the handle which, on a tennis racket, bears the maker's name and/or the famous player's autograph), so people who wanted to put their fish back could do so without ever after wondering how big they were.

The combination spring balance and steel tape measure known as a Fisherman's De-Liar lets you get the length of the fish before you release it, but it gives you the weight only at the price of puncturing his jaw with the hook of the scale, which is not the nicest thing to do to a fish that you're about to return to the society of his peers with anything like an equal chance of competing with them.

Then one day, looking through the Dave Cook catalog, vainly seeking the Zip Leader Straightener, I saw a landing net with a scale in its throat. Since I don't normally use a landing net, having long ago come to the conclusion that they are more nuisance than assistance (scaring the fish much more than your hand slipped up from behind to seize their tails), there is always the chance that this humane device has also been featured elsewhere. I saw it in the Dave Cook catalog only because I was going through it page by page from cover to cover, to make sure that I hadn't missed the Zip Leader Straightener, hidden away in some odd corner.

It wasn't, as it turned out, much of a net, nor was the scale much of a scale, though I probably shouldn't have expected it to be at a price of $4.95. So I ordered four—three for the lean-to down by the ponds at the Joe Jefferson Club, and one for Traver to keep up at his place in the Adirondacks.

It was a good thing I did, because within a matter of weeks, all three of the nets had holes in the bottom only slightly smaller in circumference than the customary opening at the top; and one of the scales was weighing two pounds heavy and another slightly less than a pound and a half light, thus foiling all but the most expert mathematician's ability to circumvent this difficulty by weighing the fish first in one and then in the other. (Somebody broke the spring on the second one, trying to change the deficiency to an even two pounds.) As for the third, we couldn't tell what it weighed, as I broke the indicator needle off, jiggling it to try to unfreeze it, one February morning.

Ricky, who is a good man to have around, remembered a Cape Cod party for which his wife had hung one wall with netting, from which he was able to salvage enough to keep the three nets in permanent and efficacious repair. Neither he nor anybody else has yet figured out how to do the same for the spring balance.

But isn't it a good idea?

SCHWIEBERT

Perennial angling prodigy . . . when bigger fish are caught, Schwiebert will catch them. . . .

Schwiebert, Ernest (1931–). Snow is falling softly outside, and we are months away from fishing except in our thoughts. I know that isn't true as I write this, and the chances are better than even that it isn't as you read it, but it's the first sentence of the nicest Schwiebert book, *Remembrances of Rivers Past,* and it's also the key to its fullest enjoyment. This is a book to be savored, daydreamed over, and even re-enjoyed in the dreams with which it is all but guaranteed to invade your sleep. So get it now, and save it for the silent obbligato of falling snow, when fishing is indeed months away for most of us, though not, thanks be, for Schwiebert. The rest of us will be sitting home reading about it, but he'll be off somewhere, anywhere, from Tierra del Fuego to Nepal or Down Under, wherever it's summer while it's winter for the rest of us, and from his incessant travels we will be the richer—as we are with this volume—by some of the best fishing stories of modern times. It's a break for fishermen everywhere that Ernest Schwiebert's attitude, throughout the long years of his often-interrupted and hence protracted schooling, was that "architecture can wait" and maybe the fish won't.

These are thinking man's fish stories, to be sure, as the Proustian overtone of the title indicates, and they leave to the outdoor magazines most of the clichés of reel-screeching and the gee-whiz aspects of how much and how many. But every page of this book is solidly based on the great angling traditions and the resultant blend of memory and learning, mixed with a near-genius for evocative detail, makes for some of the headiest vicarious fishing experience to be encountered anywhere today in print. In fact, unless and until somebody writes a definitive history of American angling (Austin Hogan could and should, whether or not he ever will), Schwiebert is our nearest equivalent to England's Major J. W. Hills. You have to read him to get, from the present vantage point, the panorama of our angling past.

Schwiebert is much more relaxed and relaxing to read now than he was in his Tom Thumb phase of *Matching the Hatch* (he was really a *baby* when that came out eighteen years ago). Then he used to come on like a juvenile Hewitt, without the saving grace of the latter's venerability to alleviate the stiffness of his know-it-all posture. The boy is older now, by the equivalent of what would be several fishing lifetimes for ordinary people. The *Wunderkind* has mellowed, and has begun to seem as human as yourself. True, you read about his fifty-one-pound salmon on the Vossa—who could keep that a secret?—but you also get the benefit of an ingratiating ploy that Schwiebert has picked up from the old-time acrobats, who always used to miss their star turn a couple of times, so the audience could appreciate how much harder it was than the rest of their stunts, and Ernie is generous with endearing details of broken-off leaders and pulled-out hooks and even, for which you could hug him, plenty of fishless days. But most rewarding of all are the set pieces, like little vignettes, that project the exotic aspects of the varied backgrounds against which Schwiebert's small tales of tall fishing are told. For instance, the story of his fourteen-pound rainbow at Boca Chimehuin, after night fell and the rest of his party had gone back to the trucks. True, the fish "engulfed the fly in a wild lunge, and the reel screeched out huge staccato lengths of line." But the rest of the story has this great difference: as he stood a moment in the road, looking at the Southern Cross, the tail of the great fish dragging in the dust, "the wind stirred and moved in the monkey puzzle trees, riffling the still surface of the lake. There was an Araucan woman resting with her children beside the shrine, and their candles flickered in the darkness."

Schwiebert is himself of that breed he characterizes as "men who carry pictures of salmon instead of wives in their wallets," but you don't have to be as nutty about fishing as he is to read his book with relish and reward. (Sara Schwiebert is the Patient Griselda of all the fishing widows of both history and legend.) Trouble is, if you aren't already that nutty about it, you might be by the time you finish reading it. The first chapter alone would drive anybody out of doors, rod in hand. So save it for winter. It will keep. You can be sure this book will be around for a long time.

Schwiebert's first book, *Matching the Hatch,* is still well worth reading, though it was written as far back as 1955, and whether or not you intend in actual angling practice to try to follow all its precepts. You don't have to become a slavish devotee of hatch-matching on a full-time basis to get some occasional benefit out of selective use of some of the things it preaches. (The same goes for Vincent Marinaro's *A Modern Dry Fly Code* and Alvin R. Grove, Jr.'s *The Lure and Lore of Trout Fishing.* The well-read angler will be a more resourceful angler, when the going is tough, for having read and remembered Schwiebert, Marinaro, and Grove.)

As for *Salmon of the World,* Schwiebert's outsize portfolio of text and drawings covering the entire range of the salmonid species, its hundred dollar price would at first blush seem to preclude its mention in the same breath with ordinary books for the average angler. But when you stop to think that by today's standards salmon fishing has itself been priced almost out of conscience, maybe it's fair to suggest that, to anybody who can even contemplate the possibility of going after salmon personally, Ernie's salmon book is a downright bargain. For salmon fishing is one of the few remaining privileges in a demotic era when privilege of every sort is either heavily in discount or already in eclipse. It is without question one of the costliest, per minute of action in ratio to total investment, of all participant sports. Certain beats on certain famous rivers now bring as much per week as they brought, within the memory of most of us, per season.

So when scaled to the proportionate costs of seeking the lordly creatures it depicts, anywhere outside the confines of an armchair, *Salmon of the World* is indeed a tremendous buy at the price.

In its thirty drawings alone, it fulfills the promise of its title. To most of us, this is six or seven times as many as we've ever either seen or heard about. Atlantic salmon and Pacific salmon, sure. Everybody knows the A. & P. Then there are the landlocks, of course, and sea trout, including steelheads. But then what? Well, better than a score of others that it would take a young fortune to go see for yourself. And given the time and the money, it would still take a lot of luck, to see so many in anything like this gorgeous close-up of colorful detail.

And as for the text, that's a reverse switch on the title, for it equates quite simply and succinctly to nothing less than *The World of Salmon.* Despite its relative brevity, it is almost encyclopaedic in the breadth of its coverage of the subject, and for those who wish to pursue any of its facets in greater depth, serves as the most knowledgeable of guides to further study.

In fact, when you look at this relatively short text in perspective, against the vast literature of those most-written-about of fish, the salmonids, Ernest Schwiebert's contribution to that already impressive literature is not only notable and definitive; it is unique.

Putting these three books together, and remembering that in his student days, with *Matching the Hatch,* Schwiebert did more for the appreciation and understanding of trout than most authors of fishing books have accomplished in a lifetime, then in his still young manhood to do as much or more for salmon, enhances the stature of *Remembrances of Rivers Past.* With these three entries already logged in a career obviously still in the ascendant, Schwiebert emerges as the triple-threat contender for the ultimate title as the complete angler of our time. His newest book, *Nymphs,* buttresses the contention.

SPORTING BOOK SERVICE

A. Aldridge Williams
Box 181
Rancocas, N.J. 08073

Despite the rapid and continual escalation of all book prices over the past decade, Sporting Book Service remains the source of an occasional bargain for the angling collector seeking to fill the gaps in his list of books wanted, and feeling neither willing nor able to pay more than ten dollars for every least and last item on it. His secondhand lists reflect the fact that when Aldy Williams obtains books advantageously he's not averse to passing the advantage on to the customer, quite evidently contenting himself with a modest profit, instead of whooping up all the prices across the boards in line with the general current trend. You'll still find items like Hewitt's scarce 1934 *Nymph Fishing* for a mere five bucks (List No. 739, 1972) and Grover Cleveland's *Fishing & Shooting Sketches*, 1906, for a measly three dollars, and even a Derrydale Press item here and there for less than half of the thirty-five-dollar price that has long been considered rock bottom for anything bearing the Derrydale imprint.

As for recent books on which the prices have been advanced a dollar or so by their publishers since publication, Williams shows a sporting tendency to go on supplying them at their original prices as long as his original stock holds out. This conveys the comforting impression that here's one bookseller who regrets and resists the inexorably rising tide of prices just as much as you do.

Orders over fifteen dollars are shipped prepaid, below which level a charge of twenty-five cents per book is made to cover postage and handling. New Jersey residents must also add 5 percent for sales tax. No charge for lists, which include a pretty broad coverage of current sporting items as well as out-of-print works.

STOMACH PUMP

How to Find Out What They're Taking, Without Killing Them First

Here's a stop-press item for the angler who has everything. How often have you been urged to open the first trout, to see exactly what they've been feeding on? We were all taught that, in conversation or in reading, but gradually got out of the habit as we stopped killing trout.

Who now carries a marrow scoop, which Skues found ideal for the purpose, these forty years and more a-gone?

But the principle is still sound. If you know what they've been taking, presumably it will increase your chances of taking more. Yet the trout doesn't live that can survive the use of a marrow scoop, in and out of his stomach, to satisfy your curiosity.

Hence the Aymidge, as manufactured by W. A. Carter & Sons, 2/3 Royal Exchange, London E.C.3. It's a "pipette," or suction pump, which consists of a plastic tube a little over six inches long, fitted with a rubber bulb at one end, and screwed into a test tube at the other. First, catch your trout. Then unscrew the pipette from the test tube in which it rests, compressing the bulb a little. Insert into the trout's mouth and release the pressure on the bulb—and out come the contents of the trout's stomach. Put the pipette back into the test tube, where you can examine the evidence at your leisure, after returning the trout to the water.

He isn't going to look or act very happy as you ease him back into the water, and you'll have to hold him upright with one hand while gently stroking his sides for anywhere from two to even ten minutes, before he'll be revived enough to shoot out of your light grasp, but if you've handled him gently enough, and have been careful not to squeeze *him* the way you squeezed the bulb, he'll be none the worse for the experience.

As for the contents of his stomach, they'll be far less damaged than they would be by a marrow scoop—in fact, often some of the insects are still alive.

I got this marvel from Dermot Wilson, the onetime creative chief of J. Walter Thompson's London Office, who now lives more sensibly in an old mill on a tributary of the Test, where he conducts a mail-order business in tackle items and provides paying guests with some wonderful trout fishing. (His kid caught a six-pounder in the shadow of the mill wheel—it was almost as big as he was, at least at the time.)

So if you're in England, or don't mind sending there for it, you can get an "Aymidge" (Ref. No. 600; length 7¾ in. Weight only 1 oz.) from Dermot Wilson.

Address: Dermot Wilson
The Mill,
Nether Wallop,
Stockbridge, Hampshire,
England

Or next time you're ordering something from Norm Thompson, ask them to get you one, as Peter Alport has an arrangement with Dermot Wilson.

Address: Mr. Peter Alport
Norm Thompson
1805 N. W. Thurman
Portland, Oregon 97209

In 1973 the Aymidge will cost $3.00 (plus 50 cents for air carriage) if imported to this country.

All you'll be giving up is your last excuse for killing a trout.

$\mathcal{T}$GF

Theodore Gordon Flyfishers, Inc.
24 E. 39th Street
New York, New York 10016
(Gardner Grant, President)

Tax-exempt, nonprofit membership organization, a founding charter member of the Federation of Flyfishermen and an affiliate of Trout Unlimited. Weekly Tuesday luncheon meetings in own furnished quarters in the Williams Club. Membership $15.00 yearly.

Founded in 1963 by Ted Rogowski, Walt Kehm, Lee Wulff, and Ed Zern, with the original aim of becoming the Theodore Gordon Chapter of TU, Theodore Gordon Flyfishers became instead the "queen bee" of the cluster of fishing clubs that swarmed together within the next two years to form FFF.

TGF never achieved its chapter status in TU because of a doctrinal dispute with TU's founding fathers in Michigan, who would not sanction the use of the word "flyfishers" in the organization's name, so after an uneasy year as the Theodore Gordon Anglers (which some felt might better have been spelled Wranglers), the application for TU chapterhood was withdrawn and TGF celebrated its first birthday by defiantly putting its old name back on and deciding to go it alone. By this time, Gene Anderegg was a TGF director, and he and Lee Wulff ignited each other with the flame of federation, which Anderegg carried literally across the country like an Olympic torch, seeking like-minded clubs that were both devoted to conservation and dedicated as fly fishermen.

It would be a nice fairy-tale touch to conclude that after a decade TGF made the first move to link TU and FFF in any way, but that had occurred a year earlier with the appearance of the East Jersey Chapter of Trout Unlimited on the roster of member clubs in the Federation of Flyfishermen.

TGF's affiliation with TU, dating from the end of 1972, does not represent chapter status, but rather a recognition on the part of TU of the value of TGF's training and equipping of several of its chapters in New York and New Jersey, which enabled them to take the field and perform important water-monitoring work. TU voted to give full monetary credit to TGF for the monies spent training TU chapters, and affiliation resulted, almost automatically, as a form of entente cordiale. This was stressed by Gardner Grant, under whose presidency of TGF this significant association occurred: "What affiliation with TU and membership in FFF represents is the joining of kindred spirits for the greater cause of conservation. Although we are not a chapter of TU, we are pleased to take this step and be joined with two national organizations involved in constructive conservation. We hope our affiliation with TU will help both organizations, TU and FFF, and ourselves."

Explaining further how TGF members do help themselves, Grant amplified:

Our members and associates, trained in the testing of certain water quality parameters and working as teams, act virtually as an arm of the N.Y. State Department of Environmental Conservation water-quality surveillance network, monitoring specific points on the waters we are most concerned about on a monthly basis, the year round—and reporting our findings on each field trip directly to the Department. With the skills we have acquired, we can act as the water-quality watchdog over our favorite waters, do the job that the state's limited manpower will not permit it to do, yet gain the attentive ear of the state's experts in the field who evaluate and store the data we furnish and can take corrective action based upon it, when required. Basically, people get the government they deserve. Rather than just complaining about what ours doesn't do for us, we are working as an auxiliary (without cost to the taxpayers) and believe we are improving its performance for the benefit of all.

Harking back to the beginnings of TGF, when the first annual meeting voted to become, and the next one to unbecome, a chapter of TU, the *TGF Bulletin* in the fall of 1972 reminisced editorially about how TGF "struck out on our own with a few basic concepts on how we wanted to improve trout fishing, protect it and pure waters, and thereby our own sport. That was long before the subject of conservation was a generally popular one.

With a handful of dedicated members, TGF formed a Trophy Trout policy that earned serious attention on state and national levels. Among other worthy projects: TGF launched the first Limit-Kill streamside poster campaign; published two books and lithographs to finance its expanding conservation efforts; established the first Arts of Angling series of seminars; sponsored worthy youngsters to the De Bruce conservation camp; aided local clubs in their stream improvement work; advanced its fight for pure waters by establishing the "Water Watchers." And as if all that weren't enough, the club continues to finance water quality testing teams from other interested and dedicated clubs.

Where can an organization of concerned environmentalists such as TGF go from there? We now number more than five hundred members . . . TGF needs the input and output of a national office in Washington to satisfy its concern for improving and protecting the quality of our sport.

If you're even the least bit concerned yourself, and you get to New York more than very rarely, membership in TGF, with its Tuesday lunches every week (except the last couple in August), should be worth your while, no matter what all else may enjoy your membership and support.

TROUT FLIES OF NEW ZEALAND

David B. Hilliard
Box 1087, FDR Post Office Station
New York, New York 10022

Three "proven trout killers," Mrs. Simpson, Red Setter, and
Parson's Glory, imported from New Zealand

Hilliard's Billiards, you pays your money and you takes your chances. All I know is that the first four or five casts I made with the Red Setter I got nothing but an unaccustomed splash on the water, as these flies come no smaller than size eight, and the same with the Parson's Glory, but on the Mrs. Simpson, I took one good fish right after another. (Traver came along then, and I gave him one, and he did the same, and has gone right on doing it ever since, world without end.) So for one evening I thought the Mrs. Simpson was the Final Solution to all my fly-casting problems, for the rest of my days. That's the night I sat down to order three dozen Mrs. Simpsons, size eight (since they don't come any smaller and besides that was the fly that proved to be such a killer-diller), one dozen for Traver and two dozen for me.

Hilliard sent them right out, in three Jiffy bags, a dozen in each, two of which came one day (so I gave Traver one) and the other the next. And he also dropped me a line, thanking me for my reorder, and saying that he was pleased to gather that I had had some success with the Mrs. Simpson. He added: "I have had excellent results with it myself. Last Sunday I took five nice browns (12–15 inches) from the Battenkill, on the New York side, all on the Mrs. Simpson. It is a deadly pattern."

Well, yeah, that's what I thought. I wonder if Dave Hilliard has been back there since, and if he has, how he did the second time. That was May 24. From then to August, my total catch on the Mrs. Simpson, of which I am probably New Jersey's leading collector as of this moment, has consisted of one (1) baby bass, approximately two-and-three-quarters inches long, or about an inch longer than the Mrs. Simpson itself. That was in the same spot, on the same water, where I took hefty browns and rainbows, and even a goodly brookie, on it that first night. (I didn't even know we had any bass in our ponds, never having seen a sign of any before, but we have a lot of birds, including a new family of Canadian honkers, and there's no telling what they may bring in.)

So who is it you want to believe, me or Dave Hilliard (or for that matter, Bob Traver)? Sometimes I remind myself of the fellow who said he was so inept, if he were dancing alone in a mirror-walled room, he'd probably bump into one of the guys on the walls.

So if I'm in the minority, which I seem to be, you can get all three patterns, either individually or assorted, at a dollar and a quarter each, or six ninety-five per half dozen, or twelve dollars a dozen, and they come in sizes four and six, as well as the eight that was as big as I felt like trying on our water. And may your luck be more lasting than mine.

TROUT UNLIMITED

4260 E. Evans Avenue
Denver, Colorado 80222
(R. P. Van Gytenbeek, Executive Director)

National, nonprofit public conservation organization, with fifteen thousand members in 170 chapters in thirty states. Founded in Michigan in 1959, National Headquarters is now in Denver, with a full-time office in Washington, D.C. and a

regional office in Portland, Ore. Nine state or regional councils
coordinate the chapters in Oregon, Washington, and Idaho,
Montana, Colorado, Wisconsin, Michigan, Pennsylvania, New
Jersey, New York, and North Carolina. Councils being formed
in other areas to coordinate other chapters formed or forming.
Contributions to TU and its associated organization, The Trout
and Salmon Foundation, are tax deductible (except the first
$2.50). Individual membership, $10 yearly.

TU has grown enormously since 1969, when it had four thousand
members in forty-three chapters in sixteen states. This doubling of
states and quadrupling of chapters has occurred since January of
1969, when retired Army Captain and onetime Princeton varsity
footballer Pete Van Gytenbeek gave up the office supplies and furniture business in Colorado Springs, where he was president of the
symphony and founder of the Racquet Club among other distinctions,
to become the full-time executive director. He made the Denver office
of TU the national office, largely by engineering the merger with the
Northwest Steelheaders that made TU nationwide and necessitated
the establishment of the first regional office in Portland.

The contrast to the old backwoods days of TU, when I held
membership card number 848, and Theodore Gordon Flyfishers
couldn't get in as a chapter without changing their name to Theodore
Gordon Anglers, and couldn't stay in even then, could hardly be more
complete. Today TU has fly-fishermen chapters, from the Boulder
Flycasters of Colorado to the Jackson Hole Fly Fishermen of Wyoming, and the once embattled TGF itself is now a TU affiliate, as well
as a founder club of the Federation of Fly Fishermen. And the East
Jersey Chapter of TU is even a member club in FFF.

The TU of today has matured into a full-fledged action organization and as of these past few years its name is truly writ large across
the land, and especially the waters thereof. Scratch a place on the
continental map where anything has actually been done, either to
rectify or to forestall the spoliation of important natural resources, and
when you untangle the players you'll find TU at the bottom of the
heap.

The best part of TU's growth, and its concomitant acquisition of truly national stature and clout, is that thanks to its structure in councils and chapters it has kept its grass-roots pervasiveness and effectiveness on the local level, where it counts. Also, despite a formidable roster of brass among the officers, the organization has retained its vertical demographic formation, and not lost the common touch. True, there are tycoons like Elliott Donnelley and grandees like Otto Teller, in the upper reaches of the letterhead's listings, but the board of directors is truly as broad as it's long, with some bartenders and plumbers still in there, and quite obviously not stifled by the presence of industrial and financial heavyweights like Robert O. Anderson and Willard F. Rockwell, Jr., nor overawed by the punditry of a Roderick Haig-Brown nor even the celebrity of a Bing Crosby. Nor has the eminence of some of its personnel ever yet tempted TU into grandstanding or hogging the limelight by going it alone, when it was evident that by united or coordinated action with other conservation groups better prospects of success could be assured. TU has worked closely with the National Audubon Society, the Environmental Defense Fund, Federation of Fly Fishermen, Friends of the Earth, Natural Resources Defense Council, Nature Conservancy, the Sierra Club, Izaak Walton League, and Wilderness Society. And on a day-to-day basis it never loses sight of its constant objective to protect and improve the cold-water habitat and support sound fisheries management. No project is too big or too small for TU's attention. (They've even got a reclamation project going on the Saddle River, that once-mighty trout stream that now silts its murky way past my own New Jersey doorstep.) TU protects water habitat for fish and humans by working for better water quality and to prevent destruction of streams and lakes by unwise land- and water-use projects (unnecessary dams, water diversions, highways, and stream-channeling projects). TU improves water habitat by organizing stream-improvement projects with local youth groups, conservation bodies, and officials from government and business. TU encourages better fisheries management by state and federal fish and game departments, which often involves a reevaluation of budget priorities, with emphasis on habitat protection, inventories of waters and fish, tailored hatchery programs, and reduced harvest regulations.

TU's philosophy is nearly identical to that of the Federation of Fly Fishermen, but for the one tremendous trifle of difference between them. Hear TU: "We believe that trout and salmon fishing isn't just fishing for trout and salmon. It's fishing for sport rather than for food, where the true enjoyment of the sport lies in the challenge, the lore and the battle of wits, not necessarily the full creel. It's the feeling of satisfaction that comes from limiting your kill instead of killing your limit. It's communing with nature where the chief reward is a refreshed body and a contented soul, where a license is a permit to use—not abuse—to enjoy—not destroy our cold-water fishery. It's subscribing to the proposition that what's good for trout and salmon is good for fishermen and that managing trout and salmon for themselves rather than for the fishermen is fundamental to the solution of our trout and salmon problems. It's appreciating our fishery resource, respecting fellow anglers and giving serious thought to tomorrow."

As an angler's testament, that's as pure as Ivory Soap. But if TU can come that close to being squarely on the side of the angels, why in heaven's name, you want to ask, can't it come the other fifty-six one-hundredths of a percent, and come clean by forswearing bait entirely? Why talk about what's good for trout, and managing them for their own sakes, rather than for the fisherman's, when everyone knows that a trout that has swallowed a minnow or a worm or a salmon egg is damaged beyond possibility of being returned to the water? And what greater respect can you have for fellow anglers than to leave the trout there for them to try to catch, after you've had your own enjoyment of them, and are ready to leave with your body refreshed and your soul contented?

All TU's philosophy needs, to pass muster with the most exigent of anglers, is the addition of the one thought that has never been better expressed than in Lee Wulff's words—"these fish are too valuable to be caught only once."

But then, who or what is perfect, in our far from perfect society? It would be curmudgeonly for any of us to refuse to support TU, over that one trifle, however tremendous it may honestly seem to us, when TU does so much to support all of us, in our continued enjoyment of our chosen sport, so constantly threatened and so precariously preserved.

TURKS, YOUNG

Selective Trout by Doug Swisher and Carl Richards, Crown Publishers, N.Y., 1971. Most talked about fishing book in years.

For those more concerned with the lure of trouting present and to come than with the lore of trouting past, there's no doubt about it, *Selective Trout* is the biggest single thing since bucktails. This book is all that everybody's been saying it is, for it is one of those innovative and imaginative breakthroughs that occur only rarely.

Billed as a dramatically new and scientific approach to trout fishing on eastern and western rivers, it is exactly that, and for once a dust jacket doesn't have to be scaled down by the removal of hyperbole. To anybody who ties his own flies, this book is a godsend, because it offers him a surefooted path to order out of chaos. And even to my fellow members of the All Thumbs Club who don't, it comes as a welcome relief from the confusion and clutter of previous hatch-matching directives, to find a way to cover 80 percent of the entomological bets with only eight patterns. And that's the relative simplicity the authors boil your choices down to for you, varying the selection only according to whether you're fishing East or West or in between.

One knows, of course, that in fishing nothing is guaranteed, and that what works one time on the stream is almost by that very token not going to work the next time, but even so, it's a wonderful feeling to turn to a new system, that is at least logical and sensible, as a means of simplifying the bewildering complexity of the challenges presented by the varying problems of imitation. It is in this, with their idea of placing reasoned bets on a small number of artificial flies, without for a moment kidding you or themselves that there's any way to shortcut nature's whimsical and mystifying abundance of naturals, that the authors have made a giant step toward establishing some semblance of sanity in the world of trout madness.

I've heard grousing that these kids are pretty commercial in their viewpoint, revealing an undue concern for selling their offbeat flies. Well, that's only commercial if you can't tie your own; if you can, just stick to the book and you needn't buy another thing. But if you can't, you may be glad to know where you can get something new that intrigues you. If that's commercial, well, so's Christmas, and Easter, and Mother's Day, and practically everything else in modern living.

My one quibble is with their title. What they're offering is not so much a book on the selectivity of trout as a system of selective fishing for trout.

That their system happens to involve some radically different flies, like the no-hackle and the paradun and extended-body nymphs, is really just so much icing on the cake. That they represent varying degrees of departure from the flies habitually used is only incidental, because their system can also be implemented with store-bought flies or your own old stock (including some of those old Hardy "parachute" flies, if you happen to have any left, as I do), assuming that your old flies are reasonably decent imitations of enough entomologically different types. The value of their system lies in their super hatch concept, and the aid it gives you in bringing some modicum of rhyme and reason, in relation to emergence and prevalence of insects at given times, into what might otherwise be a merely frantic and directionless changing of flies one after another.

That a plastics salesman and a dentist, which Swisher and Richards respectively are, should be the new wise men to come out of a small town in Michigan with the most sophisticated new approach to what has become one of the most tradition-bound of sports is the best justification our problem-plagued democracy has had in a long time. Reading *Selective Trout,* and following the precepts of its tables (whether or not you tie flies) is like turning on a mental windshield wiper, to clear away the film of confusion and bewilderment that keep too many of us from seeing the fish for the maze of our fishing tackle.

As these Young Turks say, a major theme of their book has been to reexamine the traditional ideas and advance new concepts. But their minor is no less worthy, for it is an eloquent stress on conservation and the necessity for the development of a new breed of angler, more interested than those of the past have been in the preservation as well as improvement of the sport. And here and there they achieve the level of wisdom, as when they say: "Since fly fishermen represent a distinct minority group, the best procedure is to sell clean water to the public rather than to promote trout fishing only."

Truer words than those you won't find. If Swisher and Richards be the harbingers of a new breed, may their tribe increase. They appear to have arrived in the nick of time.

UNDERESTIMATED BOOKS

Six nominations for rescue from at least relative oblivion

In an old jacket, that I seem not to have had on since around 1966, I have just come across an odd slip of paper. It's the top half of a piece of Hotel Pontchartrain notepaper, so I don't even know whether it's the one in Detroit or the one in New Orleans, but I do know it's in my handwriting.

All it says is the following:

> nominations for underestimated books—
> Charley Wetzel—
> John Crowe—The Book of Trout Lore
> Robert Venables—The Experienced Angler
> Brian Curtis—The Life Story of the Fish: His
>   Manners and Morals
> Ben Hur Lampman—A Leaf from French Eddy
> Negley Farson—Just Fishing.

That's all it says. Why it doesn't say *which* Wetzel title, I don't know, but pretty obviously the one that's meant is the bibliographical one, *American Fishing Books*, that incorporates the Goodspeed list of angling titles.

It's a pretty good list, but I've no idea whose it is. I thought it was my own, until I came to the last title. Negley Farson was a fine foreign correspondent and, I understand from those who knew him, a hell of a fisherman, but I've never read a book by him, so this can't be my list. (I'd have said *Just Fishing* was a Ray Bergman title, which of course it is, but titles can't be copyrighted, and there are several books, apart from the one by Al McClane, called *The Practical Fly Fisherman,* to cite just one example.)

Well, anyway, I came across this list just as *this* book had one foot on the press, so to speak, so I stuck it in here, with the thought that—like the chicken soup for the desperately sick patient—it couldn't hurt, and might help somebody find a book that would do him some good. If this is something I read somewhere and just jotted down, I'd hate to print it without credit, but I doubt that it is—the "Charley" instead of Charles Wetzel makes it unlikely.

The Wetzel, printed and even bound by the author, had about as many copies in its one 1950 edition—some 235—as it had pages, with the result that the price now amounts to at least that many dollars, if not more, what with devaluation. It's one of the angling books that cries out for reprinting.

As for Venables, it may seem odd for a book dating from 1662 to be included in anybody's list of underestimated works over three centuries later, but it is even more odd that *The Experienced Angler,* which formed Part Three of the famous 1676 fifth edition of Izaak Walton's *The Compleat Angler,* which was the first to include Charles Cotton's since-famous Part Two, should have been so precipitately dropped, while Walton and Cotton have been bound together ever since, almost like Siamese twins, through hundreds of subsequent editions. The one edition of *The Compleat Angler* to carry Venables as Part Three was even retitled, for the occasion, *The Universal Angler.*

Crowe's *A Book of Trout Lore,* published by A. S. Barnes & Co., N.Y., 1947, was in my list of recommended books in *The Well-Tempered Angler* in 1965, so if that's been underestimated, don't look at me. But Lampman's lovely little book had only regional publication in Portland in 1965, after my own had gone to press, so I couldn't blame myself for missing it. I could kick myself, however, in the case of Brian Curtis, as I had the Dover reprint of *The Life Story of the*

Fish among my own helter-skelter aggregation of fishing books for years, and had never even realized I had it, much less read it or even looked at it, until I stumbled across it in the course of a vain attic-to-cellar search for another book, that I knew I had, but couldn't lay hands on when I tried to find it for somebody who had an overnight emergency need for it. For this sin of omission from my earlier fishing book, I have tried to make belated amends in the entry of Brian Curtis in this section, which I suggest you turn back to now, if you haven't already read it, while I go look for a copy of the Negley Farson. All I seem to remember hearing about Negley Farson's fishing is that he was very big on the trout streams of Yugoslavia, about which I know nothing. But so potent is the power of suggestion that, since finding this list in my pocket, I'm on fire to read him. For a start, I've just looked him up in the handiest source, which is dealers' lists, and all I find under his name is not *Just Fishing* but *Going Fishing,* a book published in New York in 1943.

So not only isn't this list mine, but I'm feeling less compunction by the minute for not being able to give anybody credit for it, because obviously it's the work of some dunderhead who doesn't know his Farson from his Bergman.

Under that circumstance, I'm surprised that the list is any good. But it is. At least with the first five of the six I know you can't go wrong. In fact, if you haven't read any one of those, I envy you the experience. As for the sixth, I hope it's a pleasure for which I can be envied myself.

VOELKER

Fisherman's Fisherman
My nomination for the next dean

Since the present acknowledged dean of American angling, Alfred W. Miller, has long lived his fishing and writing life under a pseudonym, Sparse Grey Hackle, it is a nice coincidence that his obvious and logical ultimate successor to this unofficial title should also be the wearer of a nom de plume. As Sparse has been called the angler's angler, so does Robert Traver deserve to become known, if only within the fraternity which is the only place where the title trails clouds of glory, as the fly fisherman's fisherman.

It was as Robert Traver that, back in the fifties, Upper Michigan's Supreme Court Judge John Voelker became famous as the author of his novel (and movie) *Anatomy of a Murder,* and he kept the pseudonym for his subsequent books, two of which are about fishing.

It is as self-depicted in *Trout Madness* and *Anatomy of a Fisherman* that John Voelker earns my nomination, as he emerges from their pages as the curmudgeon's curmudgeon, the character's character, of the true trout-lover's world. Some welcome additional touches to the portrait were supplied in an interview with William Serrin in *The New York Times* on May 28, 1972.

Contemptuous of worms and tourists alike, referring to the former as "pork chops" and to the latter as characterized by the determination to make "their damned 500 miles a day," Voelker lives in Upper Michigan, regretting the day when it was joined to the rest of the state by the Mackinac Bridge. As told in the Serrin interview, Voelker was invited to the dedication ceremonies for the bridge, but wired his regrets: "Sorry, but I must reveal I've been named chairman of the Bomb-the-Bridge Committee."

"Voelker loves the Upper Peninsula," William Serrin said, "because of its isolation and beauty, and because of the trout fishing it affords, a kind of fishing he calls 'bramble fishing,' backwoods fishing. . . . Voelker loves to fish for brook trout because they are the native fish of the peninsula. There are also brown trout and rainbows, huge fish and to a pro like Voelker his almost for the taking, but they are planted fish. There are bass and pike, too, planted in the 1920's and 1930's so there would be big fish for the people of the peninsula to catch and to lure tourists with. Voelker finds bass and pike 'unspeakable' . . ."

As the interview opened, Voelker was "standing in a lonely, lovely place, a pond ringed by spruce and balsam. Voelker has fished it for 50 years or more, ever since he was a boy. He has not seen more than 5 or 10 people here, outside of a few friends, in all that time.

"He jerks the line to hook a trout—but it escapes. 'Hah,' he says, 'I write books about trout, but I can't *catch* trout.' "

After citing various rivers in Upper Michigan that Voelker recommends, Serrin continued the interview with some of the most telling touches, by way of attributes of this great angler's persona:

"He prefers ponds, for pond fishing, he says, is the most difficult. In rivers and streams the noise a fisherman makes is masked by the water. Fish face the current, so they can be, by a man of Voelker's expertise, easily stalked from downstream. Fishing small ponds means 'you don't get the natural protection of river fishing.'

"Why, I wondered, had Voelker never changed his fly all morning? He had hundreds of flies, $1,000 worth or more, in his vest. And why, too, had he not sneaked up on the trout ponds, as one is told to do in textbooks?

"What the hell," he replied, "he's read all the books about fishing, heard all about the scientific approach, but he just doesn't believe it. Most fishermen stick with a favorite fly, he said, and when it's impossible to make out the markings of flies and nymphs on the water it is fruitless, he believes, to tie on fly after fly. When trout are biting, you can catch them on a shoehorn. When they are not—like this day—they simply are not. Usually there is little anyone can do about it. He said, too, that he is careful, even stealthy, without crawling around on his hands and knees. 'You can be careful without this Indian belly-creeping.'

"And you do not need to catch fish, Voelker insists, to enjoy trout fishing—indeed, catching the trout, he argues, is almost incidental to the fishing. (His biggest trout has been a 17-inch one; the world's record catch, pulled out of Canada, is 31½ inches. No matter, no matter at all.) 'I had a full day' he said, 'I'm just not quite as mad at the trout anymore.' And: 'I've sort of gotten away from the full creel thing.' "

Voelker said: "I think a good deal more of some trout than I do of some fishermen." He once began an article: "Trout fishing is so enjoyable it should 'be done in bed' "; to his surprise, the line was printed.

Voelker wrote, "Fishing is one of the few pursuits left to man that is fun even to fail at." And, "Being out in the woods fishing is one of the few places left on earth where a man can find solitude without loneliness."

Gentlemen, could there be any other nominations?

ALKER REELS

Arthur L. Walker & Son, Inc.
P. O. Box 249
Hempstead, New York 11550
Tel. (516) 481–2896
(Archie L. Walker, President)

The direct commercial descendants of Edward and Julius vom Hofe and Otto Zwarg, their shop foreman, the Walkers have been making custom trout and salmon reels on the Vom Hofe patterns since 1942, and with subsequent modifications and redesign of certain elements now offer a full line of twenty trout, salmon, and saltwater reels, the only full line of custom reels made today in all sizes.

Vom Hofe, Conroy, and Abbey & Imbrie reels were all produced in the 1870s. The first Conroys, beginning in 1873, were of German silver, which by 1878 was succeeded by aluminum. At about the same time as his astonishingly early introduction of aluminum, Conroy began experimentation with hard-rubber end plates that, with his characteristic raised pillars, evolved into the famous Mills reel, which was in production until 1970. Julius vom Hofe began experimenting with hard rubber around 1874, but it is not clear whether he or Thomas Conroy introduced its use. It is certain, however, that the end plates of vom Hofe reels, which at first were chrome-plated brass, were of hard rubber from 1881 on, whereas the Conroy reel, except in its transubstantiation into the Mills reel, was mostly of metal. But all these early makes were simple click reels using a two-way dog, spring and ratchet gear. The simple click trout reel was most successfully developed by Edward vom Hofe, following the pattern of salmon reels of the vom Hofe 1889, 1893, and 1903 patent designs. These trout reels are still alive and working, but Arch Walker likens them to "little old ladies beginning to show their wrinkles" and says that "practically every one we have serviced shows surface cracks in the end plates." But with the death of Edward vom Hofe, in the opinion of both the Walkers, "the quality trout reel in America died with him." Otto Zwarg began making salmon reels in Brooklyn, but never made trout reels, and the vom Hofe reels made in Philadelphia, unlike those produced in New York, were salmon reels only, and the vom Hofe trout reel was a dead issue.

The Walkers began making trout reels from the vom Hofe patterns in 1942, but came eventually to the conclusion that the simple dog ratchet was no longer satisfactory and began seeking a formula, from about 1960 on, for an action that would be superior and might initiate a renaissance for the high-performance trout reel.

Their design, which was granted U.S. Patent on October 10, 1972, took as its point of departure the realization that the simple ratchet was incapable of meeting today's demand for high-speed running. It employs instead a compound ratchet that separates the actions of running and retrieving.

The high-speed compound ratchet system is embodied in single-action reels of the trout model and also the intermediary, the latter also incorporating a finely adjustable drag that is completely enclosed and requires no lubrication. These reels are built with two considerations uppermost—the maximum in high-speed running and long life. They are capable of handling everything from salmon to bonefish, and are limited only by their line capacity from coping with such vigorous marine quarry as amberjack and tuna or the billfish.

While not yet released, the intermediate sizes of this model are expected to be available by the end of 1973. Of one-inch diameter, with huge line capacities using the modern Dacron backing, these reels are being built in three diameters, 3⅛, 3⅜, and 5⅝ inches.

Meanwhile, the Walker salmon and saltwater reels are the old standbys, produced on the original vom Hofe patterns but really redesigned during the years 1961 to 1963, with a tough waterproof drag developed to handle virtually anything that swims. Line capacities are, 2/0–200 yards of class 20 (20-pound backing); 3/0–400 yards, and 4/0–600 yards. Available on special order are 1/0–a 3⅛-inch diameter reel that matches up with a 4-ounce, 8-foot rod and handles 200 yards of class 18, and the 6/0–a 3⅞-inch diameter reel with a capacity of 800 yards of class 50 or 1200 yards of class 30.

The major difference between the salmon and the saltwater reels is the use of a stainless steel spool in the saltwater models. This spool is designed to handle backing-line core pressures of between 45,000 and 56,000 PSI–28 tons of pressure per square inch. The aluminum spool of the salmon models is nearly as tough but not fully corrosion-resistant. The hard-rubber fully machined end plates of both salmon and saltwater models are encased in silver bands, or rings, while the trout models have rings of tempered aluminum around their end plates.

The trout reels are in full production now, and according to Archie Walker represent today "the only trout reel in the world constructed from fully machined components of certified materials. The stainless steel shaft is permanent and compatible with bronze bearings machined to a two-ten-thousandths tolerance, the stainless steel cut gears in the ratchet mechanism are impervious to corrosion, and the life expectancy of the hard rubber end plates is fifty years or more. These reels are not a static storage component in your fly fishing ensemble; we now have a fully integrated component for playing a running fish with a 6X leader. Broken leaders are a thing of the past. We are able to offer a five-year factory replacement guarantee on every reel. We expect you to own and use our trout reel for the rest of your life."

The lightest and smallest of the four Walker trout reels is the T/R 1, "The Midge," of 2½-inch diameter and 3.755-ounce weight, which balances well with one-to-two-ounce rods and affords a line capacity of 100 yards of Dacron 10-pound backing and a number 3 or 4 line. Like all the other trout models it has a ¹⁵⁄₁₆-inch width. But because it is the smallest, it is the most expensive.

Model T/R 2, Light Trout, has a 2¾-inch diameter and 4.773-ounce weight, offering balance with one-and-a-half to two-and-a-half-ounce rods, with a line capacity of 150 yards of 10-pound backing and a number 3 or 4 line.

Model T/R 3, Standard Trout, recommended by the Walkers as the best all-around trout reel, has a 3-inch diameter and weighs 5.172 ounces, balancing with rods over two-and-a-half ounces, and providing 200 to 250 yards of 10-pound backing and a number 4 or 5 line.

Model T/R 4, Heavy Trout, is for those requiring an expanded line capacity. It is 3¼ inches in diameter and weighs 5.979 ounces. It balances with rods of three ounces and more and allows 200 to 250 yards of 10-pound backing with a number 5 or 6 line.

To recap, the full Walker line includes, in addition to the above four trout reels, and the three intermediary models (3⅛, 3⅜, and 3⅝ inches by 1 inch wide) that will be ready by year's end 1973, three saltwater models, with stainless steel spools, in 2/0, 3/0, and 4/0 sizes and a special big game 6/0 model, and five aluminum spooled salmon reels in 1/0, 2/0, 3/0, 4/0, and 6/0, of which the first and the last are special order reels. Both the salmon and the saltwater reels are produced in single and multiplying (2½ to 1) actions.

The Walkers are to reels as the late Jim Payne was to rods— sworn enemies of any least semblance of compromise and passionate adherents to a standard of craftsmanship that in the old vom Hofe days might have been taken for granted but in this slapdash age seems downright eccentric, not to say fanatical.

I've known their work for almost twenty years, since they first reconditioned two little gems that they found me blithely using at Turnwood on the Upper Beaverkill—an aluminum Conroy of 1878 and a vom Hofe not more than ten years younger—and for the last decade or so I've used one of their Midges, ever since they first developed it. I'll take their word for it that their new Midge, which supplants that first model, is a better reel, but I find it very hard to see how it could be. As far as I'm concerned, they long ago made good on their promise to make a reel that would last a lifetime.

WETZEL

From pioneer entomologist and bibliographer
to tarpon-fishing guide, a triple-gaited marvel

Charles Wetzel, author of *Practical Fly Fishing* (1943), *American Fishing Books* (1950), and *Trout Flies* (1955), veteran member of The Anglers' Club of New York, has been around for such a spell that on hearing his name today most fishermen would simply assume that he's long gone. Gone away, yes, but alive and well and guiding tarpon fishers at Marco Island in Florida, where he has been for over fifteen years, Charlie Wetzel is one more living proof of two assumptions— one, that boys named Charles have a better than average chance to grow up to be anglers, and two, that anglers have a better than average chance at happy and healthy longevity.

Wetzel's name would be far more widely known than it is today if one of the reprinters would pick up any or all of the above-mentioned books, none of which had any appreciable circulation, and all of which contain information that is worth having in far more common supply. A one-volume Wetzel would be wonderful.

Meanwhile, the heartiest of salutes is the least that is due to a rare old-timer, one who has literally known and done it all.

WINCHESTER PRESS

Winchester Press
460 Park Avenue
New York, New York 10022
(William Steinkraus, editor)

A welcome "third force" in sporting publications, Winchester Press benefits by the "endowment" inherent in being an affiliate of the fiscally mighty Olin Corporation, permitting it to take a chance on items that might be a dubious risk for such self-dependent operations as the Crown Classics or Freshet Press.

Our sport is so little and seldom subsidized, it can use all the breaks it can get.

Launched by Jim Rikhoff, of Midtown fame, within the purview of his corporate public relations responsibility for the parent company, Winchester Press has added some beautiful books to the sporting library. Some of them, like a medieval horsemanship manual (that Bill Steinkraus was evidently willing to go to any lengths just to get a copy for himself, or maybe to give to other members of the U.S. Equestrian Team), or the portfolio of Ernie Schwiebert's thirty salmon drawings in full color at a hundred bucks a throw, could hardly have been done with one eye on the box office, but by and large they've been an ornament to the literature, and there's no denying that they lend a certain tone that the sporting establishment in our demotic times would otherwise lack.

Of course, this latter consideration is almost automatically guaranteed by the mere presence of William Steinkraus as editor, although up to just recently "absence" would have been a more operative word, as his long captaincy of the U.S. Olympics Equestrian Team required month-long journeys, out of the office and usually out of the country. But even if he hadn't announced his retirement from this uniquely demanding post, obviously such a commanding figure is not one to whom the ordinary rules of office deportment were ever meant to apply. Aside from being able to ride a horse like a god, he also plays violin and viola like an angel. You don't ask anybody like that to punch in and out, do you? Editors in this field who have both knowledge and taste are very hard to come by, and Steinkraus is almost awesomely qualified.

John Olin, the éminence grise behind the corporate colossus that is behind Winchester Press, is one of the men most concerned with the Atlantic salmon emergency, and this too is an auspicious augury for the continued indulgence of Winchester Press, whenever it is moved to embark on an editorial venture that it deems worthwhile but could not endorse within ordinary limits of commercial risk.

A case in point is Winchester's reissue of *Trout Streams*, by the late Paul R. Needham, Annotated and with a Foreword by Carl E.

Bond. This 1938 classic of stream biology was updated in its nomenclature and annotated to make it current in the light of all the developments in fishery management and research since its original publication, and it is now comprehensive. At the same time, it was in no way "killed with improvements" and Dr. Needham's basic reasoning, intuition and opinion, and creative approach remain as brilliantly pertinent as ever. This book is one of the keystones of angling wisdom, and if Winchester Press hadn't printed anything else in the last four years that alone would have justified its existence.

It is to be hoped that Winchester will continue to put out its share of such sorely needed reissues, along with such excellent volumes of highly specialized appeal as Steve Raymond's definitive work, *Kamloops Trout*. There are titles that cry out for reclamation from the simioblivion of occasional listing at prohibitive price in rare book dealers' lists, such as Robb's *Notable Angling Literature*, Marston's *Walton and Some Earlier Writers on Fish and Fishing*, Radcliffe's *Fishing from the Earliest Times*, Scrope's inimitable *Days and Nights of Salmon Fishing in the Tweed,* and for that matter, why not a facsimile of Bethune's first American (1847) edition of *The Compleat Angler* itself? It's still one of the best of all the nearly four hundred editions of Walton to date, and it's next to unobtainable.

As long as there are so many worthy titles awaiting restoration to currency, some of which are poor risks commercially, the presence of a third force among specialized hunting and fishing publishers will by that token alone be eminently justifiable. With all due deference to Freshet and Crown, long may Winchester flourish.

WULFF

Wulff, Lee (1905–   ). Since as far back as 1939, Lee Wulff has been the answer man, if you wanted some new dodge or wrinkle that would make your fishing easier, simpler, handier, and more efficient.

In that year, the *Handbook of Freshwater Fishing* came out and our indebtedness to Lee Wulff began. It has grown by leaps and bounds, through his articles and films as well as books, until today it is almost mountainously awesome.

Probably no other single figure in the world of participant sports is as widely known to the public at large. And as for the angling public, certainly nobody else has had as much influence on methods and tackle, nor acted as effectively, both as pacesetter and as peace-maker, among its several divergent and sometimes nearly embattled groups.

His has been that greatest form of teaching: instruction by example.

The crux of his creed has been stated succinctly in *Fishing with Lee Wulff*, so it's better to give it to you in his own words than to try to put words in his mouth: The essence of the *sport* in fishing is to take the available fish and, by the use of very sporting tackle, demon-strate an uncommon skill. If the skill required is not uncommon, neither is the angler.

That's the simple common denominator of all his exploits of the last thirty years, and especially of the last eight or nine, when by example he has broadened the range of the fly rod's utility, and given it a new versatility—setting a few new records in the process—and at the same time brought fly fishermen, of both fresh- and saltwater persuasion, closer together than they have ever been before.

"Closer" probably isn't the right word. "Close" is more like it. Because their closeness, before Lee Wulff began showing them some identity of interests, was that of strange bulldogs.

Actually, of all the high deeds of the last three decades, this last is by far the most remarkable thing Lee Wulff has ever done, but it is like all the rest in that, up to the time he did it, nobody would have believed it could be done.

But to go back a bit, Lee Wulff's name, like Theodore Gordon's, first became known to the angling world as that of a fly. The Grey Wulff, and the White, and subsequently the Brown, the Grizzly, the Blonde, and the Royal, were known for a decade even before the appearance of his first book in 1939. And since the *Handbook* came out when he was thirty-four, you can readily see that he must have been a very young man when he first began to be famous as an angler.

I know my own awareness of his name, and indebtedness to him as an angler, began back in the days before this country's involvement in the Second World War, when a trick that I had picked up from the *Handbook* began enabling me, all of a sudden, to catch a lot more fish than I ever had before. Those were the days, if you can remember back that far, when we had to carry something to keep our leaders moist, because gut was brittle until soaked, and putting on a dry-gut tippet was a guarantee to lose immediately any fish you were lucky enough to hook. Those were also the days, pre-nylon, when we had to have something, like a chairback if nothing else was handy, to dry our silk lines on overnight, because a rotted spot in either line or backing was another sure way to instant loss of any fish sufficient to give you any play at all, even if you had been foresighted enough to soak the leader beforehand.

At Lee's suggestion, via the *Handbook,* dental floss was substituted for the terminal tippet, at the all-important last length of the knotted leader, right next to the fly itself, and the difference it made was not to be believed until you tried it. Gut is relatively stiff, even when saturated, so it was always hard to avoid drag, even on 4X, which was as fine as most of us could either get or in fact had ever even heard of in those primitive times, and also it came in relatively short lengths, so you had to have a lot of knots, at the place where you least could tolerate them, near as well as next to the fly.

The next improvement, equally simple but again something that nobody but Lee seemed to have thought of, was to cut the fly line off, at the reel, after making the longest cast that a test on the lawn showed you could make with it, and then to replace with backing the space that the useless bulk of the rest of the running line preempted on the core of the reel. Suddenly a line on a reel that you'd thought was limited to stream and pond fishing was "enlarged" to become perfectly adequate for the biggest fish in the broadest rivers, and your trout outfits were overnight postgraduated to use for steelhead and salmon.

But of even more universal application, since not everybody gets to go for the big fish that are for most people also in far places, was a stunt so obvious that you kicked yourself for never having thought of it before. Most fly fishermen in this country use a rod and reel exactly the way they use a knife and fork. They cast the rod with the right, or knife, hand, and then change over to hold it in the left, or fork, hand while they use the right hand to reel in the line, just as they use that hand to hold the fork, while actually eating, after having laid down the knife when it has finished, for the moment, its "casting" function of cutting up the particular portion of food about to be swallowed.

Europeans, much more sensibly, avoid all the useless motion by keeping both knife and fork in hand until they've finished with them, instead of picking up and laying down the one and switching the other back and forth throughout the main course of the meal.

Thanks to Lee again, a lot of us who may still be stupid at the table are at least much smarter on the stream, because we leave to our stronger right arm the job of controlling the rod at the one time it might make any difference—that is, while actually playing a fish— and let the weaker left hand do the less strategic job of turning the reel handle.

Nothing could be simpler. All you do is mount the reel in what to the less enlightened seems the upside down position on the rod's reel-seat, so that when you reel in toward yourself with your left hand, the line and the backing still accumulate on the reel spool in the clockwise direction, as they should, and as they would if you were reeling right-handed only if the reel were mounted the other way.

As frequent as the slips 'twixt cup and lip have been the freedom-achieving jumps by fish that have got away between hands, so to speak, during this needless and purely habitual shifting of the rod back and forth between casting and reeling.

If a time and motion study of the average angler's day were to be made, it would show the hundreds, even thousands, of waste motions that are made between actual hookings of fish. Such a study would of course dissuade all but the least sensible from further pursuit of an activity in which effort is so minimally rewarded. But it would also convince all but the most adamantine of those who were left that anything that can reduce those wasted movements by as much as two-thirds—back and forth and back again, where forth is all that's needed—is the obvious thing to do. I know I changed the mounting of my reel the day I read Lee's advice to do so—this was years before

I ever laid eyes on him—and I have never since even thought of going back to the old way.

It's ironical, though, that I cite these tricks, learned from Lee, which all seem calculated to make things easier, when the man's influence—his achievements and his records—has always been in the direction of doing things the hardest way possible.

As far back as 1938, Lee was attracting attention by doing things the hard way, as when he landed the first tuna ever taken on rod and reel in Newfoundland, in a makeshift boat and with a crew recruited for the occasion. That was on 130-pound tackle. Almost thirty years later he was back doing the same thing, but this time on 50-pound tackle. In the latter instance the weight ratio of fish to tackle had risen to an impressive level of very nearly 11 to 1, as the tuna in question, played through daylight and darkness, weighed 597 pounds.

In other words, Lee Wulff in his sixties was doing what he couldn't have dreamed of doing—and in fact what none of us then would have believed could be done—when he was in his thirties.

But even that feat, while in writing and on film it seems a terrific test of endurance, is less significant than some of his other angling exploits, because they have involved the kind of tackle and lure the average person would think of as suited only to trout and bass. As such, they actually do go even farther out, as demonstrations.

Lee has been doing these things at an age when other skilled performers, concert musicians for example, are thinking of retirement, and many businessmen, whether thinking about it or not, have been retired compulsorily. Lee was born, in case you're wondering about this point, at the beginning of 1905 (in Alaska, as it happens, and his schooling was in civil engineering at Stanford, followed by art at Julien's in Paris—nothing is usual about this man). As he says in *Fishing with Lee Wulff*, it's lucky that the sort of thing he's been doing "requires swift movements combined with excellent judgment more than youth or strength or dazzling speed."

(Just how speedy speed has to be before it's dazzling is a question you might feel like raising when you get to the page where Lee's timed speed with a cast from one of those "toothpick" rods he uses on salmon turns out to be ninety-six miles an hour, but let's leave that.)

As he says, "It's a glorious thing that a man whose hair has gone gray and whose muscular power is not what it once was can continue to improve his abilities to take on the top challenges of angling. Few sports or games offer such a lifetime of enduring activity and challenge."

Well, the part about the gray hair is true enough; his hair looks like pewter, and his features are as craggy as if carved on granite by somebody like Gutzon Borglum. And as for the longevity angle, all of us, if we were honest enough, would admit that we fish as a cheap form of life insurance, placing our bets on such long-winded favorites as Izaak Walton, who made ninety in a day when the actuarial statistics averaged about a third as much, and such latter-day distance runners as Hewitt and LaBranche, who were stream cronies for longer than the allotted three score and ten years.

But still the key word in that statement of Lee's is none of these, but the word "challenge."

The odds against success in angling must be longer than in almost anything else you can think of. Speaking of the study of anglers' motions, as we were a while back, there was one of those studies made, years ago, about warfare, that I remember said only one out of every thousand shots fired ever found, not even its mark, but any mark at all. I'm sure the score of anglers' casts, if there were any way to keep it, would make even such a random thing as gunfire equate with total efficacy.

Yet here is Lee, now and for the last thirty years, constantly trying to lengthen those odds, as if they weren't long enough, and what's more, getting us to like it. Somewhere in his writings he likens his kind of angling to golf, and such candor is becoming, because what he has been doing to and for the fly rod over all these years reminds me of that old definition of golf that, sparing you the dialect, is supposed to be of Scottish origin: The art of getting a small ball into a wee hole, with instruments ill adapted to the purpose.

Certainly no more appropriate comparison could have come to mind, when he went after tarpon with Stu Apte, armed with a bass rod and a Beaudex reel. Not even a Landex, which at least has a free-stripping release, to let the fish take line without making the reel handles turn (I say handles because the Landex has two), but a simple Beaudex single action, single handle, no drag, no adjustable brake, no nothing but the angler's thumb on the practically smoking line, if he has the temerity to put it there.

Lee has the temerity, all right, but actually the word is out of place in reference to the tarpon exploit, because this was really act one of Lee's three-act drama of demonstration of the fly rod's range, and the beginning of his successful attempt to bridge the gap that formerly estranged the flyrodders of fresh and salt water.

As has often been remarked on in the past, each of fishing's many forms has its devotees, so passionately addicted to their particular form of the pastime as to be anywhere from surlily noncommittal to downright contemptuous of its other forms. It often seems that the contempt of the trout purist for the spin or bait fisherman is only exceeded by the dedicated salmon angler's contempt for the trouter, which in turn is only exceeded by the tarpon man's contempt for both of them. As for the tarpon man, he in turn is looked down upon by the billfish anglers. Overlooked in this vicious circle is only the contention of the great but now almost forgotten Dr. James Alexander Henshall that the black bass is inch for inch and pound for pound the greatest fish that swims.

Be that as it may, Lee Wulff set out to attempt to turn this vicious circle of contempt into a charmed circle of content, by positing this simple angling equation: It is equally hard, and equally a matter of pride, to take on a fly rod, and with a fly, a tarpon of over a hundred pounds, on a leader of twelve-pound test, or a salmon of over sixteen pounds on a size sixteen fly, or a trout over twenty inches on a number twenty fly.

Having set up the charmed circle concept, it was of course like putting a chip on his shoulder, and having set up the tarpon claim, along with the new 16/16 goal for Atlantic salmon, against the already established 20/20 par for trouting skill, he simply had to go do it.

He had already, back in the fifties, well established his ability to take salmon of substantial size on featherweight tackle, and in his 1958 book, *The Atlantic Salmon,* he had shown by many records and pictures that these fish could be taken on small flies, although he had not actually taken heavier than sixteen-pound salmon at that point on anything smaller than a size fourteen spider. To his recollection, the best he'd done on a size sixteen fly was a fourteen-pounder. But that was such a small difference that it could always wait, whereas the tarpon goal was something else.

He took the tarpon, comfortably clearing by twenty-odd pounds the 100-pound mark that he had posed, at Islamorada in April 1963, setting a new world record in the process, though one that Stu Apte, having seen it done, fairly soon thereafter went out and bettered by a few pounds; then twice in the summer of 1964 Wulff cleared his own salmon mark by taking fish of twenty-two-and-three-fourths and twenty-four pounds on a size sixteen of a new skating fly of his own devising. That was on the Moise, a river he always hopes to fish wherever his schedules may require him to be, and he named the fly the Prefontaine in honor of his host there. The fly looks like a cross between his own stone fly and the one known as Whiskers. It has a surface-riding action, like a small hydroplane, as opposed to the semi-submerged swath of the Whiskers fly. The forepart is of white bucktail with white hackle aft, and with a ring of badger hackle slightly abaft of midship.

There remained, to close the circle of contempt completely, even though the charmed circle of equal skills had been rounded, only the ticklish question of the billfish, and Lee set out to see if this gap too could be bridged.

He set the second record with a ninety-five-pound Pacific sailfish at Pineas Bay in Panama in April of 1965, making the breakthrough by establishing the fact that sailfish could be taken with fly on an ordinary fly rod, without extension butt, fighting chair, or harness, and with a dragless reel, and though the fish was only of average size for the Pacific where the sailfish run larger than on the Atlantic side, it set the pattern, no matter for how long or short a time the record itself might stand. In other words, much more important than the size of that particular sailfish was the accomplishment of the feat to show that, on this tackle and under these conditions—which amounted to the taking of the freshwater fisherman's technique and limitations to sea—the sailfish could be fought.

It was this last factor which made this taking of the sailfish more significant than that of the even larger tarpon the year before. Tarpon had been fished for from skiffs, and in fact the playing of tarpon was almost exactly analogous to the playing of Atlantic salmon which also, everywhere except New Brunswick and Iceland, were much more often fished for from canoes than by wading.

It could be argued, and often has been, that one of these two fish is much rougher and tougher than the other, but leaving that aside, the fact is they both had been fished for much the same way before.

But the billfish had always been fished for quite another way, and it was a way that gave the starring role to the handler of the boat rather than to the angler. The latter, up to the point of the actual playing of the fish, had a passive and really secondary role, sitting in a fighting chair, lolling at his ease with perhaps a cold drink in one hand and his rod in the other—if indeed the rod were not stashed away in a socket on the stern—with plenty of time to pick it up and begin playing the fish after the snapping of the "clothespin" on the outrigger signaled the taking of the trolled bait. The captain was really doing all the work, finding the fish and, in effect, even getting the fish to strike by his strategic manipulation of the bait via the actions of the boat. And even after the point of getting the fish on, the captain's role in maneuvering the boat was always a crucial determinant of the angler's subsequent success or fortune. It was, in any case, if not always credited when things went right, at least invariably blamed if anything went wrong.

The one way to remove this variable element that flawed all arguments about the relative skills involved in deep-sea fishing for sailfish and tidal or coastal small-boat fishing for tarpon (and, indeed, river fishing for salmon) was to take everything from the captain's hands back into those of the angler.

Stop the boat. Cast to the fish. And let the angler, rather than the action of the boat, play the fish to the capitulation point where it could be either landed or released.

This leaves only one argument. Which is toughest to play on a fly rod, a tarpon or a sailfish or a salmon? True, the argument could start right up again, like the band resuming play after the intermission between sets, because the tarpon man and the sailfish man could be strident, nor is the salmon man famous for taciturnity.

But there is one word that alone could shut them all up, and indeed make them scurry like Indian natives at the shout of "Tiger!" and that is *marlin*.

Wow. Not on a fly rod?

Yes. So that was Lee's next move and that was the third record, at Salinas in Ecuador in April 1966. The fish weighed 148 pounds, but again, more important than the record in and of itself was the proving of the point that it could be done. Once the way was shown, others would be sure to go and do it too. And this, rather than any need to demonstrate any further his exceptional skill as an angler, was the underlying motivation for this series of exploits.

He had one really basic point to make, and he made it—by example. He wanted to show what the fly rod could do, by way of making all kinds of fly fishermen realize how identical their basic interests are and how much more sense it would make for them all to come together rather than to remain standoffishly apart.

After all, there is only one fish, the Atlantic salmon, that must by law, at least on our side of the water, be fished for only with the fly rod. Lee has fished for them every year since the early thirties, and daily when he ran a camp on the River of Ponds in Newfoundland, and he could have stuck to fishing for them the rest of his life. There's nobody who does it better or enjoys it more. And as far back as 1962, in his celebrated match with Jock Scott on the Dee in Aberdeenshire, he settled to everybody's satisfaction the consummate mastery of this regal quarry that can be effected with a six-foot rod weighing less than two ounces.

But he was also aware, that long ago, that the Sport of Kings was steadily pricing itself out of the reach of all but economic royalists, and that the kind of sport fishing that it exemplifies would soon be unavailable to all but the very few.

He used to talk about this Wednesday noons at the Midtown angling lunches in New York, and his one constant theme, to which he returned again and again with many variations, was that it's not the fish but the fishing that counts—the kind of fishing you do rather than the kind of fish you fish for—that's the essence of the sport in fishing. We could see then that there was a method in his madness, not just a mania for ever bigger fish on ever smaller rods, but the spreading of this attitude toward angling skill—call it the Atlantic salmon attitude if you like—into other forms of fishing, and with a consequent broadened range and wider use of the fly rod.

More or less directly out of these talks, these aims and ambitions which he so long and often formulated, came the founding of the Federation of Fly Fishermen, and in the wake of his own exploits with the fly rod in salt water came the adherence of saltwater fly fishermen to that one big organization. I don't mean that he did it alone, but that he struck the spark from which others caught fire.

Thus Lee moved a mighty step nearer to the attainment of his avowed hope that a considerable body of anglers would start being "prouder of the quality of their fishing abilities than of the abundance of their catches" and that fly fishing might "spread out from the streams, lakes, and salt water shorelines onto the deep blue sea."

In this light it can be seen that his approach to the sport of fly fishing is statesmanlike, for as he says, "Freshwater fishing is limited and most of our fresh waters are heavily fished. Where fishing is private it's expensive. The best Atlantic salmon fishing, for example, can cost the angler as much as $5,000 per week. But the seas are free and open."

That certainly makes long-range sense, in a world that's three-fifths wet. And it is consistent with that tenet of his sport fishing creed that puts the stress on "the available fish" as well as on "the uncommon skill."

But this is still only a part of the total score of what Lee Wulff has done "to and for the fly rod." For one thing, he took the ultralight rod out of the toy class and showed the way it could be used, on all but the very biggest fish and waters, at an actual advantage over the heavyweight rods that had been traditionally employed and considered necessary. To do this, he had to revolutionize the whole conception of the featherweight rod's nature and the manner of its use. Leonard made the first one, and put it at the foot of their Baby Catskill class, as a superdelicate trout rod: they actually featured it as a lady's rod. And when Paul Young took the same idea and beefed it up into a stronger-backboned creation, he called it the Midge, to indicate the tiny flies and gossamer tippets to which he thought its utility was limited.

But what Lee Wulff did with the light rod can only be likened to what Paganini first did with the Guarnerius violin—he brought things out of it that the maker could never have believed he had put in. Lee did a lot of experimenting with the possibilities of ultralight rods between 1940, when he wrote *Leaping Silver*, and 1958, when he published his findings on their capabilities in *The Atlantic Salmon*. He determined, first of all, that a salmon could be played with no rod at all, by way of establishing a *ne plus ultra* in the argument on behalf of ultralight tackle. Then, as a pilot, he applied the principles that he had found most successful, as a seat-of-the-pants bush flier, in outwitting the wind. He showed that if you can just make a fast enough cast, you can often take advantage of the vagaries of even strong winds, by getting a quick cast in between puffs. Timing himself with a stopwatch, and giving his best effort in turn to two of his own rods, both made by Orvis, he found that there was a distinct advantage in speed in his little six-and-a-half-foot, two-ounce rod over his nine-foot five-ouncer. The time he needed, on the former, to straighten out his back casts and forward casts averaged only 18.4 seconds, whereas on the latter, the larger rod, the operation took 23.1 seconds. But in the course of such experiments he found he could get the maximum performance out of the little rod only by, quite literally, "throwing the book away," and not using it as fly rods were used in the past, with the easy and graceful rocking-chair motion of the forearm alone, and with an imaginary book held between ribs and elbow, but by lifting it up and treating it as if it were an extension of his forefinger, with his whole arm as upthrust as that of the Statue of Liberty.

Watch Lee on a TV sports program, as he uses the little rod, and you'll see that on his back cast his arm is fully extended, a good eighteen to twenty inches behind his head—and on the forward cast his whole body goes forward in a follow-through like that of a baseball pitcher.

The style is heretical, but the results couldn't be more orthodox, as Lee gets off eighty-foot casts from a rod that Paul Young, its foremost maker, thought limited by its size and weight to casts of about thirty-five feet, or at most, and tempting fate every time, around forty.

But the same is true, to a degree, of everything else he has done, thought up, devised, or improved. We used to fear drag on a floating fly as a fate worse than death to its fish-taking chances, until Lee introduced the Portland Creek hitch, as a means of imparting a sort of bias motion to a wet fly, with the unexpected result that a lot of us found that a riffled hitch on a dry fly, creating a wake like a toy motor boat, as it was pulled back just beneath the surface on the retrieve, provoked more strikes and took more fish than it had in the course of its natural float.

And we used to wear cumbersome fishing jackets, until Lee Wulff had the original inspiration for the first tackle-pack vest, with its blessed provision for all needed gear above the waterline when wearing chest waders.

For that matter, we all used to believe those horror stories about guys in waders found drowned, feet up and heads down, after wading accidents, until Lee deflated that myth. Again you might say he did it the hard way, by diving off a high bridge into a deep pool of the Battenkill, wearing chest waders, to prove that the air in them will not upend a man who has taken a spill.

But the innovation that best expresses Lee Wulff's fishing philosophy, which he has summarized in a sentence as "in this sport of catching fish I like to do the entire job myself," is beyond a doubt his invention of the tailer, that spring-steel device which, when looped over the tail of a large fish, obviates the need of either the clumsy and fish-scaringly awkward net or the cruelly disfiguring and often lethal gaff. It also implements another tenet of his angling creed, expressed in his words "these fish are too valuable to be caught only once," as a tailed fish, momentarily paralyzed and completely subdued, and thus spared the injurious thrashings induced by either net or gaff or even sometimes by beaching, can be returned to the water completely unharmed.

And that's another practice that Lee pioneered (though of course he didn't originate it) long before the establishment of the first stretches of public waters restricted to fly fishing only and before the first designation of areas where the Fishing for Fun concept—confining all angling to catch-and-release—is now practiced in a number of states.

It's a disservice to any man to make him sound too much like Goody Two-shoes, and I realize that any attempt to characterize Lee Wulff as a fisherman must seem like a strained effort to achieve the personification of the Complete Angler, but the best and worst I can do, to counterbalance any such tendency, is to say that to see Lee fishing is to shatter the theory, as formulated by Walton or anybody since, that angling is the contemplative man's recreation.

Lee on a stream is as constantly in motion as the pacing wild animal in a cage. As he says of himself, somewhere in *Fishing with Lee Wulff*, he's a mover. He appears to be of a restless and seemingly impatient disposition. Of course you know that no man can really be impatient who will try a hundred casts to tease a single fish into taking one of a succession of flies, and he has done this often on salmon rivers. But watching him on a trout stream I could never think of a word more suited to him than Fish Hawk. I didn't say Hog, because he puts them back as fast as he brings them in. But while you, the contemplative type, are working on three fish, say, he'll have darted around enough to swoop down on fourteen. (That was an actual and honest score card, the last time I counted.)

But the very fact that he can still get excited in the pursuit of twelve-inch trout, after he's caught individual fish weighing over a quarter of a ton, is to me one of the strongest character counts in his favor. Expert as he has become, he still has to be considered the farthest possible remove from a purist, and if my harping on the fly rod has had the effect of making him seem so, then I hasten to apologize. Why, there's even a chapter on worm fishing in *Fishing with Lee Wulff*, and if you look carefully you'll find more than one reference to spinning that is anything but derogatory.

Atlantic salmon still come first in Lee's book, and undoubtedly they always will, though he confesses an occasional sneaky yen to go bonefishing. But for all his insistence on quality fishing, his appetite for the sport would still have to be categorized as more gourmand than gourmet. It isn't that he has to yield to anybody in the ability to appreciate and enjoy the best fishing, but rather that his attitude remains the wholesome one that while some fishing is obviously much better, still any fishing is better than no fishing.

So those whose fishing haunts and habits will never take them within leagues of either trout or salmon country need not feel shut out of Lee Wulff's collected pages. They have only to leaf past the portions devoted to the salmonids and they'll find that when they came to their fish, be they bass or pike or even walleyes, Lee will be right there beside them, acting as if he'd never had more fun in his life and that a chance to go fishing, any kind of fishing, were the rarest of treats.

That he should have a wife who shares his feeling for the sport would seem to be too much to be any man's portion, combining into one incredible parlay such a triple feature as vocation, hobby, and mate. But in Joan Salvato, as no angler needs to be told, the All-American angler has found his counterpart.

Yes, you really would say that this exceeds all likelihood.

But then, as I've earnestly tried to suggest, and every page of his book attests, nothing that has to do with fishing is too much for Lee Wulff.

*Y*OUNG

Paul H. Young Co.
c/o Jack Young
14039 Peninsula Drive
Traverse City, Michigan 49684

Young, Paul H. (1888–1960). Rod maker and flytier who came originally from Arkansas and started making fishing tackle in Duluth in 1914, moving to Detroit in 1921, with a shop that was at first devoted primarily to taxidermy, Paul Young was venerated in the last decade of his life as "the Stradivari of the Midge Rod" and died enjoying near-legendary status as a cult figure. Never a fanatic on the subject of light tackle, he developed the Midge rod at six-and-a-quarter feet and an average weight of one-and-three-quarters ounces for use with HEH (Number four) line, 5X and 6X leaders, and size eighteen to twenty-four flies purely as an answer to what he regarded as the highly specialized needs of the sophisticated fly fishermen of the limestone streams of Pennsylvania. He offered it first in the early nineteen fifties as only one of a dozen different designs of fly rods that he made, spanning a wide range of lengths and weights, and was surprised and frankly incredulous when he first heard of its use as a salmon rod.

He rather grudgingly acknowledged its best-seller status in his line of rods, as for his own use he greatly preferred the Parabolic 16, an "all-purpose" rod of eight feet and three-and-three-quarters ounces weight, and regarded the use of a "toothpick" like his Midge for long casts and large fish as something of a perversion of its natural purpose. He testily refused either to claim, or even to acknowledge, that he had pioneered the small-rod craze, pointing out that the H. L. Leonard line had featured a Baby Catskill rod, at six feet and fifteen-sixteenths of an ounce, several years before he made his first Midge, and that Wm. Mills and Sons had even advertised it as "the world's smallest fly rod." Admitting that his Midge was clearly out of the "baby rod" class, which he considered "about as practical as a wet noodle," he still contended that it was being put to uses for which he neither intended it nor considered it suitable, and he was both amused and puzzled when he saw the term "midge rod" come into generic use, as categorizing all split-cane rods with light mountings, measuring under seven feet and weighing two ounces or less, and thus outgrow its original application to a specific model in his line.

Other Paul Young light rods are the Driggs, at seven-feet-two-inch length and two-and-seven-eighths-ounces weight, a much stouter stick than the Midge, the Perfectionist at seven-and-a-half feet and two-and-a-half ounces (really a Midge at extended length), and the Martha Marie (named for his wife) of seven-and-a-half feet and three-and-five-hundredths ounces when supplied with featherweight fittings. The other Young rods ranged up to the Texas General at eight-and-a-half feet and five-and-a-half ounces and the Bobby Doerr at nine feet and six ounces.

Paul Young didn't live to see the momentary craze for a still smaller category, the Bantam rods which were turned out by a number of makers in the mid-sixties at four feet four inches and weighing exactly one ounce. As made by Hardy and Orvis, and even in a couple of instances by Payne, these are treasured by light tackle devotees but are now generally no longer made except on special order.

The thing that Paul Young is best remembered by, aside from his monument, the Midge rod, is his unique creation, the Strawman nymph, an impression via clipped deer hair of the rather shaggy look of the straw housing of the caddis nymph at one stage of the process of becoming a fly.

The Paul Young Company's business locations in the Detroit area ran afoul of highway developments in the suburbs so often in the years following his death that it was finally moved to Traverse City, where his younger son John, of whom Paul always said that "he was the one born with bamboo in his blood," carries on as the family rod maker.

The outstanding attribute of the Young light rod, as exemplified most notably in the Midge and its longer mate, the Perfectionist, is the attainment of backbone and power, to permit the vigorous use of the double-line-haul for long casts, without sacrifice of the "slender ankle" effect of the last foot of the delicate tip, affording accuracy and finesse in fishing "fine and far-off." It is the exploitation of the first of those two qualities, by their use for grilse and salmon, and the ignoring of the second, which can only be brought into play in the upper reaches of trouting, that went against the artistic grain of their maker, and made him such a reluctant exponent, less royal than his courtiers, of the craze for ever-bigger fish on ever-lighter tackle, of which he was at one time regarded as the king.

ZERN, ED

The Last Word

"Exit, Laughing," as regular readers of *Field & Stream* well know, is the jester's stool, only very occasionally turned to pulpit, that Ed Zern mounts monthly. Consistently it makes you smile, and frequently it makes you slap your thigh and double up in a real old-fashioned belly laugh. The author of *To Hell with Fishing, How to Tell Fish from Fishermen* and, most recently, *A Fine Kettle of Fish Stories*, is an ex-advertising-agency executive. He was a very fine advertising copywriter when he felt like it, which he hasn't for some while now. But long-memoried readers may recall his ads for Nash cars. There's one at least that I'll never forget, which contained a passage to this effect:

"They tell me this car has a body by Pinin Farina . . . Shucks, I think I'll buy it anyway."

Kidding the product later became a more or less routine gambit, but when Ed Zern did it first it represented a radical departure from accepted advertising practice. In his monthly column Zern kids everybody and everything, but there is one subject in which his kidding is on the square, and that's conservation. His most memorable effort in this respect was the time he devoted the full page of "Exit, Laughing" to a parody that still seems to me, some years afterward, to be a better and more timely benediction for this whole section than anything I could possibly devise. With his permission, I give it to you here, just as it appeared on the last page of *Field & Stream*, minus the music, which you know by heart anyway:

America the What?

Ed Zern, 1910–   *Samuel A. Ward, 1847–1903*

O beautiful for specious guys Who piously declare,
"That's progress' price," as fact'ry stacks Spew poison in the air.
America, America, Smog smears its grays on thee;
We stain thy prime with soot and grime And strontium ninety!

O beautiful for strip-mine pit Where once the laurel bloomed;
For brooklets running sulphur-stained And rotten egg perfumed.
America, America, On bureaucrats cry shame;
For canyons dammed and us flim-flamm'd In Reclamation's name!

O beautiful for scenery Black'd out by billboard's span;
For nauseous stink of sew'rs we drink Where once pure rivers ran.

America, America, What thieves thy people be,
Who rob from earth their children's birth-Right, Nature's legacy!

O beautiful for neon sign By big dam power lit;
For carrion of countless cars On hillside charnel pit.
America, America, Whom ev'ry gully robs;
Thy landscape slopped with litter dropped By (let us face it) slobs!

O beautiful for highways broad, With beer cans tightly hemm'd;
For marshes drained and dollars gained And water fowl condemn'd.
America, America, God grant us sanity;
With wealth we're blest, yet foul our nest And then chop down the tree!

POSTLUDE

Wherein we bid each other goodbye

Well, angler, we've reached the end of this stretch. Our catch may not have been anything to get our pictures in the papers, but the time we spent together conceivably kept us out of worse mischief that we might have got into, and at least nobody got hurt.

Coming to the end of a book like this is like coming to the end of a day's fishing. I seldom hang up my rods without thinking of two songs of my childhood; one, that my Aunt Lizzie used to sing me to sleep with when I was really a tike, had a refrain that began with

> *Hang up the fiddle and the bow,*
> *Lay down the shovel and the hoe,*

and though I had none of those implements, nor even knew any who had, I used to look around to see those actions that were fixed in my mind with the meaning that it was time to close my eyes; the other, that I remember my mother singing as she sat at the piano, was a sentimental song, by Carrie Jacobs-Bond, of the era when I was only a little older, that began

When you come to the end of a perfect day.

Undoubtedly we all have little wispy chords of memory like this that are faintly twanged whenever we do some of these accustomed things that we have done for years and hope to go on doing as long as we can. And similarly for all the other moments that we spend, at a pond or on a stream, going through all the motions so long practiced that they become one with movements that are so habitual as to seem almost instinctive or intuitive, actions of which we are barely more conscious than we are of our own breathing. To some degree, but not altogether, dependent upon whether those actions of ours are rewarded with success, our thought patterns, too, like our physical motions while fishing, tend to slide into well-worn ruts, so that a lot of our ruminations over the hours devoted to this pastime are as idle and formless as humming. When asked what tune you're humming, you have to stop and think, and often you can't, for the life of you, place it.

More often than not the thoughts of an angler, at least while he's actually fishing, would be overpriced at a penny. The angler's mind, while making those countless casts, is so often lulled by the repetitive motion, that it is reduced to a state of suspended mental animation, a trancelike level of slowed-down activity, that is the next thing to that suspension of thought induced by sleep. That's why I could never really see the aptness of old Izaak's rather pretentious tag for it as "the contemplative man's recreation." Walton was, obviously, a most exceptional man, but I still think that his real "contemplating" was done at home, with purposive intent, in his study, rather than on the banks of the Dove.

The thoughts we have while fishing are, almost invariably, idle thoughts, which is undoubtedly a large part of the reason we find it such a delightful contrast to work. Most of us do more real hard work while wielding a rod than we would ever do with shovel or hoe, but the blessed difference is that we don't have to do it and therefore don't mind doing it, and don't think of it as work at all. I'd drop in my tracks if I had to do in a factory or on a farm half of what I do without a thought on the Miramichi or the Esopus.

The mind of an angler is like a large roomy attic—a room that you could call empty except for all the stuff it's strewn with, most of which is little used and seldom looked at. A lot of it is there just because it "might someday come in handy," though most of it never does. Still and moreover, it's a mighty pleasant place to get away from it all.

Farewells, I know, should not be protracted. So all I'm saying is that I'd be pleased and honored if, among the oddments that I've spread out over these pages, you will have found some things that you will now feel like keeping in mind.

Fifty Books
for a Fly Fisherman

In the chapter of *The Well-Tempered Angler* called "The Angling Heritage," I gave a list of thirty books that I thought constituted a short but comprehensive outline of angling literature and made the statement that any man who has read these thirty books could feel entitled to regard himself as a well-read angler.

The thirty titles were divided into three groups of ten each, as Classic, Vintage, and Modern, ranging in point of time from 1496 to 1963, and I still say it wouldn't hurt any angler a bit to read, or reread, all thirty of these books.

By way of supplementing and updating my basic thirty, I've added twenty more that seem to me, out of the hundreds that have since come from the presses, to be worthy of keeping the first thirty company. Two of them are old, and are here simply because I should have found some way to squeeze them into the first thirty.

Mottram is the real "sleeper" of British angling books of the past century, and Thad Norris is the cornerstone of our angling literature. There is no American counterpart to Walton, for none of our fishing books has ever achieved world stature as literature. For that matter, neither has any other English fishing book, as Walton is unique. But it is hard to cite any fishing book, Walton's not excepted, that constitutes a more engaging self-portrait of a sportsman than Uncle Thad's.

The most unjustly neglected book among the last twenty is the Brian Curtis, which deserves to be a bestseller; the most charming are the William Humphrey and the Ben Hur Lampman; the most scholarly, the McClane and the McDonald; the most innovative, technically, are the Swisher and Richards and the Leonard Wright; the most surprising, as departures from their authors' previous works, are the Brooks and the Schwiebert; the most endearingly personal are the Sparse Grey Hackle and the Robert Traver; the most arrestingly original, not only of this year but indeed of many a year, is the Sosin and Clark—in fact, *Through the Fish's Eye* is the eye-opener not just of the season but of the decade. You'll feel as if you'd never read a fishing book before.

But put them all together and I think they make a pretty good case for the old contention that some of the best fishing to be found anywhere is to be found in print.

Classic

Dame Juliana Berners: *A Treatyse of Fysshinge Wyth an Angle,* 1496.

Thomas Best: *A Concise Treatise on the Art of Angling,* 1787.

"John Bickerdyke" (Charles Henry Cook): *The Book of the All-Around Angler,* 1889.

Richard & Charles Bowker: *The Art of Angling Improved in All Its Parts, Especially Fly Fishing,* 1758.

Gervase Markam: *Country Contentments,* 1631.

Alfred Ronalds: *The Fly-Fisher's Entomology*, 1836.

Thomas Salter: *The Angler's Guide*, 1814.

J(ohn) S(mith): *The True Art of Angling*, 1696.

*Izaak Walton & Charles Cotton: *The Compleat Angler*, 1676.

Vintage

*Sir Humphrey Davy: *Salmonia, or Days of Fly-Fishing*, 1828.

Francis Francis: *A Book on Angling*, 1867.

Sir Edward Grey (Viscount Grey of Falloden): *Fly-fishing*, 1899.

Frederic M. Halford: *Dry-fly Fishing in Theory and Practice*, 1889.

*Edward R. Hewitt: *A Trout and Salmon Fisherman for 75 Years*, 1950.

*George M. L. LaBranche: *The Dry Fly and Fast Water* and *The Salmon and The Dry Fly* (together in one volume), 1951.

*"Jock Scott" (D. G. H. Rudd): *Greased Line Fishing for Salmon*, 1935.

Wm. Scrope: *Days and Nights of Salmon-fishing in the Tweed*, 1843.

G. E. M. Skues: *The Way of a Trout With a Fly*, 1921.

Eric Taverner: *Troutfishing from All Angles*, 1929.

Modern

*Ray Bergman: *Trout*, revised edition, 1952.

*Chas. K. Fox: *This Wonderful World of Trout*, 1963.

*A. R. Grove, Jr.: *The Lure and Lore of Troutfishing*, 1957.

A. J. McClane: *The Practical Fly Fisherman*, 1953.

*John McDonald: *The Complete Fly Fisherman* (the *Notes and Letters of Theodore Gordon*), 1947.

*Vincent Marinaro: *A Modern Dry Fly Code*, 1950.

*Charles Ritz: *A Fly Fisher's Life*, 1959.

*Ernest Schwiebert: *Matching the Hatch*, 1955.

*Helen Shaw: *Fly Tying*, 1963.

*Lee Wulff: *The Atlantic Salmon*, 1958.

Selective & Supplemental
(including books published in the last ten years)

*John Atherton. *The Fly and the Fish*. New York: Freshet Press, 1971.

*Joe Brooks. *Trout Fishing*. New York: Harper & Row, 1972.

Brian Curtis. *Life Story of the Fish, His Manners and Morals*. New York: Dover, 1961.

*Sparse Grey Hackle (Alfred W. Miller). *Fishless Days, Angling Nights*. New York: Crown Publishers, 1971.

*John Waller Hills. *A History of Fly Fishing for Trout*. New York: Freshet Press, 1972.

*William Humphrey. *The Spawning Run*. New York: Alfred A. Knopf, 1970.

*Edward C. Janes. *Fishing with Lee Wulff*. New York: Alfred A. Knopf, 1971.

*Preston Jennings. *A Book of Trout Flies*. New York: Crown Publishers, 1971.

Ben Hur Lampman. *A Leaf from French Eddy*. Portland, Ore.: Touchstone Press, 1965.

*Nick Lyons. *The Seasonable Angler*. New York: Funk & Wagnalls, 1970.

* Indicates reissue or current availability.

*Nick Lyons, ed. *Fisherman's Bounty* (an anthology). New York: Crown Publishers, 1971.

*A. J. McClane. *McClane's Standard Fishing Encyclopedia.* New York: Holt, Rinehart, and Winston, 1965.

*John McDonald. *Quill Gordon.* New York: Alfred A. Knopf, 1972.

J. C. Mottram. *Fly Fishing, Some New Arts & Mysteries.* London: The Field Press, 1915.

Thad Norris. *An American Angler's Book.* Philadelphia: 1864.

*Ernest Schwiebert. *Remembrances of Rivers Past.* New York: The Macmillan Co., 1972.

*Mark Sosin and John Clark. *Through the Fish's Eye.* New York: Harper & Row, 1973.

*Doug Swisher and Carl Richards. *Selective Trout.* New York: Crown Publishers, 1971.

Robert Traver. *Trout Madness.* New York: St. Martin's Press, 1960.

*Leonard M. Wright, Jr. *Fishing the Dry Fly as a Living Insect.* (The Thinking Man's Guide to Trout Angling) New York: E. P. Dutton, 1972.

* Indicates reissue or current availability.

Bibliography

SELECTIVE AND SUPPLEMENTAL

*(confined to pertinent books, published
between 1963 and 1973, but including reissues)*

Annesley, Patrick, ed. *Hardy's Book of Fishing.* New York: E. P. Dutton & Co., Inc., 1971.

Arnov, Boris. *Fishing for Everyone.* New York: Hawthorn Books, Inc., 1970.

Atherton, John. The *Fly and the Fish,* Rockville Centre, N.Y.: Freshet Press Inc., 1971.

Babson, Stanley M. *Bonefishing*. New and rev. ed. New York: Winchester Press, 1972.

Ball, John W. *Casting and Fishing the Artificial Fly*. Caldwell, Idaho: Caxton Press, 1972.

Bates, Joseph D., Jr. *Atlantic Salmon Flies and Fishing*. Harrisburg, Pa.: Stackpole Books, 1970.

Bay, Kenneth. *Salt Water Flies* (with life-size sequence photos, by Hermann Kessler). New York: J. B. Lippincott Co., 1972.

Blaisdell, Harold F. *The Philosophical Fisherman*. Boston: Houghton Mifflin Company, 1969.

Bradford, Charles. *The Brook Trout and the Determined Angler* (reissue). Rockville Centre, N.Y.: Freshet Press Inc., 1971.

Brooks, Charles E. *Larger Trout for the Western Fly Fisherman*. Cranbury, N.J.: A. S. Barnes & Co., 1970.

Brooks, Joe. *Trout Fishing*. New York: Harper & Row, 1972.

Chandler, Leon, ed. *There's No Fishing Like Fly Rod Fishing*, by L. James Bashline, Leon Chandler, Donald DuBois, Bob Elliott, Larry Green, Roger Latham, Tom McNally, Mark Sosin, Charles F. Waterman, with Foreword by Bing Crosby and drawings by Dick Jennings. New York: Richards Rosen Press (for the Cortland Line Company), 1972.

Coman, Dale Rex. *Pleasant River*. New York: W. W. Norton & Co., Inc., 1966.

Combs, Trey. *Steelhead Trout*. Seattle: Salmon-Trout-Steelheader, 1972.

Corodimas, Peter. *In Trout Country* (an anthology). Boston: Little, Brown and Company, 1971.

Cross, Reuben. *The Complete Fly-Tier*. Rockville Centre, N.Y.: Freshet Press Inc., 1971.

Davy, Sir Humphry. *Salmonia* (reissue). New York: Freshet Press Inc., 1971.

Dennys, John. *The Secrets of Angling* (reissue). Rockville Centre, N.Y.: Freshet Press Inc., 1971.

Dick, Lenox. *The Art and Science of Fly Fishing*. New York: Winchester Press, 1971.

Dubé, Jean-Paul. *Let's Save Our Salmon*. Montreal: Atlantic Salmon Association, 1972.

Fennelly, John F. *Steelhead Paradise*. Vancouver, B.C.: Mitchell Press, 1963.

Ferris, George. *Fly Fishing in New Zealand*. Auckland, New Zealand: William Heinemann Ltd., 1972

Flick, Art, ed. *Art Flick's Master Fly-Tying Guide*, by Art Flick, Ed Koch, Lefty Kreh, Ted Niemeyer, Carl Richards, Ernest Schwiebert, Helen Shaw, Doug Swisher, and Dave Whitlock. New York: Crown Publishers, Inc., 1972.

————. *Art Flick's New Streamside Guide to Naturals and Their Imitations* (reissue). New York: Crown Publishers, Inc. 1969.

Fox, Charles K. *Rising Trout*. Carlisle, Pa.: Foxcrest, 1967.

————. *This Wonderful World of Trout* (reissue). Rockville Centre, N.Y.: Freshet Press Inc., 1971.

Freeman, James. *Practical Steelhead Fishing*. Cranbury, N.J.: A. S. Barnes & Co., 1972.

Fulsher, Keith. *Fishing the Thunder Creek Series*. New York: Freshet Press Inc., 1972.

Gerlach, Rex. *Fly Fishing the Lakes*. New York: Winchester Press, 1972.

Gingrich, Arnold. *The Well-Tempered Angler*. New York: Alfred A. Knopf, Inc., 1965.

———— (ed). *The Gordon Garland*. New York: Theodore Gordon Flyfishers, 1965.

———— (ed). *American Trout Fishing, by Theodore Gordon and a Company of Anglers* (trade edition of *The Gordon Garland*). New York: Alfred A. Knopf, Inc., 1966.

Grant, George F. *The Art of Weaving Hair Hackles for Trout Flies*. Privately printed, 1971.

————. *Montana Trout Flies*. Privately printed, 1971.

Grove, Alvin R., Jr. *The Lure and Lore of Trout Fishing* (reissue). Rockville Centre, N.Y.: Freshet Press Inc., 1972.

Haig-Brown, Roderick. *Fisherman's Fall*. New York: William Morrow and Co., 1964.

———— *A Primer of Fly Fishing.* New York: William Morrow and Co., 1964.

Hewitt, Edward R. *A Trout and Salmon Fisherman for 75 Years* (boxed with LaBranche's *The Dry Fly and Fast Water* & *The Salmon and the Dry Fly*). Croton-on-Hudson: Van Cortlandt Press, 1972.

Hidy, V. S. *The Pleasures of Fly Fishing,* with a foreword by Sparse Grey Hackle. New York: Winchester Press, 1972.

Hills, John Waller. *A History of Fly Fishing for Trout* (reissue). Rockville Centre, N.Y.: Freshet Press Inc., 1972.

Horne, Bernard S. *The Compleat Angler 1653–1967: A New Bibliography.* Pittsburgh: University of Pittsburgh Press, 1970.

Hughes, Stephen Ormsby. *Tight Lines and Dragon Flies.* New York: J. B. Lippincott Co., 1972.

Humphrey, William. *The Spawning Run.* New York: Alfred A. Knopf, Inc., 1970.

Janes, Edward C. *Fishing With Lee Wulff,* with an Introduction by Arnold Gingrich. New York: Alfred A. Knopf, Inc., 1971.

————. *Fishing with Ray Bergman.* New York: Alfred A. Knopf, Inc., 1970.

Jennings, Preston J. *A Book of Trout Flies* (reissue), with a new Introduction by Ernest Schwiebert. New York: Crown Publishers, Inc., 1971.

Kilbourne, S. A. *Game Fishes of the United States* (20 Kilbourne paintings, with text by G. Brown Goode). New York: Winchester Press, 1972.

Knight, John Alden. *Moon Up—Moon Down: The Story of the Solunar Theory* (reissue). Montoursville, Pa.: Solunar Sales Co., 1972.

————, and Knight, Richard Alden. *The Complete Book of Fly Casting.* New York: G. P. Putnam's Sons, 1963.

Koch, Ed. *Fishing the Midge,* with an Introduction by Joe Brooks. Rockville Centre, N.Y.: Freshet Press Inc., 1973.

Kreh, Lefty, and Sosin, Mark. *Practical Fishing Knots.* New York: Crown Publishers, Inc., 1972.

Kroll, Charles. *Squaretail*. New York: Vantage Press, 1972.

LaBranche, George M. L. *The Dry Fly and Fast Water* and *The Salmon and the Dry Fly* (boxed with Hewitt's *A Trout and Salmon Fisherman for 75 Years*) (reissue). Croton-on-Hudson: Van Cortlandt Press, 1972.

Lamb, Dana S. *Bright Salmon and Brown Trout*. Barre, Mass.: Barre Publishers, 1964.

———. *Green Highlanders and Pink Ladies*. Barre, Mass.: Barre Publishers, 1971.

———. *Not Far from the River*. Barre, Mass.: Barre Publishers, 1967.

———. *On Trout Streams and Salmon Rivers*. Barre, Mass.: Barre Publishers, 1963.

———. *Some Silent Places Still*. Barre, Mass.: Barre Publishers, 1966.

———. *Woodsmoke and Water Cress*. Barre, Mass.: Barre Publishers, 1965.

Lampman, Ben Hur. *A Leaf from French Eddy*. Portland, Ore.: Touchstone Press, 1965.

Leisenring, James, and Hidy, Vernon S. *The Art of Tying the Wet Fly and Fishing the Flymph* (reissue). New York: Crown Publishers, Inc., 1971.

Leiser, Eric. *Fly Tying Materials*, with an Introduction by Art Flick. New York: Crown Publishers, Inc., 1973.

Lynde, John G. *34 Ways to Cast a Fly*. Cranbury, N.J.: A. S. Barnes & Co., 1971.

Lyons, Nick. *The Seasonable Angler*. New York: Funk & Wagnalls, Inc., 1970.

——— ed. *Fisherman's Bounty* (an anthology). New York: Crown Publishers, Inc., 1971.

McClane, A. J. *McClane's Standard Fishing Encyclopedia*. New York: Holt, Rinehart & Winston, Inc., 1965.

———. *Field & Stream International Fishing Guide* (annual). New York: Holt, Rinehart & Winston, Inc.

McDonald, John. *The Complete Fly Fisherman* (The Notes and Letters of Theodore Gordon), with an Introduction by Arnold Gingrich (reissue). New York: Theodore Gordon Flyfishers, 1970.

————. *The Origins of Angling* (and a new printing of the Treatise of Fishing with an Angle, attributed to Dame Juliana Berners). New York: Doubleday and Co., 1963.

————. *Quill Gordon,* with paintings by Atherton and Howard. New York: Alfred A. Knopf, Inc., 1972.

Macdougall, Arthur R., Jr. *The Trout Fisherman's Bedside Book.* New York: Simon and Schuster, 1963.

Marinaro, Vincent C. *A Modern Dry-Fly Code* (reissue). New York: Crown Publishers, Inc., 1971.

Marshall, Howard. *Reflections on a River.* London: H. F. & G. Witherby Ltd., 1967.

Marshall, Mel. *Steelhead.* New York: Winchester Press, 1973.

Melner, Samuel (with Hermann Kessler). *Great Fishing Tackle Catalogs of the Golden Age,* with commentary by Sparse Grey Hackle. New York: Crown Publishers, Inc., 1972.

Morris, Dan (and Norman Strung). *The Fisherman's Almanac.* New York: The Macmillan Company, 1970.

Needham, Paul R. *Trout Streams* (reissue). New York: Winchester Press, 1970.

Netboy, Anthony. *The Atlantic Salmon, A Vanishing Species?* Boston: Houghton Mifflin Co., 1968.

Ovington, Ray. *Tactics on Trout.* New York: Alfred A. Knopf, Inc., 1969.

Poltroon, Milford "Stanley." *How To Fish Good.* New York: Winchester Press, 1971.

Pringle, Lawrence. *Wild River.* New York: J. B. Lippincott Company, 1972.

Raymond, Steve. *Kamloops: An Angler's Study of the Kamloops Trout.* New York: Winchester Press, 1972.

Rikhoff, James, and Peper, Eric. *Fishing Moments of Truth* (an anthology). New York: Winchester Press, 1973.

Ritz, Charles. *A Fly Fisher's Life,* with a Foreword by Ernest Hemingway and an Introduction by Arnold Gingrich. London: Max Reinhardt, The Bodley Head, 1972. New York: Crown Publishers, Inc., 1973.

Sage, Dean. *The Ristigouche and Its Salmon Fishing, with a Chapter on Angling Literature.* Second, augmented, edition, with an Introduction by Arnold Gingrich and a Notice of Dean Sage by his grandnephew, Dewitt L. Sage. Goshen, Conn.: Anglers and Shooters Press, 1973.

Sawyer, Frank. *Nymphs and the Trout.* New York: Crown Publishers, Inc., 1972.

Schaldach, William J. *Currents & Eddies* and *Coverts & Casts.* Boxed set of the earlier Schaldach classics. Rockville Centre, N.Y.: Freshet Press Inc., 1971.

———. *The Wind on Your Cheek,* with an Introduction by Arnold Gingrich, Rockville Centre, N.Y.: Freshet Press Inc., 1973.

Scholes, David. *The Way of an Angler.* Brisbane, Queensland, Australia: Jacaranda Press, 1963.

——— and Neil Robson. *Tasmanian Angler.* Launzeston, Tasmania: Foot and Playsted, 1973.

Schwiebert, Ernest. *Nymphs.* New York: Winchester Press, 1973.

———. *Remembrances of Rivers Past.* New York: The Macmillan Company, 1972.

———. *Salmon of the World,* with an Introduction by Arnold Gingrich. New York: Winchester Press, 1971.

Scott, Jock (D.G.H. Rudd). *Greased Line Fishing for Salmon* (compiled from the papers of the late A. H. E. Wood) (reissue). Rockville Centre, N.Y.: Freshet Press Inc., 1971.

Shaw, Helen. *Fly-Tying.* New York: The Ronald Press Co., 1963.

Slaymaker, Samuel II. *Simplified Fly Fishing,* with an Introduction by Sparse Grey Hackle. New York: Harper & Row, 1969.

Sosin, Mark, and Clark, John: *Through the Fish's Eye.* New York: Harper & Row, 1973.

Sparse Grey Hackle (Alfred W. Miller). *Fishless Days, Angling Nights.* New York: Crown Publishers, Inc., 1971.

Starkman and Read. *The Contemplative Man's Recreation.* A bibliography of books on angling and game fish in the University Library. Vancouver: Library of the University of British Columbia, 1970.

Swisher, Doug, and Richards, Carl. *Selective Trout*. New York: Crown Publishers, Inc., 1971.

Traver, Robert (John Voelker). *Anatomy of a Fisherman*. New York: McGraw-Hill Book Co., 1964.

Van Gytenbeek, R. P. *The Way of a Trout*. New York: J. B. Lippincott Co., 1972.

Veniard, John. *Fly Dressers' Guide*. London: A. & C. Black, 1972.
———. (and Downs, Donald). *Fly Tying Problems and Their Answers*. New York, Crown Publishers, Inc., 1972.

Wahl, Ralph. *Come Wade the River,* with text from Roderick Haig-Brown's *A River Never Sleeps*. Seattle: Salisbury Press, 1971.

Walden, Howard T., 2d. *The Last Pool* (one-volume edition of *Upstream and Down* and *Big Stony*), with Introduction by Sparse Grey Hackle. New York: Crown Publishers, Inc., 1972.

Walker, C. F. *The Art of Chalk Stream Fishing*. New York: Stackpole Books, 1972.

Walton, Izaak, and Cotton, Charles. *Le Parfait Pêcheur à la ligne*. First complete translation of *The Compleat Angler*. Paris: Club des Libraires de France, 1964.

Waterman, Charles. *Modern Fresh & Salt-Water Fly Fishing*. New York: Winchester Press, 1972.
———. *The Fisherman's World,* New York: Random House, 1972.

Weeks, Edward. *Fresh Waters*. Boston: Little, Brown and Company, 1968.
———. *The Moisie Salmon Club*. A Chronicle. Barre, Mass.: Barre Publishers, 1971.

Wilson, Dermot. *Fishing the Dry Fly*. London: A. & C. Black, 1972.

Wright, Leonard M., Jr. *Fishing the Dry Fly as a Living Insect*. New York: E. P. Dutton & Co., Inc., 1972.

Zern, Ed. *A Fine Kettle of Fish Stories*. New York: Winchester Press, 1972.

Index